NEW YORK FRIARS CLUB BOOK OF ROASTS

THE WITTIEST, MOST HILARIOUS,
AND, UNTIL NOW,
MOST UNPRINTABLE MOMENTS
FROM THE FRIARS CLUB

BARRY DOUGHERTY

FOREWORD BY ALAN KING

MJF BOOKS
NEW YORK

Published by MJF Books
Fine Communications
322 Eighth Avenue
New York, NY 10001

The New York Friars Club Book of Roasts
LC Control Number 2002100596
ISBN 1-56731-513-5

Book design and type formatting by Bernard Schleifer

CONTENTS

This book is dedicated to the love of laughter!

FOREWORD

Let me warn you right now. When it comes to the Friars, there are no rules. Let ethics take a backseat here. Society has deemed that we act and speak according to certain mores—they don't apply at the Friars Club, nor do they apply in this book. Fuggetabout them. You want class, read Miss Manners. You want laughs, read about the Friars. A visit to a Friars Club Roast is like being at a brothel with your clothes on. We often say, "We only Roast the ones we love." Well, that's bullshit, because we Roast *everybody*.

I am proud to hold the post of Abbot of the New York Friars. I follow a long and illustrious cast of characters from our first, Charles Emerson Cook, to celebrities such as George M. Cohan, George Jessel, Milton Berle, Joe E. Lewis, Ed Sullivan, and Frank Sinatra. The Friars Club holds a very special place in entertainment history, and it is an honor for me to lead them into the new millennium. I often regale the members from my perch at the Club's bar with stories of Roasts and Testimonial Dinners that have come and gone. I have my own version of certain events, I admit to that. Otherwise I would not be a raconteur, I would just be a tape recorder.

This book, however, is a tape recording, of sorts. It plays for you some of the funniest, dirtiest, wittiest, and lewdest comments that have been made at some of the most hysterical events in history. It would be gloating to tell you that nothing compares to actually attending a Friars Roast or Dinner—but nothing does compare. Within these pages you are about to read, however, is the next best thing to being there. For almost one hundred years, what has gone on behind our closed doors has been only assumed, guessed at, or rumored to have happened. Now you can read them for yourself.

The Friars have honored hundreds of personalities and show business celebrities. They could all not possibly be covered in this book. Don't feel cheated—be thankful; not all of them were winners—trust me. Another reason you may not read about an event is, quite frankly, we may not have the best filing system in the world. We're humor savvy, not business savvy. As for the jokes, some of them were told at *every single event*—you will only have to read them once or twice.

You are about to embark on a journey filled with laughs and maybe even a sentimental moment or two, so enjoy the read. And remember, you read it at your own risk. I don't want you telling me you were shocked, appalled, and disappointed at the Friars' lack of class. We got class all right—it may be coming out our ass, but we got it. In retrospect, what we considered bawdy and obscene twenty, thirty, or forty years ago is nothing compared to what your kids have seen or heard on cable TV today. So either press on with the book and have a great time, or put it down and head over to the Christian Science reading room. In any case, I'll be at the bar talking about the time . . . well, I'll let you read it for yourself.

—ALAN KING

INTRODUCTION

Anytime I tell people I work for the Friars Club, I'm either met with a blank stare—which doesn't necessarily mean they're clueless, it just means they didn't ask me where I work, I just offered—or they comment, "Oh, the place that does those Roasts. Do you get to go to them?" Not only do I get to attend them, but as editor of the Friars Club's newsmagazine, the *Epistle*, I also get to write about the antics of the Club's members. Being on the inside of one of the best-kept secrets in show business is almost better than sex—another topic that elicits blank stares whenever I'm not asked, but just offer.

These events are too good to be true and too good not to be shared with anyone who loves a good laugh—especially when the laughs are at someone else's expense. Let's face it, who hasn't stifled a giggle at the sight of a person walking out of a public bathroom with toilet paper attached to his or her shoe. The Friars have been keeping people in stitches for almost a century now, so they figure they're old enough to spread their wise ways with the world. That's wise as in wise guys, by the way—their wisdom is still a work in progress.

So many jokes, and so many stories, and so many laughs have been the focal point of various Friars events throughout the decades that it would be a comedic injustice to keep silent any longer. So here they are, some funny and maybe even some not-so-funny moments from the Friars' archives. Not to mention a personal memory or two from the people who carved their own Friarly niche—like Milton Berle, Red Buttons, Carol Burnett, Ed McMahon, Jason Alexander, and David Hyde Pierce, just to name a few.

Oh, and for those of you who are thinking, "Okay, great, I get to take this trip down the Friars Club's memory lane, but what the hell is a Friars Club?" you'll find that out, too. I'll guide you down that Friarly road to fun and frolic as best I can. But if you slip on a banana peel along the way, you will be laughed at, I guarantee. I'm sorry, but that's just how it is at the Friars Club.

—BARRY DOUGHERTY

CHAPTER 1

IN THE BEGINNING

*(Who the hell are these people who make
Howard Stern seem like a virgin?)*

". . . And God said, 'Let there be comedy' . . . and there was the New York Friars Club." Okay, so maybe it is too presumptuous to say that this is how the Club was created, but press the point with any Friar and he or she will defend it until you die laughing. After all, laughter and comedy are synonymous with the Friars Club.

If you walk up to anyone on the street today and ask, "What is the Friars Club?" among the many answers (which, by the way, run the gamut from "a weekly poker game for monks" to "a culinary organization for people with tough arteries") one comment will most certainly stand out—"Oh, aren't they the comedians who do the Roasts?" Never let it be said that the public doesn't recognize a good thing when they see it.

Truth be told, the New York Friars Club did not start out as a house of cards, with an overabundance of jokers. While those historically challenged comedians would have you believing their Friarly roots are firmly planted in a pair of baggy pants, with banana cream pie coursing through its veins, the truth is far from funny. However, for those who would rather believe the tales of comedians with overactive imaginations spinning yarns of a more unorthodox beginning, allow me to suggest the following conversation between George M. Cohan and Irving Berlin:

GEORGIE: Say, Irving, I been thinkin' we need a place to hang out. Away from the goils. *(It's funnier if he sounds like he hailed from Brooklyn).* A place where we can sing and dance and drink . . . and . . .

IRV: Curse?

GEORGIE: Yea, dat's it. And curse!

IRV: You mean like a private stag club?

GEORGIE: Now you're talkin', my boy.

IRV: Yea, a place where there's no dames. Just the guys being guys. Sort of like a monastery.

GEORGIE: Exactly! Like friars!

For the rest of the planet, the real skinny is far less ludicrous, but it is a tad more honest, which would make a real monk very proud. The Club began in 1904 when a group of theater press agents were incensed over a situation that was happening in their business. It seems some men were fraudulently claiming to be reporters, thereby gaining access to free tickets for Broadway shows. The agents organized themselves to meet and discuss these "freebies," which were out of control—you see? It's always about money. The agents got together to discuss their plight and come up with solutions to their problem. The group met at Browne's Chophouse in New York City and those eleven men—Charles Emerson Cook, Channing Pollock, John S. Flaherty, John B. Reynolds, John Rumsey, Philip Mindil, Mason Peters, William Raymond Sill, Burton Emmett, Bronson Douglas, and Harry Schwab—in essence, became the first Friars. They apparently resolved the problem by forming a blacklist—how twentieth century of them!

Say? Did you really read that list of eleven or skip over it because it was just a bunch of names—of people who are long dead, no less, and how interesting a read is that? We're talking about the Friars' forefathers here, people! The real founding father, by the way, is a name you will not see listed anywhere—Colonel Marshall E. Lee. He is probably the single most important founding father—his being a crook notwithstanding. Channing Pollock, a press rep for the Shuberts, said of Lee, "Out of obscurity he came to do his great work, and,

George M. Cohan, Irving Berlin, and William Collier checking those Frolic reviews.

Above: The Friars first Clubhouse in 1908–all the comforts of home, except the women folk.

Right: The 48th St. Monastery— so many rooms, so few Friars.

Alan King and Phil Silvers renamed Times Square Friar Square in 1960–and Mickey Mouse went into cardiac arrest.

The funniest Monastery in the world—the Friars' 55th St. Clubhouse.

having done it, into obscurity he disappeared again, leaving no address." It seems Colonel Lee was one of the men who tried to pull the wool over the press agents' eyes for free passes to Broadway shows by pretending to be a reporter for the *Washington Post*. Although, depending on who you ask, the Colonel was either a really good imposter or you'd have to have been living under a rock—make that a dock—to think he was anything but an imposter. Charles Emerson Cook, a press rep for David Belasco who spotted Lee at the Belasco Theatre, said, "He might have been a living portrait of the great Confederate general himself. Such manner and dignity must grace a stage box, nothing less. He must take back a good report of us to Washington." But Pollock, when he encountered Lee trying to get into a show called *Fantana*, said, "Colonel Lee looked as much like a newspaper man as a scow looks like a battleship." Astute though he may "claim" to be, Pollock still let the man get away.

In any case, the jig was up for the Colonel and anyone else who tried to mess with the press agents cum Friars again. When Cook or Pollock asked the Colonel about his colleagues at the *Post*, he obviously knew nothing about anyone at the paper and tried to change the subject. The Colonel split the scene but as Cook said, "That was the last of this genius. His fade-out was complete." Fade-out fraudulent founding father, fade-in Friars Club.

The group discovered that they actually enjoyed each other's company on their Friday night after-theater get-togethers. "We discussed ticket frauds and Welsh Rarebits," said Pollock, who was president of this group at the time. Welsh Rarebits? "Such meetings! Good cheer, many a laugh, and friendships that have been lifelong. But the end of that season seemed to end our mission," said Cook. Almost a year would pass after taking care of their nasty little problem when the press agents decided to get together again for professional as well as social reasons. They started to meet every week, just to shoot the breeze, hang out, and have a good time. This go-around, they held their gatherings at a place called Keene's Chophouse, also in Manhattan. What's with the chophouses? Initially they called themselves the Press Agents Association (nobody ever said that press agents had huge imaginations—did they even consider "The Chophouse Club?"), but on November 15, 1907, after the group more or less came and went and came back together again, they incorporated with a formal constitution and bylaws. That's when they officially became the National Association of the Friars, AKA the Friars Club. Voila!

Why Friars Club? Why not, say, "Liars Club," which would work with a lot of these guys; or "Criers Club," which only works when they've laughed themselves to tears, and let's face it, they weren't that funny yet; or "Pliers Club," which maybe they were saving for a club for stage hands? If we want to take the word of Charlie Cook—who seems to have a lot of words to say about the founding of the Friars—it was his idea, of course, that they change the name Press Agents Association (which happened to be a good idea) because the club represented many interests. He felt it should be replaced with a "terse two-word name, like The Players, The Lambs, The Strollers." Sounds like someone was dying to jump on a bandwagon. According to Cook, the committee that was assigned to name the Club "brought back to us a report that electrified the meeting—THE FRIARS—a term derived from the Latin, *frater*, or 'brother.'" Little did Mr. Cook know just how electrifying fryers were going to be in a few years, what with the discovery of french fries and all. The two men on this committee, by the way, were Frederick F. Schrader, editor of the *Dramatic Mirror*, and A. Toxen Worm, which, if you read really fast, makes you think that the Club was named by a toxic worm. Then again, they could have named it after their very own worm—The Colonel Marshall E. Lee Club—if they had any chutzpah.

"To establish and maintain a fraternity among men engaged in theatrical enterprises" was the basis of the new Club's constitution. It also suggested, "To voluntarily aid each other in sickness or in distress," which is not to be confused with one's wedding vows. A 1911 booklet containing the constitution and by-laws listed the founders, and, in parentheses next to John S. Flaherty's name, placed the word "deceased." It's a pretty good bet that if we were to use that format today, all Friars would have "deceased" next to their names. Then again, Milton Berle—a Friar you'll be reading oh-so-much about in this book, because he is not just Mr. Television, he is also Mr. Friar—has pointed out on several occasions that the average age for Friars is "deceased." So maybe they were just listing Mr. Flaherty's age in 1911, using the new Friar math.

Also listed in this booklet were the House Rules, which contained a list of the games that were "absolutely prohibited in the Club." Among them were Basset, Hazard, and Passage. Those officers certainly knew their stuff. These games must have been so diabolical that they have been totally eradicated from the gambling world. Or maybe they just made them up to fill the page, which is basically what I'm doing right now. But it is House Rule number VII. Article (3) that stands out as the most intriguing and, we're assuming, least important: "The use of profane, improper or indecent language in the Monastery, or any conduct in any way subversive of the good order or decorum, or serious interference with the personal comfort, enjoyment or safety of another person is absolutely forbidden. Any member who shall violate this rule within the limits of the Monastery, may be suspended by any member of the Board or the House Committee, pending action by the Board of Governors or House Committee." That clearly explains the vacant dining room the day after every Friars Roast.

Already in place at the time of their incorporation was the Friars newsletter, the *Epistle*. A fascinating read, the December 5, 1907 issue shares Club business under the headings, "First Lesson" and "Second Lesson." This particular issue, which announced the formation of the organization, is chock-full of pronouncements. One particularly engaging one, with the headline, "Smoke Up," announced that soon "The Friar Cigarette" would be on the market. "The cigarettes will be put up in an attractive form and each box will display the emblem of the Friars. The Friar Cigar will be ready for delivery January 1st. While waiting for the cigarettes and cigars Friars should create a preliminary demand by asking for them at the cigar stands, and getting their friends to ask for them also. This would start a very effective endless chain and ensure a big sale from the beginning." There's no business like smoke business. Funny thing though, in the June 10, 1909 issue, which included the Club's financial report, there is no mention under "Profits" or even "Losses" of any Friar Cigarettes and Cigars. So much for the fraternal bros getting out there to drum up all that demand.

Allow me to jump, briefly, to the present. One reason is to give you a breather from your history lesson and another is that, I just thought of something funny. Because the Friars Club is constantly moving and shaking and organizing events and generating tons of ideas and information, they keep their members up-to-date through a plethora of mailings. Not a week . . . make that, not a day . . . actually, not an hour goes by without some envelope from the Friars Club ending up at the doorstep of each and every member. Comedian Jeffrey Ross says, "I only joined the Friars Club because I was lonely and I like getting mail." Jason Alexander says that it took exactly one week after he was informed of his honorary membership status for those cards and letters to come cascading down his mail chute. Now, he can't stop the deluge until his membership ends which, being an honorary member, means he's stuck with it for life! Well, Jeffrey and Jason, you are not alone. Even as far back as 1907, the Club was obsessed with its mailings. They would list in the *Epistle* the names of Friars they could no longer locate under an "Addresses Wanted" section: "Any Friar knowing the correct address of any of the following members, will confer a great favor by forwarding same immediately to the Treasurer John W. Rumsey, Lyceum Theatre, New York. Mail sent each week to those Friars at the only address known is always returned by the Post Office Department." Wonder what the "great favor" was for ratting out the members who obviously went on the lam to avoid their daily dose of Club mail? A free pack of Friar Cigarettes, perhaps?

Okay, break over, back to your lesson, kids! By 1907, a man by the name of Wells Hawks, a press agent for the Hippodrome who later became Mary Pickford's press rep, was president of the club. Word quickly spread among the theater set—vaudevillians, nightclub performers, minstrels, monologists, and basically anyone who was rejected by the Lambs Club—that the Friars was THE place to be. This was when song-and-dance sensation George M. Cohan and music men Victor Herbert and Oscar Hammerstein started to join the boys in their fraternal fun. When you add performers to any mix, things are bound to get interesting—not to mention they put the Friars name up in lights. For years the Friars have touted George M. Cohan as the founding father; then again, can you blame them? Have you ever heard of Philip Mindil or Bronson Douglas? And, until this book, they never dared call Colonel Marshall E. Lee "daddy!" The current executive director of the Friars Club, Jean Pierre Trebot, while not a comedian by trade, is partial to tossing out this bon mot, which he admits he stole but can't remember from whom: "There were three popular theatrical clubs in New York. The Lambs were actors who would like to be gentlemen; the Players were gentlemen who would like to be actors; and the Friars were neither of them." First lesson: never expect a pedestal at the Friars Club.

The Friars quickly began to organize Testimonial Dinners and special outings. These guys had so much fun together that it was apparent they needed a permanent home. Moving around to various locations in New York City, places such as the Hotel Hermitage and the Café des Beaux Arts, didn't exactly scream stability for the fledgling Club. At one point they moved into a room at the Knickerbocker Theatre Building. The rent was twenty-five dollars a month and the members panicked with worry, wondering if they would be able to afford it. Milton Berle's take on the nomadic life of the Friars is, "We kept moving because it was cheaper than paying rent!" Second lesson: don't ever expect a straight answer from any of them.

Once they hit their stride, the Friars eventually found a residence in 1908. It was actually to be the first of four buildings the Club would own. This one was located at 107 West 45th Street. The four-story brownstone had all the comforts of a home-away-from-home that included a bar (naturally), café, pool table, small rooms for lounging, and a huge room for meetings, as well as for their soon-to-become infamous Dinners. They bought the building with money they made from the First Annual Festival. That event, held at the New York Theater, featured the comedy of Weber and Field—you remember them, don't you? They performed their famous "The German Senators" routine, featuring a billiards table. Aha! Now it all comes back to you! Actress Louise Dresser also performed and Victor Herbert led a chorus of the Friars anthem, which he composed. All these riotous high jinks earned the Friars $10,000. The key to that clubhouse was as good as in their hands. The Clubhouse, by the way, was called the Monastery, and that namesake carries over to their current digs as well. Why a Club, which has been linked to some of the funniest borscht-belt comics in history, adopted that particular name, no one knows. Nor do they know why the head of the Friars is called the Abbot, followed by the Dean, Prior, and Scribe—so don't even ask.

The members held elections at their new Monastery, and Charles Emerson Cook became the president—that's the title that was later changed to Abbot—the grand pooh-bah, the head honcho, the guy in charge. Comedian/actor Alan King holds that title today, but he just prefers to be known by the more sedate "The Big Kahuna." Cook was one of the original eleven press agents who formed the Club. But if the truth be told, his management skills in running a private organization were a tad under par, rumor has it, though, he was a heck of a nice guy. This was new territory for Cook and for the other officers of the Club—in other words there wasn't a financial wizard in the bunch.

By 1909 the Club's financial affairs were so bad that when the new Abbot, literary agent John Rumsey, took office after an election that was not pretty, the Club had a deficit of $18,000, which rapidly grew to $22,000 four months later. This was not exactly a drop in a bucket for the early part of that century. The records for that year show a loss of $70.00 under "Memorial Committee"; it would seem the members would rather die than pay their dues! The Friars took their woes to heart and acted like any faction would in such dire straits—they held a banquet at the Hotel Astor. The kicker was that Charles Emerson Cook, the man responsible for basically putting their finances in the toilet, was the guest of honor. They even presented him with a loving cup. This proves more than anything that this Club, regardless of the personalities or dissension among the ranks, has always held firm to their fraternal instincts. They pride themselves on always being there for one another and standing by their motto, "Prae Omnia Fraternitas." Well, you have to have a motto. Every club has a motto. Even the *Little Rascals* He-Man Woman-Hater's Club had a motto: "We promise not to fall for this Valentine business because girls are the bunk!" Okay, that's more of an oath, but same difference. Of course, one would expect the Friars' motto to stand for "And let seltzer be sprayed down every member's pants," but at the risk of knocking down yet another Friars myth, it actually means "Before All Things Brotherhood." This motto, as written in their original constitution, is contained within the Friars Club's logo, "The seal of this Club shall be circular, with a Friars head in the center." Who knew the Friars head would resemble Don Rickles?

It only took a year for Abbot Rumsey to put the Club back on the straight and narrow. By June 1910 the Club was on its feet and $8,000 richer. Time for more celebrations! On June 23, 1910, they held a Jubilee Dinner at the Hotel Astor, with Rumsey as the guest of honor. He, too, received a silver loving cup—presumably it cost less than $8,000, or it would have been time to examine his financial expertise as well. Rumsey must have had a great time at the Jubilee Dinner because he threw his own "Dinner Gathering" the following month. The July 29, 1910 *Epistle* reports, "As a personal, living human illustration of the real meaning of our motto our Friar Abbot took advantage of the presence of many out-of-town Friars to entertain them all at dinner in an informal way at the Monastery on Friday evening, July 16th." And what a hoot it must have been, by this hysterical account: "Because of a sudden rainstorm, Friar Eugene Kelcey Allen and his smile did not attend the dinner, but appeared in time for the gathering. When he was informed later in the evening that the room was so crowded that Friar Governor Louis Nethersole had 'to sit without the prandial,' Friar Allen opined that it was for the best, as it was a warm night. Since then Friar Allen has accepted the advice of his side partner in comedy Morris Jones, and is studying the dictionary." Don't get it? Well, put yourself in the same boat as Friar Allen—"prandial" may have escaped today's lexicon (and most likely that of 1910 as well), but basically what happened was that it was so crowded that Louie didn't get to eat his meal. Ladies and gentlemen, you were there!

The Friars Frolics—or Frolic, as it was originally known (apparently at some point in their history someone added an "s" and nobody bothered to question it)—began as a fundraiser. Remember that First Annual Festival with the riveting performances of Weber and Fields and Louise Dresser? That was basically the first Frolic, and in 1909 they staged a second to help pay off some of their debt. For this show Louise Dresser was again dusted off and teamed up with Douglas Fairbanks, Sr., in a scene from "Nellie The Beautiful Cloak Model"—that's what their records say, I swear! One can only wonder how Louise felt performing in all these Friars Club fundraisers, not allowed to actually BE a Friar. Maybe she just chalked it up to that He-Man Woman-Hating club mentality, or maybe it was just because those guys thought that "girls are the bunk." That's really not fair; these guys liked women—probably a little too much, in many instances—that is, they did until 1988, but we'll get to that in due time. In any case, Ms. Dresser was a good sport about helping them out in their time of need. And they were damn lucky to have one of the superstars of their time on the bill. (A little digression here—note the use of the word "damn." It gets a heck of a lot worse, this being a book about the Friars. Just wanted to get your feet wet a bit, that's all.)

By 1911, the Friars were financially solvent. Rather than throw a bash, this time they decided to move on up . . . three blocks up to be exact. Some people buy new cars every two years; the Friars purchase new buildings every three. They found property at 106–110 West 48th Street that would be just perfect for hanging up their cowls, racking up their billiards balls, and eating their prandials. How to pay for it would be another story entirely. This time they figured they could make a killing if they toured the Frolic—let's face it, if the savvy New York crowd went bonkers over that German Senators billiards routine, you can only imagine the howls it would play to in Peoria!

By this time George M. Cohan and Irving Berlin were making beautiful music together for the Friars and their audiences, and Cohan asked Berlin to prepare a song specifically for the 1911 Frolic. It was to be Irvy's contribution to the event, and rumor has it he started and finished it all in one long night. The song was his famous *Alexander's Ragtime Band*, and it was the musical smash of the Frolic that year. They toured through Atlantic City, Philadelphia, Baltimore, Pittsburgh, Cleveland, Cincinnati, St. Louis, Chicago, Detroit, Buffalo, Rochester, Boston and New York. Audiences went wild for the music, jokes, and specialty acts, the likes of which they'd never seen before, and $40,825.56 later, the Friars realized their new building was as good as remodeled and almost ready for occupancy. They toured another Frolic in 1912 and by 1915 the new Abbot, George M. Cohan, was ready to raise the rest of the bucks needed to remodel the new digs. The members dug a hell of a lot deeper into their pockets than Cohan and the officers imagined, and with $100,000 staring them in the face, they decided just to build a new building from scratch. Sort of like what Phyllis Diller did with her face.

On October 21, 1915, the cornerstone of the new building was laid. Needless to say, this event did not pass without the Friars' already trademark bombastic fanfare. They gathered at their 45th Street Monastery and then marched en masse to the site of the new one. Cohan broke a bottle of sparkling American wine on the stone saying, "I dedicate this club to art, literature and good fellowship." Art? Literature? Oh, brother!

Finally, on March 22, 1916, that damn building that the Friars had been going on and on about for five years was completed. They marched from their old stomping grounds, up Sixth Avenue—with a military police band escort, no less—to their spanking new 48th Street Monastery. And what a Monastery—a bar (naturally), billiards room, grill room, library, gym, wine room, and barbershop. As if that wasn't enough to keep the ol' boys happy, the new Club also had forty-two bedrooms—each with a private shower! These guys really had come a long way since their nomadic days. And they owed much of it to founder George M. Cohan—oh, right, he wasn't the founder, but he sure was the man of the hour. When Cohan, who led the march, entered the new Monastery he threw the key into the street to symbolize that the building would never be closed—then got locked out. Nah, he made it inside and hosted a banquet where over five hundred Friars attended. According to one account, there was also a show, "A program rendered by the stars of the stage and concluded a never-to-be forgotten day." Only there doesn't seem to be any mention of that event in any of the Club's archives, so I guess everybody forgot about it. (Speaking about forgetting great things—is this the part where it should be mentioned that the McGraw Hill Building now stands on this site?)

The new Monastery boasted a wonderful, state-of-the-art gymnasium. Friar Bob Edgren, who was apparently the chairman of the Gymnasium Committee around 1916–17, couldn't boast enough about this place. "Folks who imagine that an actor only exercises his lower maxillary would be surprised to know the number of Friars who take their exercise otherwise than in capsule form. The gymnasium under the ridgepole of the Friars' roof is the most unanimously patronized cell in the entire Monastery. While some of the boys are exercising on the horizontal bar in the buffet, the horizontal bars in the gym are getting their share of customers. Weights, medicine balls, wrestling, boxing, and handball are the more popular sports, although stalling, puffing, and asking for time-out are also greatly in vogue." The Friars' gym today continues to be the most popular room in the Monastery—only they had to remove the horizontal bar to make room for the television set.

The 1916 Friars Frolic was by far the most successful of the Friars early Frolics. It opened at the Amsterdam Theatre in Manhattan and then toured sixteen cities in fourteen days. They closed at the New York Hippodrome in a benefit performance for the Actors' Fund. The tour earned the club over $55,000 and helped put a dent in their escalating bills for their new half-million dollar home. George M. Cohan, Irving Berlin, and

Will Rogers were all on the bill. They were three of the biggest stars of that era and here they were, dropping everything for their fellow Friars—which begs the question, "Didn't these guys ever work?"

President Woodrow Wilson attended the performance at the New Academy of Music in Baltimore and was the butt of most of the jokes. Political satirist Will Rogers naturally had a field day with his lasso and wit, talking about the war, German submarines, and American military preparedness. Irving Berlin wrote a special song to honor the Prez:

> We're with Mr. Wilson,
> Yes we are, yes we are;
> He's the only candidate in the swim
> Abraham Lincoln would have voted for him.
> Give three cheers for Wilson
> As Americans can,
> Let every man remembers, when he votes
> Sometime in the next November, sending notes
> Is safer than a fighting plan.
> Mr. Wilson, we know you're the man!

Does anyone else smell a Grammy? Irving seems to have spent a little too much time in the new Clubhouse bar whipping up this nifty ditty—but maybe the tune was to die for!

The finale, which was the talk of the tour, was a sketch centering around Pancho Villa and his own personal war with the U.S. Army. Seems at that time, President Wilson, with the consent of the Mexican government, sent General John J. Pershing to crush the revolutionary, but Persh didn't exactly walk away with the trophy. Oh, the field day the Friars had with this little bit of American history. What they didn't expect was to perform the skit in front of the president himself—who took a hilarious hit or two from the Friars. When the tour made its way to Baltimore, however, the president had a ringside seat to his own comic destiny.

According to one of the performers, Sarry Saranoff, a vaudevillian who was a regular around the Monastery well into the '60s, "Backstage there was some doubt among the show's personnel as to how the president would receive the finale, which was a 'rib' on the Villa incident. But their fears were groundless, for as George Sidney, in the role of Villa, and the entire company played out the travesty, Mr. Wilson was just as convulsed with laughter as any one else in the theater. In fact, so delighted was he, a secret service agent was sent forth to tell Mr. Cohan of the president's desire to meet the cast." Nothing like a good Pancho Villa sketch to put the commander-in-chief in stitches! The Friars were so taken with Wilson that Cohan, "Ever the dramatist and never one to miss a golden opportunity such as this, huddled with some of the officers and Board of Governors and introduced a resolution to make the president an honorary member of the Friars right then and there!" says Saranoff. Since this Friars' scribe has a flair for his own dramatics, it's only fair to let the rest of his rant be played out: "Thus on the stage of the Old Ford Theater, in the quaint City of Baltimore, in the year 1916, 'a President of the U.S. became a member of the Friars Club!!!'" Wow, Sarry gave that three exclamation points. By the way, don't think this was overlooked—what the hell kind of name is Sarry Saranoff?

While the Frolics were a wonderful mishmash of songs, sketches, and even dramatic interludes with the best of the best in show business, a large portion of them were in the form of minstrel shows. Those shows amounted to jokes and songs performed by men in blackface. Al Jolson leads the pack of minstrel performers, and he made several appearances at various Frolics. Frank Tinney was also a popular entertainer of the time who plied his wares donning blackface. When it comes to the Friars, everything, of course, needs to be put into perspective, and for those Friars of 1916, who stood at the dawn of the twentieth century, it was one of the most popular means of entertainment. Now, as we stand at the precipice of the twenty-first century it represents a notable travesty. This is not the place to judge, criticize, condone, or condemn—it's just a vehicle to pass along some fascinating tidbits about some very fascinating people who have their own agenda—to entertain. Now, about Ted Danson . . . oh, sorry, not yet!

Believe it or not, the Friars have always put their philan-thropic hearts before their caustic tongues, and by the time World War I arrived, they were more than ready to do their part to help the cause. They used their popular Frolics to raise money for the war effort and to perform for the soldiers. Not that every venture was a successful one. Take, for instance, the Friars Frolic that Henry Ford attended. Seems Al Jolson spot-ted the auto tycoon in the audience with the missus and their son Edsel and before you knew it, dollar signs appeared in the Friars' eyes. Marshal McCarthy, a Friar, pressed Ford to donate $10,000—it was for the boys overseas, after all—but Ford wouldn't budge. Wouldn't even speak. The show went on with acts that included Irving Berlin and comedian William Collier, but Ford eventually walked out with his family.

The war was often a huge topic of debate at the Friars "grill," with members arguing well into the early morning hours. Sarry Saranoff remembered one such morning, around 1:30 A.M. to be exact, in 1917. Sitting around the Roundtable . . . it's imperative to digress here a moment. The Roundtable is a table that still exists today at the Friars Club. It's the main table in the dining room where the Friar elite sit and dispense their witty wisdom. From Cohan and Rogers to Berle and Henny Youngman to Red Buttons and Sid Caesar to Robert Klein and Richard Lewis, it is the funniest piece of furniture in the joint (some Friars would have you think it's the funniest in all the world—and on some days, it is). Let the Algonquin have their literary wits, the Friars have their shining clowns!

Back to Sarry's tale. He claims that Cohan, Will Rogers, artist Harrison Fisher, William Collier, World Heavyweight Champion "Gentleman Jim" Corbett, journalist Harding Davis—who had just returned from the war front—and a few others whom Sarry can't recall (Sarry's sorry, though) were sitting around that famous table talking about the war. As Sarry writes, "The conversation waxed hot, since some in that group were in favor and some were against." Be honest, don't you get goose bumps anytime you hear that a conversation "waxed hot?"

According to Sarry, while the talk was heating up, Cohan

and his music director Charlie Gebest "ducked away from the roundtable and went to the piano. They seemed to be going over some sort of tune. After twenty minutes of that Cohan turned and addressed the boys, asking them if they would care to hear a little ditty he had just thought of, written around a bugle call. He sang it, as only the great Cohan could. Pandemonium broke loose in the Monastery—they loved it! The boys joined in and wouldn't stop singing. For there, in the Friars Monastery, that early morn, a wonderful war song was born. In the next few weeks, every band was crashing it out with blaring brass. Soldiers, sailors, and all the armed forces marched to the music of *Over There*."

The Friars hosted a Thanksgiving dinner at the Monastery for "our boys." On November 29, 1917, their banquet hall was overflowing with uniformed men. The *Epistle* noted that, "If all the men in the service of Uncle Sam measure up to the standard of the crowd that were here on that day, Germany is in for a terrible licking." As for the meal, "The lads were entertained at a luscious and sumptuous turkey dinner in the Great Hall of the Monastery and after it was finished they enjoyed a program of interesting 'movies' and vaudeville acts. The Friars' martial guests were given the freedom of the Club and many of them monopolized the billiards tables during the evening." This billiard room, by the way, had five. . . that's right, *five* pool tables. It even had a white strip on the floor, "To test the mental and physical balance of players who have circled the table, more than three times for a single shot. " These men really needed to get a life outside that Monastery! Or at least let a woman or two in to test their real mental and physical balance.

Each soldier was presented with a photograph of himself and his companions at the end of the evening, which, the *Epistle* noted, "They sent home to their mothers, wives, and sweethearts to commemorate the eventful day." Who wants to bet that most of the soldiers just kept them in their attics and their descendants are now making a mint selling them on ebay.com.

You're probably wondering by now when you'll be reading those jokes the Friars are famous for telling. Beware of what you wish for; it just may come true. Here's an offering from Friar Joe Feibleman in 1918: "A gentleman and a couple of ladies were sitting in front of a friend of mine at a recent performance of Ruth Chatterton in *Come Out of the Kitchen* at the George M. Cohan Theatre. As the curtain went down on the last act, the gentleman said to the ladies, 'What did you think of the show?' 'Oh,' answered one, 'I think it was very good, but I don't like George Cohan in this show nearly as well as I did in his last one.' 'Neither do I,' chimed in the other lady, 'he isn't nearly so funny'!" You asked! How about this one, also from 1917: "Friar Ed Bruns was being congratulated upon his gift of the new clock to the Club. 'Do you imagine anyone will object to the chimes?' he asked. And then, as though answering his own question, he added, thoughtfully, 'After all, they will help to keep the employees awake.'" Had your fill yet? Here's a wartime hoot from Friar Al Sanders:

"('Twas the day when diplomatic relations with Germany were broken off)"
"I've just heard a horrible rumor!"
"What is it?"
"Heard the German employees of the Club were up in the Gymnasium drilling!"

Now you know why you haven't read any jokes yet. Never trust an era that starts a joke with the word "'Twas." But fear not, the funny ones will start flowing as soon as their spats morph into loafers.

Friar Charles Grapewin showed his disdain for the enemy with this poem, published in the January 1918 *Epistle*:

Here's to the Kaiser—the great big stiff!
May his nose swell up so he can't even sniff.
May he burn to a pulp
In Chloride of lime
And go to h--- singing,
"I may be gone for a long, long time."

Now them's fightin' words!

Not that there weren't any wits hanging around the Monastery to make truly funny jokes. Actually, some of the quickest and most brilliant minds were a daily source of entertainment. In January 1918 the Club published a list of the membership along with what they would have liked to have seen in their stockings that past Christmas. While some, such as Edward F. Albee, who wished for "Peace," were quite admirable, others meant to amuse, while still others bordered on downright disturbing. Some speak for themselves, and some you're on your own to figure out what the heck they're talking about: "Felix Adler—A Maxim Silencer; Roscoe "Fatty" Arbuckle—A Slapstick; Roy T. Barnes—A New Gun; Irving Berlin—An American Name; Francis X. Bushman—Mash Notes; Frank Carter—Nut Tootsie Rolls; George M. Cohan— Imitators; Wm. Delany—A Rubber; female impersonator Julian Eltinge—Reducing Parlor; Douglas Fairbanks—Less Jumps; Frank A. Fay—A White Slave; Wm. Randolph Hearst—More Circulation; Al Jolson—A Corking Show; George S. Kaufman— BVDs; Lew Kelly—Dope; Channing Pollock—Green Books; John Ringling—Spring Circus; Will Rogers—Fred Stone's Jack O'Lantern; Adolph Zukor—Chaplin, Pickford, and Fairbanks." Nut Tootsie Rolls does sound like an interesting concept, but a white slave? Is that supposed to be more PC?

When the twenties roared into town, they headed straight for the Friars Club. The war was over, fun was in the air, and the Friars bellied up to the bar and partied hearty. Their Frolics were more popular than ever, with Cohan, Berlin, and Rogers leading the pack. Other names popping up on the Friars' roster were William Frawley—long before his Fred Mertz of *I Love Lucy* fame bellowed from television sets—W.C. Fields, Florenz Ziegfeld, and Eddie Cantor, to name a few. Their irreverence was being honed through skits such as The Japanese Actor: "With a scene behind the German lines during the war. A man shot down in an English plane is condemned to the firing squad, but his place is taken by the General's cook, long a servant in the household of the captured man, a prince in his own land." And then there was A Quiet Afternoon in Chicago, "Where Leon Errol and Harry Kelly shot down everybody in sight, including each other."

But can I just say the funniest bit of entertainment news for this decade came from a 1926 *Variety* and happened to be on the same page as a story about the Friars Club. Its seems that "Anna May," the elephant, was missing. Missing! In broad daylight! "The Luna Park elephant took a walk while on location near Santa Monica and has not been seen since. The animal was being used in a picture. It just strayed to get a bit of air. Several hundred men started an elephant hunt, but were not able to locate the pachyderm." How hysterical is that? Oh, the Friars' item was that they made George M. Cohan Abbot Emeritus, automatically making him a member for life. Big deal, the guy was Abbot for almost a gazillion years anyway. Wonder if Anna May is still AWOL?

Just in case you thought the Friars hadn't found their "mean streak" yet, see what Bernard Kamber, the historian of the Club, has to say about those 48th Street days. (Bernie is a former press rep—remember when the Friars were just press reps? See how everything that goes around comes around?): "Comedians can be kind of cruel. I remember I was a sucker for them. You'd get guys like Groucho Marx sitting around a table and they would tell a joke that had no punch line in it. Somebody like me, I thought I was an idiot because they would all laugh after they'd tell these jokes. So I laughed because I was afraid they'd look at me funny. The more I laughed, the more they'd laugh. Somebody else would tell a story without any punch line and you just laughed because you really didn't know what was going on. They did that to anybody who was not in show business." Good Lord, not only did you need to pay the Club dues, you also needed to pay an analyst to get over the trauma from the pranks of these childish comedians (but it is pretty funny).

Alan King has his own practical joke moment: "The first time I walked into the old Club, Eddie Davis, Harry Adler, and Milton Berle brought me there. Sound asleep, in a big chair, up front was the legendary comedian Willie Howard. He was a giant. Milton's laughing and everybody's chewing gum. They put a piece of chewing gum on his nose, a piece of chewing gum on his ear, and they stick a match in between them with the phosphorous on the outside. Then they light the fucking thing and holler, 'Fire!' Willie wakes up and he's surrounded by all this, rubbing out the fire. I said, 'This is the coolest thing!'" Good heavens—don't ever fall asleep around King, that's for sure.

Things weren't so amusing for the Friars in the thirties. Not that funny things didn't continue to happen. They went bankrupt and lost their beloved Monastery—that's not funny. But in October 1932, four Club employees sued for back salary. One of the employees was listed as "bartender." Can anyone spell PROHIBITION? From 1919 to 1933, that sticky little no-drinking law was in effect, and this guy says in 1932 that he was a bartender—now that's funny! What really put them over the edge, though, was an unpaid bill for $1,130.00 for butter, eggs, and cheese. Funny enough, they seem to have been paid up in their liquor bills. The bank foreclosed on the mortgage in 1933, which was the same year more employees tried to sue for back wages. When Abbot George M. Cohan was served with the papers—oh, a year after he was made Abbot Emeritus, he then went back to work as their Abbot—he denied having any connection with the Club. But he did "express affection for the Club and was sorry to see it pass." Wait a minute? What about the Abbot Emeritus for life bit? Oh well, Jesus had his Peter and the Friars had their George.

Contrary to Cohan's assumption, the Club did not pass, although it did seem to take a breather, sort of like what I'm about to do now. Remember the episode of *Seinfeld* when Jerry was being proposed as a member of the Friars Club by Pat Cooper? He met Pat for lunch at the Monastery—which they recreated on their set in California—and didn't have a sports jacket, so he had to wear one supplied by the Club. Then he left, wearing the jacket. From the Club he went with Elaine to see a Broadway show called the *Flying Sandos Brothers*, which was based on a real production, *The Flying Karamozov Brothers Do The Impossible*, and that cast played themselves in the episode. The Friars in real life actually had a theater party for the play. I walked out, but in *Seinfeld*, Jerry stayed long enough for the brothers to take his Friars jacket. The irony is that while his television persona didn't get into the Club, the real Jerry became an Honorary Friar because of it, so go figure. He, too, would most likely deny his membership, a la Cohan, if he were served with a summons—not that there's anything wrong with that.

Seinfeld isn't the only production to use the Friars Club in a story line (and film the outside for that "realistic" look). In 1975 a scene in Neil Simon's *The Sunshine Boys* was shot in the Monastery. George Burns and Walter Matthau, along with their lights, cameras, and action-shouting director Herbert Ross, entered Friar history when theirs became the only film to ever actually shoot on the premises. For three days the second floor Milton Berle Room was turned into a Hollywood soundstage. Matthau was thrilled to be on location in the Monastery—where else can you find a venue that comes with its own card room? (Named after his co-star George Burns, no less.) The first words out of his mouth when he arrived were, "Is there a poker table?" Always ready to accommodate a fellow Friar, their custom-made table was brought down to the second floor. Matthau played poker all day long between takes. He loved the table so much he asked if the Club could replicate it and have it shipped to his home in California, but unfortunately the cost was too prohibitive. Maybe he picked one up at Kmart?

Billy Crystal also wanted to film a scene at the Monastery for *Mr. Saturday Night*, his directorial debut. He checked out the same Milton Berle Room where Burns and Matthau had filmed seventeen years earlier. Unfortunately the cost of shooting a California-based film at a New York location was too exorbitant for Crystal, so he did the next best thing—recreated the room using all of the furnishings. The Club shipped tables, chairs, photos—everything but the kitchen sink (of which there are several to choose from)—so the look would be as exact as the real thing. The movie may not have done all that well at the box office, but the Milton Berle Room looked sensational!

Now, where was I? Oh yes. Just because there was no home to speak of after Cohan's dismissal of the Club it didn't mean there weren't still Friars who wanted to get together, play cards, and drink themselves into oblivion. They skipped around to various hotel rooms, and even entertainer Ted Lewis opened up his basement for a party or two. Why does veneer-coated balsa wood paneling and green linoleum come to mind? They still somehow managed to put together a Frolic here and there. In 1935 *Variety* reported that they "Represented heaven, with the boys all sporting wings and leaning on a lily-white pool table. That it was the Friars' own version of heaven, nobody doubted and that it is the nearest the Friars will ever get to playing there, everybody agreed." Ouch! Another review from 1940 mentioned, "Berle went back to his kid-actor days and did an imitation, reprising his strip-tease bit and peeling down to gold-spangled briefies. It was a closing roar." Now there's an image you don't want to conjure up too often.

For the Friars, 1936 was a wacky year. It seems they were in hot water with the government for failing to pay their taxes for 1934–35. Oops! This, in spite of the fact that the members paid those taxes individually along with their dues. To add insult to injury, $2,000 of a gym fund was also missing. All fingers collectively pointed toward their executive secretary, Charlie Pope, who would have seen those fingers wagging had he shown up at the emergency meeting that he was asked to attend along with the Club's books, which he was asked to supply. The last they heard from Charlie was a telegram he sent to the membership, "explaining that he was forced to close down the clubroom atop the Hollywood Theatre Building, New York." Brilliant maneuver, Charlie! Close down the place where a meeting about your taking money is going to be held. That way, no one will even notice. But it didn't work. They met anyway, at the Edison Hotel, and decided to just put the mess behind them and start fresh by legally reorganizing the Club into the "National Association of Friars, Inc." (Not to be confused with their 1907 corporate handle "National Association of the Friars"—but as none of this affects your life one iota move along.) George Jessel had been the Abbot at the time—he was the first to be replaced.

That year also saw a slight glimmer of hope for the floundering Club. They found a permanent space, sort of, at Edison Hall, adjacent to the Edison Hotel on West 47th Street. They sent out a letter to those diehard members who were left, excitedly informing them of the new place, "Our new quarters consist of the entire tenth floor and the exclusive use of the roof. Work has already started on the equipment and decorations. Among the facilities of the roof will be a solarium tastefully decorated, a handball court, dressing rooms, showers, lockers, and a summer garden. The club will be equipped immediately with a card room, lounge, billiards room, and grill. Our landlord will give us complete dining room service at reasonable prices and will also install a bar" (naturally).

Funny how words on paper can make anything sound sweet. Allow Buddy Arnold, an event producer for the Friars throughout the 40s and 50s, to give you a reality check: "It was a large room and adjunct to it was another smaller room that was used as a meeting place and you could watch television." End of subject. But what about the solarium? The billiards room? The showers? What about the goddamned summer garden? Allow Berle to burst that bubble, "We had a pay phone. It wasn't too decorative. We were busted. We were just starting from scratch." Even Red Buttons, who joined the Club in 1946, which would have been ten years after they moved in—plenty of time to grow a petunia or two in that garden—noted, "It was just a card room. They were struggling." Oh well, every day a kid somewhere finds out there's no Santa Claus, so why should the Friars be any different.

Regardless of the surroundings, it was still the Friars Club, which transcends any cozy furnishings. "I felt like I belonged. I belonged somewhere. I was part of show business, and it was a feeling of a Club," remembers Buttons. "There was a cadre of people who made the Club. Made the Club and kept it alive," says Buttons, who gives due credit to the man who would be Abbot. "I would say foremost and up front is Milton Berle. We all helped in those days. There were a bunch of us who were around, who gave our time and our talents and kept the Friars going." But it was Berle who had the name, the venue, and the love of the Friars Club to put the wheels in motion to rejuvenate it. He was, after all, Mr. Television, and one mention of the Friars on his show was worth a million gold briefies!

"I gave my life to the Friars because I believed in it. I believed in the fraternity, in the fellowship," says Berle, who laughs about the transition the Club was forced to make to stay afloat. "It started out as a theatrical club. Then one day I walked in there and got measured for a suit! . . . Joke. Meaning, that we had a lot of laymen because that's the way we started to get more members. Members that were not show business members. They had offices right near our building so they came lunch time, dinner time, and to all those events that I was very much a part of." Oh boy, was he a part of them! Berle Toastmastered and Roastmastered more events for the Friars than Jessel presided at funerals! (For the generation that has no idea what that means, try replacing that last part with . . . "than Madonna has failed movies!". . . And if that doesn't work . . . "than Disney has dalmatians!" If you're still clueless, put down the book—you're too young to be reading it!) He became Abbot of the Friars in 1940 and held the office until 1945, then again in '47 to '53 and once more in 1956. He now serves as the Friars' Abbot Emeritus, "which means they put me out in the field." He has another explanation of the title, but you'll just have to wait until you get to the Red Buttons Dinner in '87 to read it. Hey, he's not known as the Thief of Bad Gags for nothing!

"I don't want to say this about myself . . . I was hot as a pistol, and why not. I had the popularity and everybody knew me, and I was the head of the Club, so I did it for the Club. I really did it for the Club, for the membership, and we gained more memberships," says Berle, prepared to challenge anyone who thought otherwise—only no one can, because he's right. Except for the part about not wanting to say good things about himself—yeah, right.

With a new Abbot comes a new home. Thanks to Berle's euphoric promotion of the club, their roster of members had escalated—and their events were once again headline-grabbing news. By 1949 the Friars were back on track and solvent enough to go house hunting again. They bought and renovated a two-story brick garage and dance studio—for all those twinkle-toed Friars you've no doubt read about in *Variety*. This one was on 56th Street in Manhattan and while it doesn't sound as huge as their cherished 48th Street Monastery, it was still a step up from a couple of rooms in a hotel annex.

On May 12, 1950, ceremonies were held outside to formerly christen the new clubhouse. Comedian Jack E. Leonard opened with, "Brother Friars, I'm now addressing you in the street and that's where most of you belong," as he stood under a sheet covered plaque. Berle then presided, saying, "Okay, boys, let's get started. I wanna uncover this so I can get my handkerchief back." When Berle picked up a champagne bottle to break over the facade the Friars yelled, "Why break it? Let's drink it!" So they trooped inside to the "lavish semi-circular bar" (naturally) on the first floor. According to one newspaper account, the new place also boasted murals "showing well-fed frocked Friars squashing barefoot thru tons of grapes."

The Friars celebrated their 50th Jubilee in 1954—can you believe we've hit the halfway mark here? Our little Club is growing up so fast! It was such a monumental milestone for them that they shared the event with the general public by televising the Anniversary Frolic on CBS' *Colgate Comedy Hour*. You have one guess as to who hosted the show. If you didn't choose Milton Berle, then what the hell have you been reading all this time—'cause it hasn't been this book! The show featured Smith and Dale—remember them? Joel Grey also performed in the show, which paid homage to the Club and its heritage through old-time vaudeville routines and imitations of some Friars gone by. But then they go and have Mitzi Green imitate Fanny Brice, neither of whom was a Friar, so who can figure these guys out. They don't want the women in, yet they feature women in everything they do. Such a fickle bunch these Friars can be.

The year 1957 brought the Club to its final resting place— oh, sorry, Freudian slip—to its current location on East 55th Street, in Manhattan. Are real Friars this antsy about their Monasteries? They moved into a five-story English Renaissance house because their former Monastery was much too small for the highly successful Club and more room was needed to fit their ever-increasing membership.

According to Berle, he saw the house, which was up for sale, when he walked past it one day and considered buying it for him and his wife, Ruth. When she saw it, she nixed the idea because it would take a staff of fifteen or twenty to keep the place in order. Berle then brought the idea up to the Club's board to buy it as a new clubhouse, since they were looking to expand anyway. He even offered to guarantee the loan for them. What a swell guy. And what a swell story.

Or, try this scenario on for size: The Club found the property, which, according to then Executive Director Carl Timin, "resembled a monastery and contains marble and paneling imported from many countries throughout the world." While they were mulling over purchasing the place, Fred Hill, a Friar and realty operator, walks into the picture and decides to buy it first. Hey, every real estate tycoon knows, you snooze, you lose. Hill then, in turn, resells it to the Friars (at a personal profit, of course).

The Berle tale has that homespun flavor you want in your private club's folklore; yet the Hill story is so much more scandalous that why wouldn't the Friars jump at the chance to tell it over and over.

The new building had it all. The arched entranceways, that imported wood paneling, a stained glass window four stories high, and winding staircases all created the perfect ambiance for the male-only institution. It was originally built and occupied in 1909 by investment banker Martin Erdmann, a bachelor. After his death in 1937 the house changed hands, winding up in the glowing paws of the American Institute of Physics. Not only is it home to the Friars, but it was also home to the Manhattan Project. This building has seen more bombs than Europe, Asia, and Chevy Chase combined. But the man of the millennium himself, Albert Einstein, shuffled around the very same rooms that, say, Harpo Marx would a few years later (that would explain the similar hair traits). So, if they ever manage to figure out what exactly is inside Einstein's brain—isn't it hanging out in New Jersey somewhere?—they just may discover a cell or two devoted to the Friars Monastery. Of course there weren't as many laughs echoing through the halls at that time. Hill purchased the building from the Institute and soon the Friars were picking up Geiger counters along with their jokes at the door. When Mr. Erdmann, a collector of valuable English mezzotints, had the house designed he made sure that it was completely fireproof. According to the architects who designed the structure, "It is the most fireproof residence in Manhattan." Which is perfect for the Friars, what with all that hot air blowing around. (This probably wouldn't be the appropriate time to mention that much of the Club's historic records were lost in a fire at some point in the sixties, would it? It was just a little fire. But there's no record of the fire since the flood in the laundry room damaged anything that survived the first disaster. Well, don't you keep all of your valuable papers in your laundry room?)

When they moved into the new Monastery, the Friars held a street performance similar to their Frolics—minstrel shows and comedy routines. Comedian Joe E. Lewis, the Abbot at the time (who remained Abbot until his death in 1971), led a parade around the block to their new home. He flung the key into the street the same way that George M. Cohan did back in 1916. This, too, was to symbolize that the doors would always be open. That is, until they locked up the wrought-iron gates every evening. Interesting man, this Joe E. Lewis. Alan King says, "I think that the greatest guy we ever had in this Club in the fifty-five years I'm here was Joe E. There was no one like Joe E. He was a unifying figure—he was here and he came here to play cards and he was always at the bar." The bar was Joe E.'s favorite spot in the world. One night Frank Capitelli, the current maitre d' at the Friars, had to put the Abbot into a car. Joe E. took out a wad of cash and peeled off a hundred-dollar bill and handed it over to Frank. The next day, thinking that Mr. Lewis wasn't in his right mind, Frank went to the Abbot and said, "I think you made a mistake last night." To which Joe E. responded, "Kid, I never make mistakes. I gave you a hundred-dollar bill. You deserved it." Oh, to be a waiter at the Friars Club in those days!

With the new Monastery came new prosperity for the boys. They continued to hold Testimonial Dinners and Roasts and made plenty of headlines in the process. They also never lost sight of their philanthropic side. A good way to lure guests of honor for their events was to tell the honoree that a portion of any money raised would go to a charity of their choice. When all things were considered, it was easier for the honoree to be a chump for a few hours and have a chunk of change in their hand at the end of it to give to their favorite cause than have nothing at all. Along with these donations, the Friars also set up their own foundation in 1977 for the sole purpose of creating grants and scholarships for those organizations and students interested in fostering the performing arts.

Don't you hate it when naughty boys do good things—it's never as funny as when they're up to no good. Fear not, the Friars inevitably manage to combine the best of both worlds. Take, for instance, their Friars Foundation's 1996 black-tie gala held at the Plaza in New York City, to honor Ted Turner with their prestigious Applause Award. He and then-wife Jane Fonda showed up to the exclusive soiree for the festivities that included cocktails, dancing, dinner, and a show. If only the entertainment mogul had bothered to stay for his own affair. He and the Mrs. cut out sometime between the steamed mussels and the chicken fricassee. They also didn't bother to share their hasty exit with anyone, leaving the Friars dumbfounded as to where they'd gone. He sure should be sorry that the emcee for the event was Alan King, "Fuck Ted Turner! Murdoch was right. You are a Nazi. And Jane, you got a big ass!" Surely Alan had planned finer things to say had the Man of the Year not made such a sneaky retreat, but isn't he so much funnier when he allows the proverbial shit to hit the fan? Not to mention comedian Joy Behar, who asked the question on everyone's mind that night, "So she had her face done, right?"

If the Club were to have a saying they could call their own, they might adopt, "Behind every great Friar there's a great joke." But the joke would be on the Friars, because as everyone who's ever played the home version of *Jeopardy!* knows, the tenor of their saying has already been taken by, "Behind every great man there's a great woman"—and there's the rub! For almost a century the Friars held firm to the belief that a woman's place was anywhere but in the sanctity of their cigar-scented, gin-soaked, carefree-cursing Club. Oh, sure, they would allow the occasional female on stage with them for a Frolic or two (that's Frolic as in variety show for any wise guys out there), and had even presented them as guests of honor at Dinners and Roasts. But their Monastery was sacrosanct—as opposed to sappho-sanct—then again, they didn't want straight women there either.

Women were persona non grata, end of subject. "The whole Friars thing, when it started in the early years, was just a place for the guys to get away, have a cognac, smoke a cigar, and if they wanted to talk dirty, they could do it. Because in those days it was not the fashionable thing to do," admits Red Buttons. "You couldn't say hell or damn in front of women. You wouldn't. It was off-limits because show business was very, very clean, too. Backstage in vaudeville houses there was a sign, 'Hell or Damn, instant dismissal.' Hell or damn?" Wow, the sign backstage at today's Friars Roast says, "Hell or Damn too tame—use them and you're off the fucking dais!"

Given a choice, the Friars of 1929 would most likely choose the stock market crash over what the Friars of 1988 had to endure–the inclusion of female members. Gloria Allred, a California-based civil rights attorney, became the first female Friar in the California Friars Club. (Say, did I mention that there is a Friars Club in California? Well, there's a Friars Club in California. They started in 1947 when some of the guys like Jessel, Burns, and Benny missed the camaraderie of the New York Club and started a West Coast branch. But they do their own thing and the New York one does theirs, and everything is kept separate.) So they let Gloria become a member and when she tried to use her reciprocal dining privileges in the New York Club, all hell broke loose. She filed a complaint with the New York City Commission on Human Rights. It got real nasty. But somewhere in there, the Supreme Court told private clubs if their members wanted to retain the right to deduct their club dues on their taxes, they'd have to open their doors to women. The Friars sent a letter to the membership basically telling them that they had a choice: no women and pay higher taxes;

or allow the women in and keep their tax returns status quo. Guess what the overwhelming decision was? That's correct, money talks.

When you consider the Friars' history with women, you really can't blame them for not giving in all too readily. In the twenties the Club considered allowing women in on a "ladies' night" basis. But those stodgy studs wanted no part of it. In 1927 one of the newspapers headlined, "Friars' Vote Says Nay To Women Folk." Womenfolk? No wonder the measure never passed. But a year later, under pressure from the members' wives and girlfriends, the Club decided to reverse its decision and indeed held a Ladies' Night—on New Year's Eve of 1928. Those ladies must have had a good time because later that year the Club set aside a small room to permit women to congregate in the Monastery while they waited for the menfolk. It was in a place they called the "Boxing Room," where the telephones and mailboxes were located. The women were expected to "whiz in and out and were not to park themselves for long intervals within the Monastery precincts." The setup lasted for about a year; apparently by then the boys couldn't take any more of this whizzing. They were so rattled by these women that they rescinded their policy of letting women on the premises and just kept them to their occasional Ladies' Nights. Can you imagine? It's 1929, people are jumping out of windows left and right because they lost their life savings, and here the Friars are all in a tizzy over the ladies sequestered in the mailroom. You gotta love these guys!

Bernie Kamber will tell you about the "women-as-outcasts" days, "The old Friars Club had a little cubicle as you entered the Club. No women were allowed in the Club at any time. I remember the only time I saw Gracie Allen in those days was when she and Mary Benny would come in and they had to wait for George and Jack. They had to sit in that cubicle for about a half-hour. Women were not allowed to come in at all. Times have changed." Not overnight, Bernie, that's for sure—we're talking about Gracie Allen and Mary Livingston, for heaven's sake! That's like barring Lucille Ball! But the Club did become more liberal when they moved into their current address; the newspapers even picked up on this little item, "The structure will enable the Club to have Ladies' Nights a couple of times weekly and maybe admit femmes in the public rooms of the first two floors." You go, girls!

Still in all, Ladies' Nights and a floor or two is a far cry from seeing a woman on the Club's roster of members. But try as these guys might, the ladies room signs were hung just as the tampon holders were being unloaded off the truck. As the Friars' current president (but you can call him Dean) comedian Freddie Roman points out, "All in all that was long overdue. We're delighted to have the women here. 'Cept for about four old guys that really can't stand it. But they'll come around." And they did. Liza Minnelli became the first dues-paying female, and today the Friars could hold their own version of the dating game if they wanted to, in their very own home.

So there you have it, the official history of the New York Friars Club—with a smattering of some unofficial trivia thrown in for your reading pleasure. Sure, you get through all this and all you have to say is, "What about these dinners they keep jabbering on about?" And "What about those filthy-four-letter-strewn Roasts that everyone is dying to hear about?" Well, goddamn it, turn the fucking page!

CHAPTER 2

THE EARLY YEARS: TOASTS RULE!

*They may have worn tuxedos, but their tongues
were dipped in venom!*

TESTIMONIAL DINNERS

1907	CLYDE FITCH	1924	NELLIE REVELL
1907	VICTOR HERBERT	1925	CALVIN COOLIDGE
1908	OSCAR HAMMERSTEIN	1925	ALFRED E. SMITH
1910	WILLIAM HARRIS	1926	ARTHUR "BUGS" BAER
1912	IRVING BERLIN	1927	JIMMY WALKER
1916	ENRICO CARUSO	1929	FRED BLOCK
1918	AL JOLSON		

This is one of those times when I wish that video and audio equipment were available from, say, when the Big Bang changed the course of history (not to mention it would sort of put the kibosh on its just being theory, having all that proof). In any case, between fires, floods, fading memories, and the fact that anyone connected with the Club from 1907 to 1938 is basically dead, you'll be able to put the night-light out sooner than you expected. Well? What do you want from me? You want me to disinter these people and interrogate them? Besides, it's a proven fact that you can't believe a word these Friars say anyway, so what's the point?

For those early Friars in 1907, fraternal friendship and club camaraderie only went so far. As Channing Pollock was to note years later, "Enthusiasm began to wane and our meetings to be sparsely attended. We needed an object in life." Apparently of all of the Members at that time, Wells Hawks (who was the first Friar to bear the title Abbot) was the most desperate to get a life—I mean, find an object in life. Which may explain why he had the time to go around telling everybody, "Hey, guys? Rather than calling me president, let's call me Abbot instead. Would you mind? I'll give you a dollar?" Ego stroking aside, Hawks did have a brainstorm and his idea became the bread-and-butter of the entire organization. "Giving public dinners would fill a long-felt want and many an aching void," he reasoned. Good grief, was this man lonely or what? While the Friars loved the idea, even Pollock, fond for taking credit for original ideas, had to admit, "There were only about three hundred clubs in New York that were giving public dinners, and we all agreed that a three-hundred-and-first club was a crying necessity." As you can see, that Friar sarcasm was there from the start.

Unlike their famous Frolics, the Dinners were lavish, black-tie affairs that served to honor a particular individual. Sarry Saranoff, our nosy Friar who had the wherewithal to jot things down as they occurred, said, "The dinners were tendered to outstanding theatrical personalities. By virtue of the names honored and those who were eager to pay homage, each of these affairs attracted the crème de la crème of gay New York"—good heavens, that's all these ol' boys needed. They have always included a dinner and a show. Oh, you gotta have a show. It's almost as if Mickey Rooney and Judy Garland were the Friars' first event producers, shouting, "Let's put on a show!" at every board meeting.

The premier Friars Club Dinner was held at the Café des Beaux Arts which, according to Sarry, was "one of the most fashionable dining salons of its era." The event was to honor a man who holds a very special place in all Friars' hearts: Clyde Fitch. That would be *the* Clyde Fitch. Clyde to his friends. Mr. Fitch to his paperboy. Clyde the Crybaby to his fellow third graders. Fitch the Snitch to the boys he played stickball with. Okay, admittedly the jig is up here because even the Friars of today have no idea who the hell Clyde Fitch was. So maybe the bit about the special place in Friars' hearts was a big fat lie, but that doesn't negate his exclusive position in the Club's history. If you ask Berle, Clyde was a "brilliant actor." Which he may have been. Then again, if you ask the Friars, Berle is a "brilliant bull-shitter," and they love him all the more for that. In this instance, however, Clyde Fitch was a renowned playwright who died in 1909. (Maybe he never recovered from the kasha varnishka they served at the Dinner.)

In any case, the Friars realized they had a winner on their hands, so says Pollock, "Our first dinner was a great success. For some reason the dinner was different"—sure, it was free for the guest of honor and the performers. "There was a freedom, a wit, and a comradeship uncommon in public dinners. The next day this feast was town talk." And today, almost a hundred years later, the feast is six feet under along with the rest of the participants—providing they haven't been dug up to make room for larger quarters for New York City's town hall.

Still in all, Pollock in his philosophical way (or like any good Friar, in his egotistical way) noted in 1917, "The dinners were widely discussed and we have kept on giving them. We shall keep on as long as guests of honor hold out. Just now the stock is getting low! There are not more than a dozen celebrities within traveling distance of New York who have not been dined by the Friars. And they all have enjoyed it." Luckily the art of procreation has been so perfected that the well of guests of honor will never run dry. Who knows? In another half century or so Madonna's kid Lourdes might be chowing down on tarragon chicken and profiteroles, listening to Kathie Lee's Cody serenade her. Just a topical thought.

Now quit bitching about having to once again read quotes from people you never heard of, with phrases that haven't been used since prandial was popular. See? Thanks to the Friars, you know what that means now, don't you? Put your fears aside; we'll be in the thick of funny modern things before you can say Georgie Jessel . . . a thousand times.

Most of the people they honored in those early years have long been forgotten, as have most of the records about those events—lucky you. But a few snippets of information managed to survive amidst the moth balls, musty boxes, and matted hairpieces. Take, for instance, the Dinner held in 1907 for popular composer and conductor Victor Herbert. We'll ignore the fact that the program for the event reads "Supper." You would think an aristocrat like Herbert would at least have the more sophisticated "Dinner" stamped on his souvenir journal cover as opposed to something Ma Kettle would whip up for Pa and

Al Jolson Testimonial Dinner Program cover, 1918—this is as PC as they get folks.

Nellie Revell Testimonial Dinner Program cover, 1924—look ma, a girl!

Jimmy Walker Testimonial Dinner Program cover, 1927—the "good times" rolled.

the kids. (That's probably not really fair. For that time period, "Supper" referred to late meals, which the Friars loved to have. Sometimes these events didn't begin until 11:00 P.M., after their theater gigs—but when you hang around with Friars long enough, you can't help but be a wiseass every other minute or so.)

It was a momentous Dinner/Supper for the Friars Club. Apparently Mr. Herbert, in spite of his celebrity status, was petrified at the thought of speaking before an audience of his peers and admirers. Something he would be called upon to do at the end of the evening—after all, it wouldn't kill him to say something nice to everybody who shelled out big bucks to be there. Herbert's fear, however, was that he would start stuttering, as was his affliction in such situations. These things run long enough as it is; throw a stutterer into the proceedings, and that's all these people would need. If he wasn't careful they would end up forming a mass exodus to the Lambs Club's dinner up the block. Charles Emerson Cook came up with a solution though—when you can't speak it, sing it.

Cook wrote words and Herbert added the music to what became the Friars own song, *Here's to the Friars*. When the moment of truth came and Herbert rose from his place on the dais, he turned his back on the audience, to the bewilderment of everyone in the room, and faced the stage located directly behind the dais. If they didn't choose Friars Club as the name, perhaps they should have considered Drama Club because nothing was done without flaunting and embellishing and using larger-than-life actions. With his back turned, the curtains parted and revealed the male chorus from Herbert's Broadway hit at the time. He raised his glass and managed to sputter, "Ladies and gentlemen, this is my Toast to the Friars!" Suddenly the orchestra broke out into a cacophony of music as the chorus, dressed in monks' robes, began to sing:

Here's to the Friars, here's to them all:
Out on the road, or here in the hall.
Raise high your glasses with cheers that inspires:
    And drink a deep toast
    To the boys we love most:
A toast to all other good Friars

And on, and on, and on, and on, and on it goes. It's a wonderful tribute, but ask any Friar today and he or she will have no idea what the heck you're talking about. The song still exists and continues to be played at events on occasion, although the campiness of Friars donning monks' robes and serenading audiences (or, more to the point, unnerving them) petered out between the Johnson administration and Nixon's resignation. In spite of the fact that it is still being printed in several of the publications available to the Friars' membership, the song remains a baffling phenomenon among each and every one of them. No one ever remembers the words and the tune is a cross between a dirge and an even slower dirge. It's no *Mack the Knife* that's for sure. But, it was a brilliant way for Herbert to thank everyone for the great honor he had just received. Makes you wonder if Cindy Brady were ever toasted by the Friars, would she come up with a cute song that she could sing without lisping?

For musical genius Oscar Hammerstein's Dinner in 1908 the Friars outdid themselves. Held at the Hotel Astor, the Friars staged a burlesque grand opera with a full chorus and orchestra. The opera was called *Burning To Sing Or Singing To Burn, A "Very" Grand Opera In One Act.* The title is probably as long as some of the arias, but for the Friars of 1908 even their music was tongue-in-cheek. Take for instance the fact that the part of Madame Margurita Tremolini was played by their fellow Friar Neal McCay—enough said. There was also another treat in store for Oscar: Charles Emerson Cook whipped up yet another specially written song, just for him:

> There was a man in our big town
>   And he was wondrous wise.
> He put it over, right along,
>   All would-be wiser guys
> He worked all day; he worked all night;
> He never stopped to take a bite
> Until the Friars got him right;
>   So fill your glass, and rise to
>   HAMMERSTEIN!

(Shout) O, you Oscar!
HAMMERSTEIN!
How we love to have you with us!
HAMMERSTEIN!
If the question's rude, forgive us–
Say!
But *where* did you get that hat,
HAMMERSTEIN!

Let's hope that at some point in Mr. Cook's long and loquacious career, someone took away his pen and piano. With lyrics like, "But where did you get that hat?" you can see why the only dinner they threw his way was the pity-party bash when they demoted him from his post as Abbot while presenting him with a silver loving cup.

It's interesting how the entertainment of these early Dinners was supplied mostly through music. When they weren't performing serious songs they were presenting parodies in song. But don't think that these affairs were without their stinging jokes. On the contrary—they skipped the training-wheel portion and moved right into the Harley phase of Roasting. Even at this point the Friars were being hailed as the bad boys of the industry. "FRIARS KID MR. HARRIS: Veteran Theatrical Manager Butt of Jokes at Dinner," hailed the December 10, 1910 issue of the *New York Tribune* the day after William Harris was eviscerated at the hands of his fellow Friars. If you're under the illusion that dishonoring a guest of honor at a black-tie event is a sign of today's unorthodox times, guess again. The New York Friars have always had their own set of rules when it comes to tributes, and apparently no man or woman was ever safe from their tart-tongued performers.

One speaker at the Harris dinner said, "His record speaks for itself and, personally, I wish it had the lockjaw." This is a mild mouthful by today's unbridled standards, but when one thinks that this was said in an era of high-hats and spats, it becomes headline news. Today, of course, the remarks go something like what Steve Martin asked to have read at the Chevy Chase Roast in 1990: "Marty [Short] and I were in the dressing room with Chevy and we saw this thing. This soggy twig was only good for mixing drinks and we felt we could legitimately drop the soap and not worry." Mr. Harris and his entire dais are collectively turning in their graves.

The *Tribune* also observed of the Harris Dinner, "When a man subjects himself to being honored at the hands of the Friars he needs a steel corselet to repel the jabs of his kidders." Whatever the hell a steel corselet is, the fact remains that the Friars, all through the years, have never held back when the promise of a good laugh, albeit at someone else's expense, was at hand.

But back to the music. Along with all the musical tributes, it's interesting that many of those early guests of honor were in the music biz. Herbert, Hammerstein, Enrico Caruso, and Irving Berlin were all given the Friars' highest shout-out. At Berlin's Dinner, George M. Cohan said, "Irvy writes a great song. He writes a song with a good lyric, a lyric that rhymes; good music, music you don't have to dress up to listen to, but it is good music. He is a wonderful little fellow, wonderful in lots of ways. He has become famous and wealthy, without wearing a lot of jewelry and falling for funny clothes. He is uptown, but he is there with the old downtown hard shell. And with all his success, you will find his watch and his handkerchief in his pockets where they belong." Huh? Okay, so I could have left it at "Irvy writes a great song," but when you come across an entire spiel from George M. Cohan, from 1912, on a topic that you're writing about, you're gonna use the whole damn thing whether it makes any sense or not. Besides, I'll lay you ten-to-one that George made the speech at some point *after* cocktails had been served, so we have to cut him some slack.

As for Irving's own spiel, he wrote a song, of course—Victor Herbert, if you're listening, "Do you see what you started?" Berlin also panicked when the thought of making an acceptance speech entered into things. What's with all these famous performers? Are they all Friarphobic? (That's the fear of speaking in front of a group of Friars, as opposed to the more common Fryerphobic, which is a fear of deep-frying fish in front of Martha Stewart.) Irving's song is much more hummable than

Victor's was, and certainly far less confusing than Oscar's: "Friar Abbot, Brother Friars, ladies and gents / Don't expect too much of me / I'm confined to melody / And further more, I must confess / I don't know just how to express / The depths of my appreciation just why you honor me, in vain I try to figure out / I don't know what it's all about." Irving weaves a tale of imploring another Friar for help, who had written for other honorees, "The speech he wrote was like the *Morning Telegraph* / It didn't have a laugh / The jokes he wrote were all so solemn." Then he got carried away with his iambic pentameter, "The minute that I begin ragtiming / I've got to keep on rhyming / My rhymes if there are any / Are not so very many / You bet I'd keep on going / If I could rhyme like Cohen / But now I must be stopping / Before my speech starts flopping." Smart move, Irv.

Needless to say, for Al Jolson's do in 1918 the program is a veritable racial assault—by today's standards, at least, but certainly not for their time. Along with actual photos of Al in blackface, cartoonist Ryan Walker sketched his little heart out, filling the pages with various displays of blackfaced characters. The guests who attended the event pored over the menu of "Velouté of Chicken, Reine Margot and Supreme of Bass Sauté Chevreuse" amidst a backdrop of a Jolson caricature and several of those tiny cartoons. Across the page read, "With many a merry quip and a jest, and song to cheer, an entertainment arranged by Friar Jack Mason. To be followed by dancing." You just know what the entertainment Mr. Mason arranged included. Did they mean any harm? To be sure, they did not. So let's give their 1918 sensibilities a break, and not mention blackfaced Friars again. I haven't gotten to Ted Danson yet, have I? Well, then maybe we will touch upon this sticky wicket again.

Hold on to your bonnets everybody, because 1924 became the year of the woman for the Friars (for now, put 1988 out of your head). Whatever got into them remains a mystery, or maybe the Wizard of Oz gave them all hearts—who knows? But the fact is that on May 25, they gave a Testimonial Dinner for Nellie Revell at the Hotel Astor. Lordy! Had they gone mad! Both men and women attended the event to honor this very special lady. Nellie was a reporter and vaudeville publicist who had overcome a serious illness, much to the relief of her friends at the Friars Club. It was a "serious affair," so you can assume that all of those penis jokes that usually flew around the room at these dinners were kept for the men's room breaks in between the "Petite Marmite with Noodles and the Braised Sweetbread a la Chevreuse." Or, more to the point, it could have been after the "Silver King Mineral Water, Canada Dry Ginger Ale, Red Wine and Brew."

But the evening couldn't have been that serious, seeing as practical jokester Eddie Cantor presided over the show as the Master of Ceremonies. The program featured the likes of Olga Cook and Eric Zardo; Avon Comedy Four; the Pasqualis Brothers; Beth Beri; and Baby Sylvia Froos. Shall I repeat those for you, in case you actually do know who any of them were? Or we can move along to an act that should have a familiar ring, "The Four Marx Brothers." Just don't ask if the fourth brother was Gummo or Zeppo, okay-o?

With comedian William Collier as the evening's Toastmaster and the likes of Edward Albee and Will Rogers billed as "Speaker," it's a good guess that the evening, while a serious milestone for the Friars, was anything but a sullen affair. Unless of course they kept singing "Here's to the Friars" every so often to wipe the laugh lines off the audience's faces. If that didn't do the trick, George M. Cohan's touching tribute that was printed in the program very well may have:

> The Friars are assembled here tonight to pay their respects to Nellie Revell, one of the gamest little women in the whole wide world.
>
> The Dinner we are giving Nellie is a small token of the love and affection in which she is held and to celebrate her victory over a five year hospital sentence, through which she passed with a smile in her heart and a laugh on her lips.
>
> Nellie Revell has been tried as but few of us have: Faith, fortitude and sense of humor are the attributes that won the battle and her example should be a lesson to all of us who are prone to worry over the trifles of life, when after all, the only thing that really matters, is the blessing of good heath.
>
> Nellie Revell, we salute you!

Wow! How awesome must this woman have been, to rate such kudos from Georgie boy and, more importantly, to rate a Dinner from the Friars. Let's hope they didn't make her eat her Buche Glacee Fraisette while seated in the vestibule. (And where on God's green earth did they find these foods?) To think that it only took them another seventy-three years before inviting Joy Behar to act as the Roastmaster for the Danny Aiello Roast in 1997—now, that's progress (or maybe Joy is just pushy).

Either their seemingly endless glut of entertainment personalities began to wane, or they discovered what many knew all along—that entertainers can be such bores sometimes. Regardless, in 1925 the Friars moved on to politicians. (Did I say they discovered actors were boors? These guys never learn.) That year they held a Dinner for Alfred E. Smith, the governor of New York. If the newspaper account is accurate, the governor was afforded the respect due any politician in the presence of Friars, "He was introduced by William Collier, Dean of the Friars, with these words: 'It is the Friars' great good fortune to meet here tonight, to do honor to possibly the greatest name and the greatest figure in the United States, the Honorable Governor, Alfred E. ———' Here Mr. Collier hesitated, looked blank, reached into his pocket, drew forth a paper and read: '———Smith.'"

The political-banner year of 1925 for the Friars continued with a Dinner in honor of President Calvin Coolidge. Let's face it, once you've gotten the go-ahead to throw a Dinner for *the* man, you've made it. Yet, ask if they've got any information about the event and they'll tell you, "No." Here's a group of guys who can keep records on how their Club was formed almost a century ago, know that they once had their own brand of cigarettes and can tell you how many billiards tables they had in a place they haven't owned in over sixty years, but ask them for information and memorabilia from a Dinner honoring the thirtieth President of the United States and they just shrug and say, "No idea. But did you hear the one about the First Lady and the congressional page?" In their defense, though, Coolidge was known for being a man of few words and high moral standards—the Friars probably figured if the guy's not funny then it's not worth remembering him.

We'll get back to the politicians in a bit, but first you have to hear about the Arthur "Bugs" Baer Dinner in 1926. Oh, hush! Before you start flipping pages because you think you're going to have to read more geeky songs by Irving Berlin or outdated quotes from unknowns—which, by the way, brings up a very interesting point. The Friars had all these honchos running things in the early part of the 1900s who are revered by today's members as their forebears; meanwhile, even in 1907 the general public probably never heard of Channing Pollock or Charles Emerson Cook. Just a thought—but stick Bugs' Dinner out because it's sorta funny/interesting.

Bugs Baer was a journalist/cartoonist who was known for his puns. Just to get you more intimate with the man, here's a sampling:

> A good neighbor is a fellow who smiles at you over the back fence, but doesn't climb over it.
> It was so quiet, you could hear a pun drop.
> A newspaper is a circulating library with high blood pressure.
> It is impossible to tell where the law stops and justice begins.
> If you do big things they print your face, and if you do little things they only print your thumbs.

Well that's what they say—he was known for his witty puns—so don't shoot the messenger.

Bugs also took his wit to the vaudeville stages, and this particular night he was running late because he was making an appearance. The Dinner was held in the Great Hall of the Club's 48th Street Monastery, which was enormous and included a stage for such events. Jimmy Durante was on the dais that evening, and since there was some resemblance between the two men, he jumped into the Guest of Honor's seat. Can you imagine going through life resembling Jimmy Durante? That's a lifelong Roast in itself. Surprisingly enough, most of the audience fell for it, which probably was not his intent—what good is a joke if it's not followed by a laugh. When Bugs finally arrived, the Toasters, who by 1926 were already well on their way to being Roasters, worked their saucy magic on the crowd of five hundred. One newspaper account noted that Bugs was "panned to a frazzle." When is the last time you heard that happen? If you have heard it then either you're a hundred and ten, in which case you're eligible for a free Friars lifetime membership, or you are really into these old Friars tales, which is even more frightening.

Speaking of free lifetime memberships—this has nothing to do with Bugs, by the way, I just thought it was time for a tidbit—the Friars can be very funny without even trying. They offered jazz great Eubie Blake an honorary lifetime membership when he turned ninety-five years old in 1978. It was sort of their little joke, except the joke was on them because Eubie lived to be a hundred. So they had to give Eubie a free ride each and every time he used the Club. Just when you think they would learn their lesson about these tough old dinosaurs, they go and offer ventriloquist Señor Wences the same deal when he turned one hundred. Cut to two years later: they were still covering his meals.

All right—back to Bugs: Many of the speakers had a field day with his war record, but Bugs himself had the last laugh on that subject, "I once received a citation for the 'Bugs Baer Salute.' I was the only private who ever saluted an officer with his hands in his pockets."

At some point during the evening a couple of uninvited guests entered the proceedings. Two cops arrived and escorted Jimmy Durante off the dais. It seems Mr. Durante, who was co-owner of a speakeasy called Club Dover, was in a little hot water with the law—or, more to the point, with the liquor law. An article in *Variety* that covered the story about Bugs' Dinner mentioned Durante's run-in, but interestingly enough made a point of omitting Club Dover's location, writing, "address intentionally deleted." They probably figured that most of the show business types who read *Variety*, and who were at this Dinner frequented Jimmy's joint anyway and protection was needed all around. While the cops were picking up Durante, they should have looked around for that Friars "bartender" who would be suing the Club for back pay in a few years.

Now about those politicians. The Friars held a Dinner for Jimmy Walker—no, not J.J. from the TV show *Good Times,* who made "Dy-no-mite" the catchphrase of the seventies. This Jimmy was mayor of New York City in 1927. He was also a bit of a character—a former songwriter who penned "Will You Love Me In December As You Do In May," and one of the more quick-witted mayors of the Big Apple: "A reformer is a guy who rides through the sewer in a glass-bottom boat." Who cares what the hell it means; you can just bet that J.J. couldn't have come up with it. Jack Lait wrote a poem for the proceedings, adding yet another notch to their belt of ethnic irreverence:

> From the wigwam of the lowly sprang a youth name Jimmawalka
> Handsomest of all the tribesmen, eloquent at feast and pow-wow
> Brave and dashing and a great scout, with a twinkle in his bright
> eyes
> With a chuckle in his laughter
>
> But the tribe of Brothafriars, wildest of Times Square hard riders
> Fierce and deadly, famous scalpers, kibitzers and big-time layoffs
> Known to pass the Squaw of Spades on and to deal out other
> poisons
> In their weird and mystic tepee—
>
> Thirsty for the blood of someone, these same savage Brothafriars
> Hurled a wardance at the Astor and invited Jimmawalka
> Making him the guest of honor, craftily the meanwhile plotting
> There to gently tomahawk him

There's more—much, much more, but you get the idea without needing the rest, which includes headpiece feathers and peace pipes. Say what you will about the Friars, but don't say they're not equal opportunity slanderers. Walker was such the actor's friend that it's rumored they even taught him how to use his left hand to take his handkerchief out of his left breast pocket. Just another useful trick of the trade by Friars who had a little too much time on their hands.

The mayor also happened to be on the dais of the Bugs Baer

Dinner when Jimmy Durante was carted off. I mention this only because Walker was so against prohibition that he once opined, "This measure was born in hypocrisy and there it will die." That being said, he most likely headed off to Club Dover for a nightcap. History does love to repeat itself, though. Not exactly the same situation, but when the shoe polish hit the fan at the Whoopi Goldberg Roast in 1993, former New York City Mayor David Dinkins was seated on the dais, enjoying the proceedings, proving that mayors and other politicians have always loved joining the Friars along their merry nonconformist way. And the Friars love a politician with a good sense of humor, so it makes for a nice marriage.

Vaudevillian Fred Block was asked by Friar S. Jay Kaufman, chairman of the Friars "Arrangement Committee," if he would like to be the guest of honor at a Dinner in 1929. If you think about it, the boys had been honing certain skewer-like skills for two decades, so trepidation seemed to be the best way to accept such requests. Fred wrote the following:

My Dear Jay,

I received your wire telling me the Club wants to give me a dinner on the 17th of March, and I tried to reach you at the studio, but they said you left word not to call you from the set while you were working.

I really don't see—on the level—why I should be given a dinner—unless it's because you want a Patsy to kid. If that's it, go ahead; but let me warn you, I have a lot of knockers. I am one of the original Friars, and I've made them knock because I am almost—not quite—as erratic and high strung as you, but I'm like you in another way—we both love the old Club, & we don't care much about how they Roast us, so long as there is something doing in the Club. The Miami trip wore me down, but anytime anything can help bring the bacon in laughs into my club, I'll take the slap. So thanks to you, even though it is kidding—because I know that through your kidding & your temperament you have the spirit of the Friars.

Your Pal,
Fred

P.S. Can it be arranged so I don't have to speak?

Again with the Friarphobia! Don't you just feel another song coming on? This seems to be the first unofficial, official use of the term "Roast" in the Friars lexicon—a word that would eventually become synonymous with the Friars. But for now it's just a zygote—wait until it grows up. (Oh, and don't think the word "knockers" escaped my smart-ass eyes.)

While anyone would be intimidated to accept honors from the Friars, most of the celebrities and personalities eventually managed to put their fears aside and just let things happen. Mr. Block's dinner arrived, much to his delight, with just the right amount of jokes plus the perfect blend of music thrown in. Bugs Baer, Eddie Cantor, George Jessel, and Bert Lahr were among the performers. Also on the roster was comedian Harry Hershfield. What is so amazing about Mr. Hershfield's appearance is the fact that almost fifty years later he would still be performing at a Friars Club Dinner, when they honored Carol Burnett in 1973. It must be something in the water at the Monastery that keeps these guys going—or maybe it's just the gin.

Another interesting point about Fred's soiree was that it was broadcast over the radio, courtesy of WMCA. Donald Flamm, a Friar and president of the station, cooked up the idea and it proved to be a huge sensation for the listeners at home. It was the first time that civilians were privy to the usually exclusive shenanigans of the Friars. They would dabble with the broadcast idea on and off throughout the years, and to this day the internal struggle still wages as to the pros and cons of letting the laughter out and the public in.

With the depression and a mass entertainment exodus west, the Friars were entering a new era and it wasn't a terribly pleasant one. They spent more time trying to fend off creditors than scarf down lobster thermidor at fancy banquets. Between financial straits, legal hassles, and a lot of really cranky people contemplating suicide, there wasn't a whole lot to celebrate in a tuxedo. Their events were pretty much contained to a few Frolics that earned them enough money to . . . well, let's see, they lost their building, they lost their members, they lost their credibility . . . what exactly did they do with that money? Maybe they bought bonds. In any case, they must have done something right because they emerged from their rock-bottom skid row status to become bigger, better, bolder, and downright nastier than before—that's nasty, as in brutally funny. If you're ready to face the new and improved Friars, then turn the page—but I warn you, it's at your own risk. There's no room for sweet and sappy within these pages; well, there may be a teary tidbit or two just to show their human side. But for the most part, when it comes to brutal honesty, the Friars have elevated it to an art form. They sprinkle it with unadulterated sarcasm, litter it with venom, then bite it off with wit. They didn't just write the book on Roasting, they carved it into the egos of anybody they deemed worthy to sit in their revered hot seat. The early years you just read about merely served to open the musty doors to the Friars' quirky beginnings. If you want to witness those doors blown off their hinges, then move along. There are many more funnier feasts ahead.

CHAPTER 3

1950s THROUGH THE 1970s:
LET THE ROASTS BEGIN &
THE CHEERS CONTINUE!

*You've heard the laughter from behind closed doors—
now take a look through the peephole!*

CELEBRITY ROASTS		TESTIMONIAL DINNERS	
1949	MAURICE CHEVALIER	1958	MIKE TODD
1953	SOPHIE TUCKER	1960	DINAH SHORE
1955	HUMPHREY BOGART	1962	JOE E. LEWIS
1959	JIMMY CANNON	1965	JOHNNY CARSON
1959	MILTON BERLE	1969	BARBRA STREISAND
1960	GEORGE BURNS	1973	CAROL BURNETT
1961	ALAN KING	1976	FRANK SINATRA
1968	DON RICKLES	1978	DAVID BRINKLEY
1976	JOEY ADAMS		WALTER CRONKITE
1978	NEIL SIMON		HOWARD K. SMITH
1979	NORM CROSBY		

*All the playwright is required to do is throw an occasional hump into
the leading lady. You don't have to marry all of them, you schmuck!*
—MILTON BERLE, at the Neil Simon Roast, 1978

*Carol is obviously a woman. She's soft, white, tender, delicate . . . but
so is Wayne Newton.*
—HARVEY KORMAN, at the Carol Burnett Testimonial Dinner, 1973

After a nice long sleep, the Friars emerged, not only ready to
take on show business, but to reinvent it. The first celebrated
event to put them back on track was a luncheon for Maurice
Chevalier in 1949. (1949? You ask. Oh aren't you the smart one.
True, it wasn't really in the '50s, but I wasn't going to put the
'40s in the chapter title just for one friggin' year.) This was no
ordinary lunch, my friends. This was pure gold, this was an offi-

cial Stag Roast—okay, so it was pure golden brown. With all of their troubles behind them, the Friars literally jumped from the frying pan into the fire—and it was hot enough to roast an ego. For years the Friars could not help noticing that they were crossing certain lines at their highfalutin Dinners; the demand for more risqué opportunities supplied the need for a whole new ball game. They changed the hour to lunch, they changed the tone to bawdy, and they changed the course of entertainment history beyond belief.

For the traditionalists out there don't panic, the Roast didn't affect the Friars' legendary Dinners at all. If anything, it helped loosen them up a bit. And, with no disrespect toward those original Friars and all their goofy songs, this new era shook the cobwebs out of their goddamn top hats. Okay, so maybe a little disrespect won't kill a skeleton.

MAURICE CHEVALIER ROAST – 1949

(Why serve Welsh rarebit when you can have New Jersey tongue?)

MILTON BERLE, *Roastmaster*
BUDDY ARNOLD
GEORGE JESSEL
ALAN KING
SAM LEVENSON
PHIL SILVERS
Probably a whole lot more, but this is what you get for now

Chevalier, that fancy Frenchman with the suave accent, had yet to star in his famous film, *Gigi*, but he already had a career made for Roasting. He started as a circus acrobat, then turned to acting after being injured. He was captured by the Germans during World War I and, after the war, became a huge hit in Hollywood. Jerry Lewis would kill to have this guy's vocal cords. When Chevalier's career fizzled in the '30s he hightailed it back to France and was accused of collaborating with the Nazis after he entertained the occupying German troops during

World War II. He had the perfect mix of ingredients for a Roast: a suave and debonair countenance worthy of a little bruising; a juicy personal life that would sizzle when prodded; a sporadic and often maligned career that could easily be singed. In other words, as succulent a feast for wits that befits the status of the Friars Club's first Roast.

The affair, from the start, was very different from the Friars' formal dinners. Where the Dinners massaged the ego of the guest of honor, the Roast pummeled it. If the Dinners applauded the accomplishments of the guest of honor, the Roast mocked them. The Dinners had music, the Roast rapped. Sometimes the Dinners allowed women in; not only was that out of the question at a Roast, but the waiters were even ordered off the floor. Comparing the grace, elegance, and sophistication of the Dinners to a Roast is truly a lesson in futility. With the Chevalier Roast, "class" was stricken from the Friars' vocabulary. "What do you think I had sent over from the deli, put in a champagne bucket?" asks Berle in that mischievous way of his. "A tongue! And when Chevalier got up and I introduced him as the guest of honor—of course we put him down terribly, talking about licking and all of that—we didn't give him an award. We brought out this big tongue. 'This is your award!' It was uncut." Talk about speechless!

Alan King, who today is the patriarch of the Friars, was just barely out of knickers at this event. "The first time I was asked to be on a Roast was Maurice Chevalier's. Jessel was there. Sam Levenson had just come on to the scene; he was a schoolteacher who became a big-time comedian. And, of course, Chevalier, a Frenchman, so everything was about sucking, sucking, sucking. They had a dais and in front of every speaker they had a beef tongue, a butcher's beef tongue, on a hook." A slightly different version from Berle's but you try remembering things from a half-century ago and see how your tales compare; just enjoy the read. "So here I am, my first time," says King. "I had a few remarks, but you know they never put the lightweights—the new guys—on until the end. Everyone had a pencil in front of them, and I made notes. It was the first time, I think, I made a list of all the words that were not used. All the dirty words. And I did three, four minutes on it." To hear their conversations around the Monastery, it's amazing King was able to come up with any words at all that hadn't already been used.

There isn't much more to tell about this milestone event in the Friars' history—although Berle did have everyone wear straw hats, which was Chevalier's signature chapeau—but even what little we know is proof that they accomplished their mission to make mincemeat out of Chevalier's self-esteem. As for the tongue, let your own dirty little mind figure out the symbolism on that one.

SOPHIE TUCKER ROAST – 1953

(She is woman, hear her roar!)

MILTON BERLE, *Roastmaster*	FRANK GALLOP
JESSE BLOCK	GEORGE JESSEL
RED BUTTONS	AL KELLY
JACK CARTER	JACK E. LEONARD
MYRON COHEN	TED SHAPIRO
CHARLIE DALE	JOE SMITH
BENNY FIELDS	FRANK SINATRA
ALAN GALE	HENNY YOUNGMAN

You're not seeing things. The Friars once again broke with tradition and honored a woman. Sophie Tucker was the first female to be Roasted by the boys and seeing as she was practically one of them herself, she seemed the best choice to break the gender barrier. While Sophie probably never spent any real quality time in the Monastery, she had participated in several events and joined in their Frolics antics enough to earn her an Honorary Friar status. However, her ex-husband, Al Lackey, enjoyed more fruits of her Friardom than she did, as a frequent visitor to the card room.

By 1953, Tucker was known as "the last of the red-hot mamas," and her career was not only worthy of her being a Friar but was filled with enough quirky fodder to fill several Roasts. She began as a singer, but when she first started out burlesque theater managers made her wear blackface because she was "so big and ugly." And this is by her account! (Was it a requirement that every Friar had to have performed in black-face?) When she finally ditched the grease paint—only because she found herself without her makeup and luggage one night— the audiences still loved her brash humor and silly songs, "I Don't Want to Be Thin; Nobody Loves a Fat Girl, But Oh How a Fat Girl Can Love"; and her signature, "Some of These Days."

Seeing as Sophie was nearing seventy, the guys took it a little easier on the lady than was their normal practice. Although judging by her comment afterward, it's hard to imagine what they considered "holding back" to be: "It's nice to hear to my face what you've been saying for almost fifty years behind my back." She wore a purple bird of paradise hat with feathers that measured almost two feet high, which the guys had a field day with, especially Roastmaster Milton Berle, who kept referring to it as a "Berle of paradise." Ted Shapiro, Tucker's pianist for thirty-three years, deadpanned about his career with her, "It was all a waste of time. All I got to show for it is a home, a car, ownership in a restaurant and bar, and eight oil wells. You can call her Soph or Sophie, but to me she's my boss. I call her Miss Tucker."

Vaudevillians Joe Smith and Charlie Dale, who were celebrating their fifty-fifth anniversary in theater, did a routine about two angels in heaven discussing showbiz and Sophie. George Jessel pretended to be a movie producer who apparently wasn't too keen on his "star." And comedian Al Kelly, in a scripted parody, played the lawyer who handled Sophie's first divorce; her three ex-husbands were represented Roastingly. Myron Cohen read an excerpt from the Talmud. Is that a funny book?

Berle wrote a parody of the song M-O-T-H-E-R. You know that song: "M is for the many things she, whatever; O is for the only person who, something, something; put them all together they spell MO . . ." well you get the idea. Only Berle's song was appropriately titled, S-O-P-H-I-E. He had Frank Sinatra sing the song, which Sophie just adored—at first:

> S is for the sweetness that's within her,
> O is for the others she loved so much,
> P is for the people that adore her,
> H is for her honesty and touch,
> I is for those that idolize her,

The E is for the endless curtain calls,
Put them all together they spell Sophie,
The only Friar without balls (and we're not certain),
The only Friar without balls.

Throughout the song, Sophie stared lovingly at Sinatra. As Berle pointed out, "She was appreciating that someone she admired finally had gotten up and said something nice about her, without a put-down. I heard her utter, 'God bless Frank.'" When he got to the punch line she let out a big scream, slapped Sinatra on the back, and said, "I knew there would be a switch in there somewhere, you son of a bitch!"

Looking around the room of almost four hundred men, as Tucker made her speech, she said, "It's the first time in my life I've ever been in a room with so many men. The hell of it is, it comes too late." She also managed to get in a jab at one of her ex-husbands, "I've contributed plenty to the Friars. I see it in the endorsements on my alimony checks I send to Lackey. There were lots of things he could do, but card playing wasn't one of them." Roast or no Roast, the very special guest of honor was visibly moved by the accolades, in spite of their left-handed delivery, saying, "No one should delude himself into thinking he alone is responsible for his success; it is God who runs the big booking office upstairs." And Berle who seems to run it downstairs.

HUMPHREY BOGART ROAST—1955

(Here's pokin' fun at you, kid!)

RED BUTTONS, *Roastmaster*	ROCKY GRAZIANO
LAUREN BACALL *(sort of)*	LOU HOLTZ
GENE BAYLOS	ALAN KING
PADDY CHAYEFSKY	JOE E. LEWIS
MAURICE CHEVALIER	JAN MURRAY
CHARLES COBURN	BARNEY ROSS
HARRY DELF	SOLLY VIOLINSKY
JACK DEMPSEY	ED WEINER
JOE DIMAGGIO	EARL WILSON
BENNY FIELDS	

"Everybody down!" ordered Humphrey Bogart after receiving a standing ovation as he was escorted onto the dais at New York's Hotel Delmonico for his infamous Roast. "Barney, you cover that door over there. Jack, you cover the ladies' room, we don't want no broads gettin' in here." Sounds like one of his movies. The joke is, the guest of honor doesn't speak until the end of the event—but would you tell Bogey to sit down and shut up? Of all of the Friars' Roasts, this one has become the definitive one, thanks to pop-culture buffs. Or, more realistically, thanks to the person who sneaked in a tape recorder and sold bootleg copies of it. It's only fitting, though, that yet another milestone in the Friars' sordid past was the result of unsavory antics.

Writer Ed Weiner was the Friars' historian at the time and he read a few telegrams for Bogart, although you be the judge of just how legitimate they were: from Clark Gable: "Congratulations on your comeback. We thought you were too old to come again." From Bob Hope: "Fuck you and the seven little Foys." From Liberace: "Congratulations and continued suc . . ." The beauty of the Friars, then and now, is that they never really let you in on if something is a joke or not. Rumor has it the phrase "poker face" was first uttered in the Friars Club's card room. (You'll never know if that's true or not, now will you?) Weiner did, however, make Friars' history when he announced, "We hope that Humphrey will keep in mind something the late Damon Runyon once wrote, 'When we rip a friend, we do it with the deepest of our affection.'" That catchphrase, or variations on that theme, has been handed down as a soothing salve to all Roast honorees. And the assholes actually buy into it, thinking it's a really sweet thought.

Red Buttons was Roastmaster, whom Weiner introduced as "The find of 1954 who got lost in '55." Don't let his size fool you; this little guy had no fears leveling with the man who made a killing playing mobsters and murderers. "I've seen you in all your pictures, Mr. Bogart. One picture in particular I remember, I loved you in that. Do you remember? It was that picture in the South Pacific where you hit the beachhead and you got off that LST and you were climbing, and you went under the barbed wire, and you had the revolver in your hand going all

Sophie Tucker wishes she were anywhere but listening to Frank Sinatra tell everyone that she has balls.

Humphrey Bogart's 1955 Roast with Joe E. Lewis, Phil Silvers, Red Buttons, Bogey, and Bacall—and of course, the cuff links— play the bootleg tape again, Sam.

Neil Simon is thinking, "I wonder if Milton Berle knows I'm relieving myself right now."

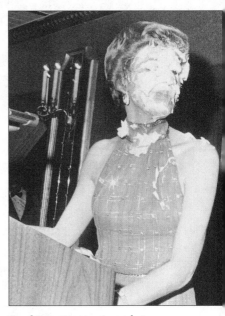

Carol Burnett gets pie-eyed at her Dinner in 1973.

Heere's Johnny Carson and Ed McMahon!

Left: Red Buttons and Jack E. Leonard in the usual Friars event pose—cracking up!

Below: Ed Sullivan, Barbra Streisand and Don Rickles can't wait for the cameras to leave so they can get some brewskies.

Milton Berle, Howard Cosell, and George Jessel about to sing "We May Never Pass This Way Again."

Boys will be boys: (*Top row*) Joey Adams, Eddie Fisher, Red Buttons (*Middle row*) Gene Baylos, George Raft, Joe E. Lewis, Sam Levenson, Morey Amsterdam, Henny Youngman (*Front row*) Sid Caesar, Milton Berle, Jan Murray.

Buddy Hackett tells Johnny Carson the one about the guy peeing on the dais.

William S. Paley, George Jessel, George Burns, Jack Benny, Fred Allen, and Adlai Stevenson create some Friar magic.

Ed Sullivan and Joe E. Lewis—God knows what that's about?

Phil Silvers, Jack E. Leonard, and Milton Berle—do you think they all share the same optometrist?

the time, do you remember? And then the Japanese in the tank pinned down the division and you ran on and opened the turret and all the Japanese blew up, do you remember that?" Unfortunately for Bogart, he acknowledged that he did indeed remember. "You're full of shit! It was John Wayne!" yelled Buttons, "Just want to give you an idea of what a lying cocksucker we got here today." Well, since Buttons survived the afternoon, it's safe to say that he won that round.

If only Bogart had ordered his goons to check places other than the ladies' room, his own broad would not have been able to sneak in the following recording: "This is Lauren Bacall. Mrs. Bogart. The uninvited guest. You rat bastards. When he informed me that the Friars were giving a luncheon in his honor, I was delighted. But when he told me that I couldn't attend because it was a stag, I sure was disappointed. I said, 'Bogey? Why can't I go?' he said, "Baby, it's gonna be a little rough. You know how men act at a stag, that's why women aren't allowed, see?' I was furious. In fact, I was goddamn mad! What the hell can the Friars say that you haven't called me?

"I must tell you of an incident that happened to Bogey before I met him. He was keeping company with a girl and one day while he was waiting in front of her house, she wanted Bogey to go to the store for her. So she opened the window and called out, 'Hump-free, Hump-free,' and twenty guys ran up to her room. Guys, don't think this guy Bogey is easy to live with. When Bogey gets his script for a picture, especially where he plays a tough guy, he studies his part with so much sincerity, you'd think our home was a hide-out and he was really on the lam. When he has his script memorized, he puts so much realism into it, he really believes that he's a tough guy. Why, Bogey even fights in his sleep. He wakes me up three or four times a night and says, 'Baby, hold my gun.' Hey, gentlemen, that's a stag.'" So much for worrying what the ladies will think about these all-men affairs. Buttons turned to Bogart and asked him, "You fucking a nice girl like that?" The smooth guest of honor quipped, "Just lucky, I guess."

"One of the fastest comers in show business. If you don't believe me, ask his wife," is what Buttons had to say about Alan King. It's more than King had to say about Bogart: "I don't know anything about Mr. Bogart. If they had given this luncheon to [Casey] Stengel, I would have had an hour and a half of beautiful fucking things to say to that miserable prick." Speaking of which, "Mr. Bogart plays a prick in most of his pictures, and I think it was a fair exchange. We sent Berle to the coast, who was the biggest prick we had, and they sent us Humphrey Bogart." While we're on the subject—and usually these Roasts are never far from the subject—not a Roast has gone by where Berle's legendary appendage was not referred to in some vein or another. This is only the beginning.

When Buttons introduced actor Charles Coburn he said, "To give you an idea what kind of gentleman he is, he always removes his monocle before he takes a piss." The Friars seem to have an unwritten rule: when you can, always one-up the guy who introduces you. Mr. Coburn obviously learned his Friar lessons well: "That is not the reason I remove my monocle—I'm ashamed to look down." He proceeded to enlighten the crowd on dirty minds and censors by telling the following joke: There was a minstrel show which was touring the East. And when they came to the town of West Chester, Pennsylvania, a man who presented himself as the self-appointed guardian of public morals said to the manager of the show, "I understand you boys have got some dirty jokes." The manager said, "Oh, that's very strange, we pride ourselves on having a very clean show." So the man says, "Well, I want to tell you, I'm going to be in the first row tonight with my wife and the first one that pulls a dirty joke, I'll stop the show." So there he was in the first row, and everything was going along fine. At one point one of the actors asks another, "What is the best thing about a woman?" To which the other man replied, "I don't know, tell me, what is the best thing about a woman?" At this point the man in the audience jumps up and says, "If he says 'cunt,' I'll stop the show!"

Jack Dempsey said that Humphrey had to "jerk off twice this morning just to get his heart started." What, I should go back to quoting Channing Pollock?

I guess nobody told Phil Silvers that he would be performing that day, "I am unfortunately unprepared. Sometimes you hit a mental block when the guest of honor is of a more spicy nature. I couldn't even prepare any ribs. There's usually a little more honesty in our guests of honor, like Berle; if he was here, he would show us his cock, something warm that you can talk about. What can I say about Humphrey Bogart? I have great Jack E. Leonard jokes." But he finally, sort of, rose to the occasion: "We did a picture together, I had a small part, *All Through The Night*, but what can I truthfully say about him, that he pissed from a balcony in Rome?" Oh, let this serve as a warning to anyone who is squeamish in the peeing department: this pissing joke is nothing, you just keep reading and those waterworks will really start flowing.

So many people in this business love to pretend they're chummy, chummy with all the stars. Jan Murray is an exception to that rule: "I don't know this man. We have nothing in common. I mean, Kutsher's Country Club, you never worked, am I right? We have no background. Were you ever in Paul's Hotel in Swan Lake? No, right? See, there's no reminiscing with Mr. Bogart. But Mr. Bogart has tremendous courage on stage and off. You must be, well, let's be kind, fifty-three, fifty-five? Fifty-five. Well, it takes plenty of guts to marry a girl like twenty-three. You know what heroism you need for this? I'm married to a girl only six years younger. He married a girl twenty-three. He's looking at me strange, like, who is this putz getting up there talking about me? He never saw me in his life. One thing I know is, you never worked the mountains. What kind of a name is Humphrey for a Jewish boy? Chevalier, he has been coming here for a hundred years and his accent gets thicker each year. What the hell is that?"

Murray also left his audience with a joke: A fairy walks into the bar, the best-looking queen you ever saw, and he says "Hello, Harry," and the bartender always says, "Hi, ya cunt." And every day he goes into the same bar and the bartender always says, "Hi, ya cunt." So one night he walks into the bar and says, "Hi, Harry," and the bartender says, "Hi, ya cunt," and this big fag says, "Listen, if you ever call me that again, I'll smash your face in." The bartender says, "Are you crazy? Every night you come in here and every night I say 'Hi, ya cunt.' How come all of a sudden you're so insulted?" He said, "Today I saw one!"

Lauren Bacall was sequestered elsewhere during the event, but they brought her out at the end of the proceedings when they presented Bogey with his Friars' gift. "The same cheap crap everybody gets. Gold-plated cuff links with a picture of Lenny Kent on the link," said Buttons. Lenny, if you're out there, please tell us who the hell you are so we can laugh at the joke. Those gifts have morphed over the years into TV sets, watches, and whatnot, until today when they receive a Friars' crystal statue. Who are they kidding? You can be damn sure the guest of honor would rather have money.

Bogart's remarks were short and sweet, "You've all used up all of the four-letter words that I knew. I've never been the guest of honor before of anything, but if there is such a profession I think I might take it up and travel around the country being a guest of honor wherever anyone would want me because I've never had so much fun in my life. I'm highly flattered, and I'd like to thank you all for being so nice to me." So much for Mr. Tough Guy. Surprisingly, the Friars let the lady have the last laugh, since they allowed Mrs. Bogart to say a word or two, "I have nothing to say to you rat bastards except that finally at long last I have four hundred men in a room and he's got to be here!"

Today Buttons remembers, "He had a good time. When the Roast was over, off the mike, he put his arm around me and he said to me, 'Redsy, this is the beginning of a beautiful friendship.'" (In case anyone keeps track of these things, the price of a ticket to this Roast was a whopping six dollars.)

JIMMY CANNON ROAST – 1959

(Well, it's one of the few they still have on tape)

JACK E. LEONARD, *Roastmaster*	ROCKY GRAZIANO
JACK BARRY	AL KELLY
JOHNNY BRODERICK	ALAN KING
JACK CANNON	JULIUS LaROSA
MAX CASE	TOMMY RICHARDSON
HARRY DELF	FLOYD PATTERSON

Journal American sports columnist Jimmy Cannon was honored with a Roast—well, as honored as one can feel when the Friars say to you, "Jimmy. We really love you. We love you so much we want to burn your ego in effigy, beat your self-esteem into submission, and crush your pride so badly you will wish you were never born." Now, that's love. This particular Roasting took place at the Copacabana which, if Alan King was correct, was one cruel joke for the recovering alcoholic, "Jim, I think it's very symbolic that a testimonial in your honor is given in a saloon. For a man who saw the light eighteen years ago and stopped drinking, I think you're to be commended on it. I think you're a schmuck, but I think you're to be commended on it. Jimmy stopped drinking, not so much for his health, but somebody gave him a tab." It is sort of cruel when you think about it—those Friars love it even more when the guest of honor is wrestling with his or her own personal demons. (Just ask Kelsey Grammer his opinion on the subject.)

When Jack E. Leonard was in the room, no one got a word in edgewise, even if the person was Friars' Dean Harry Delf, trying to introduce the Master of Ceremonies, "Gentlemen, it's my pleasure—" to which Leonard immediately cut in, "I think so." But Delf, back on track, continued, "—to introduce the emcee, and by now you know whom he is . . ." Leonard, apparently hanging onto every consonant of Delf's, said, "Whom? He's an executive of the Club and I get 'whom he is.' Who's whom? So far, you're the first flop of the afternoon. Go ahead, kid." It's a safe call to say that Harry Delf probably wasn't aware that Mr. Leonard was a professor of English. Whom knew? But Delf finally spit it out, "That bumptious, balding . . ." and after a few more tongue-twisting moments, he managed to just say it— "Jack E. Leonard."

"If Jimmy was Jewish, he'd own his own paper by now," said Leonard, who took several shots at Cannon's non-Hebrew ways. "Jimmy, I want you to know that there are going to be a lot of nasty things said about you this afternoon, and I think I'll start at this particular moment and wish you a very happy Ash Wednesday. Of course a lot of us fellas don't know what that is, but Jimmy, we're pretty liberal about the whole damn mess here."

For anyone who has ever experienced Jack E. Leonard's delivery, it amounts to a machine gun spewing out words at a hundred miles an hour. They also sound as if they are shot out of the side of his mouth, which makes him sound like a cross between W. C. Fields and the fast-talking Federal Express commercial guy. You either catch his jokes the first time, or you sit in stunned confusion as the crowd around you convulses in laughter.

Jimmy Cannon's brother, Jack Cannon, held his own among the heavyweights of that time—specifically, Leonard. "You think he lost all this weight by dieting? You're crazy. They removed a forty-pound insult." He then moved on to his big brother, "You know, Jimmy, this Club is strictly for professionals—actors, writers, pimps—there must be some category you fit into." To which Leonard interrupted, "Keep punching, Jackie, and I'm sure you'll get knocked out in about a minute." Jimmy's comeback to that was, "Jack, you got wonderful cracks, but they're all in your ass."

"Jimmy is now writing his autobiography," noted Alan King. "It's called, 'I Was An Irish Fag.' I know he's queer for schoolteachers because he can get laid and they will help him with his spelling, too." That's all we got, folks, before the tape fucked up. Oh, sorry, I'm still in Roast mode.

MILTON BERLE ROAST – 1959

(This would be Roast number 5,003!)

JACK E. LEONARD, *Roastmaster*
Lots of funny people

In case you haven't caught on about the Friars' archives, well, there really are no Friars' archives. They had better things on their minds than to worry about saving things, like coming up with new dirty words. So basically you're left with a smattering of events which, in the case of Milton Berle, is all you really need. For his 1959 Roast, the only surviving snippet is his thank-you speech at the end of the luncheon. The beauty of this is you get Berle in all his uncut glory—literally.

"Firstly, may I say it's a great pleasure to be seated here on the dais in front of you gentlemen, being honored so supremely. I do want you to know one thing before I continue. No matter how many fucking parties you give me, I will not get out of show business. I'm very glad you called on me now, Jackie, because one of your balls was in my jockey shorts, you know? The turnout for me tonight proves one thing—everybody loves a very big prick. Jackie, I've never seen you funnier than you were this afternoon, I really mean that sincerely. I haven't had so many laughs since Jessel's toupee got in Lois Andrew's snatch.

"Do you realize, gentlemen, while we are sitting here enjoying ourselves and sitting here getting laughs and sitting here so complacent, that somewhere in Spain, right now Eddie Fisher is getting his cock sucked—by a Jewish girl, yet? I know she's Jewish—one of her tits was circumcised. Sorry I had to resort to that, but when you top off the afternoon after following all of these greats such as Arnold Stang, little cocksucker, this boy doesn't go down, he goes up. I've enjoyed the whole afternoon tremendously. Mr. Barry, I am not going to make any remarks about your observations about my book. I'm not going to do that. I wish you would read the book, though; it's very good, there are a million laughs. It's in its third printing; the first two were blurred."

Okay, yet another lie for you. I did cut Berle's thank-you speech, and you'll be glad I did—trust me. Besides, that was the funny part. Then Berle sort of brought everybody down by being serious and since this isn't a serious book, you won't be subjected to it. Then again, we did mention there may be a touching moment or two, and when was the last time you heard about Berle being touching—since you haven't read about Steven Seagal's Roast yet—so here's a little bit of Berle being grateful: "I've had a very nice career in this. I'm hitting fifty-one years old, and in the last forty-six years when I started, I think I might be a little boring now, but I think I want to get something off my chest. When I was eleven years old, I made my ninth comeback. I got up off the floor quite a few times, and sort of succeeded in doing the right thing again, luckily." He then goes into a really long tale about William Demarest, teaching birds to say "Fuck you." "In conclusion, it's been a very long afternoon," Berle continued, but not nearly as long as this speech—and you're getting the shortened version. "But it's been a very great one. It's a fine fraternal feeling in my heart to know that all you guys can be here. We could have had the Waldorf-Astoria Ballroom or Madison Square Garden. It's a big kick to me to see all you guys here to pay homage and respect to me. If I had any success in my long span of show business life, a lot of it is due to a lot of you guys. They may say that in show business there's a certain friction. You can find that true in certain cases, but in my case as I look around the room today I see a lot of guys here, a great percentage who have encouraged me over the years and I want to thank you.

"And, above all, I want to thank the Friars. Being the Abbot Emeritus of the Friars makes me very proud. And what is also gratifying is to think of the days, and I think Mr. Delf and all of the people who are members of the Friars, we had it pretty rough back about thirteen, fourteen years ago. We were at the old Edison Hall and we had maybe one room, 'cause we were in dire trouble. We failed, but everyone pitching in made it what it is today." He then blathers on about dead people. But in yet another conclusion: "The time is getting so short that the friendly feeling we should have, man toward man, should continue and these festivities where we are sitting next to each other and enjoying the festivities and finding happiness, as you get older you say, 'Well, it's pretty short, let's live, let's enjoy.' This is one example of it today. I want to thank this comic genius for being so smart and witty and jovial, Jack E. Leonard. And may we continue to have functions like this, and may God bless you." Now stop asking what it was like to sit in the audience and listen to the Master of the Roast—now that you've read him, you might want some Visine for those bloodshot eyes.

GEORGE BURNS ROAST – 1960

(Even then he was close to a hundred!)

GEORGE JESSEL, *Roastmaster*	SID GARY
DAVE BARRY	HARRY HERSHFIELD
JACK BARRY	DON RICKLES
JACK BENNY	JACKIE ROBINSON
AL BERNIE	JOHN RUMSEY
MYRON COHEN	ARTHUR MURRAY
BOBBY DARIN	PHIL SILVERS
MEYER DAVIS	

According to George Jessel (you remember him—he was the Abbot during the '30s, when it wasn't the best time to have been even the doorman), this was his first time as Roastmaster. How is that possible? Wasn't he considered the Toastmaster General? Either his act was far too clean for the likes of a Roast, or the Friars really held a grudge about his shaky reign during the depression. But here he was, presiding over the event for one of the funniest Friars in entertainment history. "I'm told by my confreres that there's a rule, there is a, well, shall I say a Rabelaisian tenor to these luncheons. However, your Toastmaster will do his best to be immune from any such contamination. I will stick to the more sentimental side." Oh no, not another Berle tour de force! Thankfully, Jessel then read a telegram he claimed was from movie tycoon Adolph Zukor: "Dear George Burns, wish I could be with you today, but I cannot travel as I have the clap." Just to put things in perspective for those out of the loop, in 1960 Adolph Zukor was eighty-seven years old.

There was a young whippersnapper on the dais that day who did not speak, but the elder Roastmaster introduced him this way: "We have a gentleman here, I'm told, who is quite a raconteur—in the lingo of today, he's a big heckler. Mr. Don Rickles. He will bow and keep his goddamn mouth shut." It's not that surprising that the Friars would adopt the age-old philosophy of "children should be seen and not heard." What's frightening, though, is that Don Rickles is the child in question. If Rickles was the "pup," then John Rumsey was the "old dog" on the dais. Remember Rumsey from cleaning up the Friars' act in 1909? Here he was, seated on the dais, one of their original founding fathers. Such respect a man like that commanded. When Jessel introduced him, people weren't sure if he really was on the dais, so he quipped, "He's not? Well, then he died!" So much for that commandment that says, "Honor thy founding fathers."

Sid Gary was one of George Burns' vaudeville partners who, one would hope, had some very funny stories about Burns. Instead, he told the same goddamned William Demarest joke that Berle told at his Roast. Only in Gary's version, we found out that the birds were part of an act called "Lucille's Cockatoos" and they were parrots. Afterward Jessel commented, "He said to me, I'm not going to make any jokes. I'm a singer, but I want to be sentimental. Fine sentiment for George Burns, a parrot hollering, 'Go fuck yourself.'" Hey, maybe they should have considered Roasting William Demarest and having the parrot speak.

For some reason, Jessel introduced Phil Silvers as "Sid." In his capacity as Prior of the Club, Phil/Sid noted, "We have gotten quite a few complaints in the few days George has been here. At various times, at the bridge table, he has called various members cocksucker, prick, and fascist. We've looked into it, George, but nothing will be done, because in each case you were right." Old-time comic Dave Barry said, "Like all comics here, I came up here totally unprepared. But my writer didn't, and he hates George Burns. I have a home in Beverly Hills that overlooks George's home, which is a lot better than living at George's home, overlooking the dump I'm living in. George, I hope you will accept this little bit of advice from me: why do you leave your wife, Gracie, at home and go out on the road with a young boy like Bobby Darin? Your friends are worried about you, George." Fear not, he got back his senses a few years later, palin' around with Connie Stevens and Brooke Shields.

Harry Hershfield refused to Roast Burns, "I don't care who you're honoring—George Jessel becomes the guest of honor." He then proceeded to tell Jewish Jessel jokes—but they're not very funny, so we'll just move along. What little Harry did say about Burns was chillingly eerie, not that anyone knew it at the time: "I say this to you, George. May you live to be a hundred years old and thirty days. And you're gonna say, 'What's the thirty days for?' I certainly don't want you to die suddenly." Well, George did die suddenly—at a hundred years old and two days.

Speaking of not funny—which is not to be mistaken for not good, it just seemed misplaced, that's all—Bobby Darin sang "Mack the Knife." (There's no winning here. First I complain that the Friars' song had nothing over this one, and now I'm complaining that this song was sung at a Roast.) But why sing anything? Although Darin did take a page out of George Burns' book of quotes, saying, "Whatever your business is, do your business and my business certainly is not telling jokes so I don't want to try to compete on this dais." He then grabbed a mike, and took his place by the piano. "He will be accompanied by Mr. Mel Morris, who also accompanied General Grant," said Jessel. Wow, this kid must have had some great press agent to get him to work a Roast and sing, no less. (Bobby Darin is one of those icons whom you're not supposed to mess with, but if the truth be told, he sounded off-key.)

"George Burns is a notorious cigar smoker," announced Al Bernie. "In fact, many of our great comedians smoke cigars— George Jessel, Jack Benny, Phil Silvers—and they all have one thing in common, bad breath. I want to point out one thing to George Burns. According to Freud, a cigar is a phallic symbol. This may come as a shock, but for years, you have been smoking your cock." Even in 1960, George Burns was considered old by some, in spite of his only being sixty-four. Interesting, since he later became a young one hundred. For Bernie, Burns was old, "It is not a coincidence that we honor George Burns the same week in which we honor George Washington. There are similarities. It was Washington who said, 'I cut down the tree,' and it was George Burns who said, 'Father, I cannot tell a lie, I took her cherry.' It is well-known that George Burns is always willing to give a helping hand to any young, struggling, ambitious, beautiful nymphomaniac. I happen to know a young actress who applied for a part on one of George Burns' shows. This was a very nice girl, a very classy girl. I bumped into her the next day. I said, 'How did you make out?' She said, 'George Burns had the nerve to offer me the part, but the salary was only seventy-five dollars.' I said, 'What did you do?' She said, 'What did I do? I laughed right in his balls.'"

There is not one Friar who had the privilege of experiencing Jack Benny in person at a Roast who doesn't cherish it. He was one of the greatest American humorists to ever live, but to see him perform at a Roast was an incredible sight. Not because of that expected deadpan delivery. Not because of that quick wit. But because no one ever expected him to, well, to be dirty. "They told me to be here at twelve o'clock. I have been sitting here, and so far the speakers have left me with two words—cunt and co-habitate. My wife, Mary, hates these stag luncheons. I didn't even dare tell her that I came here today. She thinks I'm in a whorehouse. She figures, what harm can there be just looking, ya know? 'Cause if I don't get a hard-on from this luncheon, I'll never have one."

George was given a clock with his picture in the center of the Friars' logo. Why do I think he outlived that clock? "Friends and Friars, I want to thank you for making me the guest of honor this afternoon. And in my entire life, I have never heard nicer things said about me. It's too bad Gracie wasn't here." That's when the tape cuts out, but then it comes back as riotous laughter is in progress. He probably had just said the funniest thing of the afternoon—oh well. To continue, "It's not a compliment to be the guest of honor. You're not the guest of honor because you're a nice fella or a big personality. You're the guest of honor because you're good subject matter. If you're a nice fellow, there's nothing to talk about; if you're a tired schmuck, the luncheon is a success. It looks like I'll be held over for a week.

"Take a fellow like Milton Berle. It's true you can talk for twenty minutes about his dickey—have you seen it? It's a beauty. Of course, Jack Benny is good subject matter, but in reverse. I've seen his, too. It's not big, but it's sweet." By the way, if you're keeping a tally of penis jokes, specifically Berle penis jokes, may I suggest using a solar-powered calculator? "I was never a sex man. When I was a young fellow, I never worked at it, I was a Peabody dancer. If you gave me two dames, one I could win the silver loving cup with and one I could go to bed with, I'd take the one I could win the cup with, 'cause the other thing I could do myself. And when I got into the money, I used felt gloves. Make sure that the buttons are on the outside. I just hope that all these speeches were put down on tape because I can't wait to take them all home and play them for my grandchildren. Thank you." No, George, thank you, for a century of fun!

ALAN KING ROAST – 1961

(But what about me?)

JACK E. LEONARD, *Roastmaster*	BEN JACOBI
GENE BAYLOS	DURWOOD KIRBY
JOHNNY CARSON	CORBETT MONICA
MYRON COHEN	GARRY MOORE
HARRY DELF	ANTHONY PERKINS
HY GARDNER	PHIL SILVERS
BUDDY HACKETT	RUDY VALLEE
HARRY HERSHFIELD	EARL WILSON

Jack E. Leonard wrote the book on nonsensical non sequiturs, so it was only fitting he serve as Roastmaster at this particular event because everyone that afternoon seemed to be in the land of the lost. Their barbs flew around the room in search of a victim, Alan King being the least-hit target. From the moment Leonard approached the podium, he began firing away: "Year after year, this guy wins the Olympic championship for boredom. While we're having a good time I can bet you right now, Gary Morton is having a piece of Lucille's ball. I want to compliment the Hotel Astor people for this very beautiful décor. It looks like early house of ill repute. Sammy Davis won't be here, he has to prove to me—I haven't seen him in the locker room yet—I don't know if he's one of us or not." Translation: Harry Delf, the Dean of the Club, gives one boring introduction;

Lucille Ball and Gary Morton were on their honeymoon; those cheapskate Friars paid scale for the hotel space; and Sammy Davis, Jr., had converted to Judaism. About King, Leonard did have this to say, "This guy is so neat, he steps out of the shower to take a leak."

Ben Jacobi came in all the way from Israel just to say, "This man you're honoring is known for three very important things he has accomplished in life. Number one: crabgrass. We'll skip number two. Number three: We'll skip that one, too." Let's skip Ben for Garry Moore: "I don't know why I'm here"—do they ever? He eventually figured it out, but it was more of a testimonial on how King has saved his show during appearances: "When you book Alan King, you know that the second spot with the guest comedian is going to go and the whole show stands a much better chance of surviving." To which Leonard yelled out, "Damn it!" "When wide screen comes in, Jack!" retorted Moore. So he roasted the Roastmaster; at least he finally got the idea.

The speaker at the podium, it would seem, isn't necessarily the funniest guy at that precise moment, so reminisces King, "It was big-hit guys like fat Jack E. Leonard, Jack Carter, they could always guarantee that there would be heckling. We all used to heckle each other, and when the heckling became so popular they put microphones in front of everyone." That way, you get fifteen jokes a minute for the price of one.

Durwood Kirby, who opened with, "I'm really Carol Burnett in drag," tried to be nice. "Alan is one of the most wonderful gentlemen in the business. I mean that sincerely, congratulations," and what did he get from Leonard for his chivalry? "Thank you, Durwood. You're also Indianapolis' biggest liar." So just to put things in perspective here, the Roasters are saying really nice things about the guest of honor and they, in turn, are being fried by the master of ceremonies. This was one wacky Roast.

Harry Hershfield took the easy way out: he just told jokes. "This wrestler in the hospital is explaining the situation as to why he's in the hospital. 'Oh, it was a tough match. He had his knee in my belly and I had my belly against his knee, and he had his leg around me, and we're like a pretzel. I looked up and

I see a pair of balls and I bit 'em. But they're mine.'" And this one: "Three little babies are discussing the food that they're on. One little baby says, 'They are giving me oatmeal, and it's terrible.' And the other one says, 'I'm getting pabulum, and it's awful.' And the third one says, 'How'd you like to share a tit with a guy who smokes White Owl cigars?'" Gene Baylos followed Hershfield's lead: "I've never been on Garry Moore's show. Twenty-two years in this fucking business, and I *just* made Jack Paar." And this one: "In the words of the great Abraham Lincoln, who said to his wife on his deathbed, 'You and your damn theater parties.'" Guys? Remember Alan King?

This next speaker was the new guy on the block in 1961(not to mention, it would seem, was his network), as confirmed by Leonard's intro, "This next fellow has had his own afternoon show, which nobody has ever seen. He's with a very peculiar network, ABC. I know that you'll try to be entertained by him. Here he is, Johnny Carson." Johnny blew the cover off these tried-and-true ad-libbers, "I love these things because nobody ever comes prepared. I don't know whether you know this, but somebody says, 'Gee, I don't like to write anything for this. I just like to kind of go out and feel the situation. I never prepare.' I could do eight minutes from that goddamn tablecloth right now with what's written down!" But finally, somebody remembered Alan, "I keep reading about Alan King in the papers. You must have a wonderful press agent. 'Alan King has twelve Sullivan guest spots. Alan King has eight Garry Moore spots. Alan King has his own situation comedy. Alan King has the old Rodgers and Hammerstein estate in Great Neck. Alan King has a Rolls Royce.' Just once, I'd like to pick up the paper and see 'Alan King has the clap.'" But that's not to say Johnny didn't like Alan, "I've seen Alan probably fifteen or sixteen times, and I've always enjoyed his joke.

"I understand, Alan, that you're going to start your own comedy show soon. I only wish you the same success I had with mine, Alan. Over at CBS, a few years ago. I was on for Jell-O for thirty-nine weeks out there. The only reason I went off is they found out that Jell-O was causing lung cancer. So, I want to wish you the same kind of luck." But Johnny also followed suit in ribbing others, "I went on for CBS five, six years ago and I said, 'Gee, I don't know whether I'm ready.' And they kept saying, 'Go on now, because Jack Benny can't live forever.' Which I found out is a lot of shit. Jack Benny is going to be on television when Orphan Annie is going through menopause, let's face it." But, ultimately, it is about the King, "Alan has so much success. A lovely family, a lovely home, his own show coming up, and he'd give all of that up in a minute for one thing—talent."

Myron Cohen put down the Talmud long enough to tell a joke, "I'll tell you a story about a fellow who comes home and finds his wife in a compromising position with a stranger. He says, 'What the hell is going on here?' His wife turns to the stranger and says, 'Didn't I tell you he was stupid?'" Which ranks up there with Rudy Vallee's joke, "There was a bald fellow who sold hair tonic, and a guy said to him, 'How do you dare to sell hair tonic when you have no hair yourself?' He replied, 'I know a guy who sells brassieres.'"

Corbett Monica also remembered that the Roast had a guest of honor, "Alan's success in England is not some Johnny-come-lately. If you realize, his whole life has leaned towards royalty. His name is King. He's done a Command Performance. He's played the Palace. All this from a guy who once thought that the Earl of Concord was Phil Greenwald." (Phil was the legendary talent booker at the Concord in the Catskills, for anyone who joined the living after the untimely demise of the Catskills.) "When you hear about London, you hear about Danny Kaye, but since I was there, I can tell you that Alan is top man. He plays there a dozen times a year. Either that is a sign that they like his work, or he's fucking the queen." Well, he is King.

The afternoon went on and on, causing an exasperated Buddy Hackett to yell from his seat on the dais, "Anyone that leaves before I go on is a prick." Alan King got up to leave. But there was still more to come. As King remembers, "I was a big baseball fan and a big Brooklyn fan. In the front they had a Dodger table and seated there was Jackie Robinson, Duke Snyder, Gil Hodges, and Ralph Branca. Jackie Robinson became a great friend, and when Phil Silvers got to the podium, he grabbed a rather large gavel which they had used to open the proceedings and said, 'Nice of Jackie Robinson to loan us his cock for a while.' Now I've heard laughs here, but five minutes, you could not believe the screaming that went on." Silvers also took a jab at King's record of television hits, "This boy has lost more pilots than the Luftwaffe."

As for Buddy, well, maybe they did lose an audience member or two, but it seemed to fit in with his macabre description of a visit to a cemetery with Phil Foster and King, where he asked permission from the groundskeeper to erect a show biz sign on his plot, "Coming—Buddy Hackett." And so it ends with a joke that has nothing to do with the guest of honor. Maybe King will reign at his next event.

DON RICKLES ROAST – 1968

(It's called payback, Don)

JACK E. LEONARD, *Roastmaster*	ELSTON HOWARD
YOGI BERRA	BUDDY HOWE
AL BERNIE	PAT MCCORMICK
CAB CALLOWAY	PAT PAULSEN
JOHNNY CARSON	ED SULLIVAN
DICK CAVETT	JACKIE VERNON
NORM CROSBY	WILLIAM B. WILLIAMS
JOE FRANKLIN	EARL WILSON
JACKIE GAYLE	FLIP WILSON
PAT HENRY	

For Don Rickles, insulting people made him rich. For the Friars, insulting people made them rich and famous. Having a Roast for Rickles took about as much brainstorming as combining chocolate and peanut butter into a Reese's—who am I kidding; for the Friars, it's as obvious as putting water in Scotch. Jack E. Leonard was the perfect choice to serve as Roastmaster, seeing as he was doing Rickles' act long before Rickles had an act. "Don has been doing my act for about twelve years now, and I'm here to make a citizen's arrest. I don't mind the guy stealing my act, but he stole my hair, too," bellowed Leonard, who bore a striking resemblance to the guest of honor.

Flip Wilson thanked Leonard for his kind introduction. "When we take over, I'm gonna look out for you," he shared. Just to get things off his chest, Flip announced, "Fuck Don Rickles and fuck Jack E. Leonard." So much for lookouts. But in all sincerity, Flip did acknowledge, "I have to say that Don has never said anything about me. Don has never made a negative remark about Flip Wilson. I mean, he knows that you guys will take that shit, but if I ever hear that Don Rickles said one word about me, I'll stand in the goddamn alley with a brick one night and I'll dislocate his head."

At one point Wilson turned to Leonard and asked for a cigarette, to which the Roastmaster asked, "The kind you want to fly around with or just the regular ones?" Well, this was the '60s, after all. "He's bad. You're gonna make a hell of a father-in-law," quipped Wilson. "And you're gonna make a hell of a little bastard, I tell you that," was the quick comeback. After Wilson finished, Leonard said, "Thank you, Reverend Martin Luther King. Remember the words of Abraham Lincoln, who once said to his colored servant, 'Stop that goddamn tap dancing and give me back my high hat.'" Um, yes, the '60s.

Jackie Vernon took the adage that if you hit them with both barrels, then maybe they won't have time to shoot back—and, when dealing with Rickles, that's not a bad stance to take. "I don't care what anyone says, Don, I like you. Although, if Will Rogers ever met you, he would have punched you in the mouth. . . . If I had a head like yours, I'd have it circumcised. . . . I never thought I'd see the day the Friars would honor a lounge act. . . . In closing, I'd like to leave Don with two words; one is a verb and the other is a pronoun."

Poor Ed Sullivan. No matter how many appearances he made at Friars' events—and he made many, especially during his time as Abbot from 1972 to 1974—they always gave him a hard time. Whether it was about his speech or his pole-up-the-ass stance, the comedians had an endless supply of jokes at his expense. At this Roast, Leonard introduced Sullivan this way: "We have a nice man here called Ed Sullivan, who came up from down there to come up here to see you today. How do you feel, Ed—was the ground cold this morning?" Today that comment still breaks Norm Crosby up, "You realize how funny that was, because he looked like a ghoul." As if that wasn't enough, Leonard added, "I think we ought to have a few words from the late Ed Sullivan."

Sullivan ranks up there with Walter Cronkite and Jack Benny as one of the people you most want to witness at a Roast, because you will never hear them utter obscenities anywhere *but* at a Roast. Even the Pope has got to admit, it's funny. "Fuck you. You bald-headed bastard. You've made your last appearance on CBS," was how Sullivan greeted Rickles on the dais. But Ed could only pull it off for so long—well, as long as it took him to say it—before launching into a more serious tone, "If ever the world needed comedy and a sense a humor and the great artists to deliver it, it's now. And certainly this array here of great comics represents the best of our country." He did add, "Sylvia sent you her love." One minute they're saying "Fuck you" to your face, and the next they're sending their wife's love.

Pat Paulsen noted, "There's things about Rickles that you don't know. He has a rather bad kidney problem. You can tell from his rusty zipper and his yellow tennis shoes." Paulsen proved beyond a shadow of a doubt that any kid in a schoolyard at recess has the makings of a professional Roaster, "Don is the living proof of the desire to go with the constant use of contraceptives in the home." He then closed with a demonstration of finger shadows.

For Johnny Carson, whom Leonard blamed "for creating a monster" by having Rickles guest host his show, a Roast gave him the opportunity to work an audience and not have to worry about network censors putting red lines through his blue material. "The first time I met Don, his head was covered with thick, curly black hair—he was going down on Kay Armen." He then proceeded to backtrack with a dissertation on just why Don was gay, "I'm his friend and he holds his friends very dear, queers need friends." Johnny also scrutinized Don's acting abilities: "Don's act has all the subtlety of an elephant's prick. He couldn't ad-lib a fart after a Boston baked bean dinner. And now this schmuck wants to be an actor. He's made sixty-two television appearances this year, and one was starring in a whole hour segment of *Run for Your Life*. Dramatically, it was about as thrilling as watching Kate Smith take a douche." He closed with apparently what was becoming an old favorite of his, "I've seen Don entertain fifty times, and I've always enjoyed his joke." But it's still funny—providing you don't think it's a typo.

Radio personality William B. Williams said, "Don has all of the charm and all of the warmth of an unflushed toilet. Our Roastmaster and our guest of honor are twins. In fact, they were Siamese twins joined at the cock. So the big problem in making the severance was who to make the bigger prick—Mr. Rickles was victorious."

Norm Crosby's attendance on this particular dais was unexpected. He happened to be in New York for an *Ed Sullivan Show* appearance, "I got an emergency call from the Club and they said that there was a flu epidemic in New York. Everybody was really, really sick and they desperately needed me to be on the dais because they had a dozen cancellations." Crosby was not initially able to do the Roast because of his regular stint on the *Dean Martin Show*, which taped in California; however, after the Friars pulled a string or two, the comedian found himself on the dais. Hey, if Dean Martin can't help out the Friars with one of their Roasts, then who can? "I had nothing prepared, nothing. I didn't have time to think about anything. I'm sitting there on the dais and we're starting the lunch and I said, 'By God, I haven't even thought about material. What am I gonna do?' I'm sitting next to Jackie Vernon and Jackie had about four or five pages of material that he had written for the guest of honor and he said to me, 'Here, take what you want. We'll share it. And he gave me the papers. 'What you don't do I'll do and what I don't want, you'll do.'

"It's so unusual because comedians, by virtue of what they do, are so highly competitive, so extremely jealous of each other. 'That's my joke, that's my line.' Did you say 'Good evening, ladies and gentlemen?' I've been saying that for years now!' I thought it was just so wonderful, so really Friar-like and so brotherly and so good, 'Here, help yourself.' And I took a couple of things and then I managed to ad-lib a few things and it went well. I don't think there's any other place in the world that a comedian would do that for another comedian except at a Friars' Roast."

Rickles spent the entire Roast slamming his fist on the dais, he was so hysterical over the proceedings. You can only imagine what he felt when they presented him with a television set at the end of the afternoon, "I want to thank the Friars for giving me my tenth portable television set, all of which, as soon as you plug them in, they blow out. So to clear it right up now, it was definitely a cheap gift, which I won't forget. It was a very cheap gift." He wasn't any kinder on the boys either, "Ed Sullivan, I say this from the bottom of my heart, you're not a well person, you need care and help. You dribble all over yourself, you wet your pants. How long can you walk around the street touching yourself and think this is normal. I was supposed to be on your show once, my bear died. I'm sorry, Flip, about the seating arrangements, originally they wanted you out in the hall with a broom. Johnny Carson is so classy, he takes a leak on his own brother. William B. Williams, you made a fool out of yourself as usual. I've had a lot of great afternoons in my career, but this one will not go into the scrapbook."

JOEY ADAMS ROAST – 1976

(Here's to the Friars' crier!)

MILTON BERLE, *Roastmaster*	GEORGE JESSEL
GENE BAYLOS	LIONEL HAMPTON
AL BERNIE	DON RICKLES
PAT HENRY	JOE SMITH
LOU JACOBI	HENNY YOUNGMAN

"This is the first Friars' luncheon where the audience is better known than the guest of honor," said Milton Berle, opening the Joey Adams Roast. Joey, literally, wrote the book on Roasts and to celebrate his newest publication, *Here's to the Friars*, they threw him a Roast of his own. It was a way of giving him a taste of his own medicine. It's a given that by the end of the day, he was probably sorry he ever heard of the Friars Club and their damn Roasts. The jokes were pretty much consistent with Joey's stature, demeanor, and wit—short, sweet, and funny. Okay, who am I kidding? But they were definitely short.

Milton Berle: "Today we are here to Roast Joey Adams, and there is nothing like the aroma you get when you are cooking shit. . . . I sacrificed a lot to be here; for one thing, my self-respect. . . . Being a Roastmaster at a Friars' Lunch is like balling your own wife—you make believe you're enjoying it, but you try to get it over as quick as you can. . . . Getting honored by the Friars is like hemorrhoids, sooner or later every asshole gets one. . . . After reading your book, *Here's to the Friars*, I'll sum it up with the words of Eugene O'Neill, 'When the iceman cometh, I hope he cometh all over you.' . . . Adams writes like Jessel fucks."

Lou Jacobi showed up to the Roast wearing a tux. Nobody goes to a luncheon Roast wearing a tux; it just makes you look stupid. Sorry, Lou, but you did, you looked stupid. Then again, looking and being are two different things, "At least I made $12.50 in tips," he defended.

George Jessel: "This is my second engagement today. I spoke at a circumcision this morning. . . . George Burns had a very good year; he flushes his toilet and an oil well falls out. . . . Arnold Palmer has made a fortune out of his putts and mine has broken me completely. . . . I left Dolly Madison for Pocahontas. . . . Tonight we honor Fiorello LaGuardia's niece."

Joe Smith read excerpts from one of Adams' books: "Nature has blessed me with a big schmuck," but it was Berle who stood up.

Pat Henry: "Joey is so patriotic, he once went down on Bess Truman and nobody even asked him."

We won't bother quoting Lionel Hampton, because he was the perfect gentleman. He talked about Joey helping him with several children's projects in Harlem—yeah, whatever.

Al Bernie: "Joey Adams gives great political advice. He said to Nixon, 'Tape everything! It will come in handy.'"

Henny Youngman: "Berle makes a comeback with every joke. . . . In your book, Milton, you claim that you slept with Marilyn Monroe. She was dead at the time." Henny? The Roast is for Joey Adams. "Joey and his wife, Cindy, go to bed, and instead of fucking they write books." Now you're talking!

As for Joey, after sitting through hours of this, his snappy comeback was, "LaGuardia once told me, 'Don't worry about people knowing you, make yourself worth knowing.' Tonight, I feel that for the first time in my life. Thank you." Man, with remarks like that at your own Roast, you can only imagine what a hoot *Here's to the Friars* must have been.

NEIL SIMON ROAST – 1978

(He left holding the bag!)

MILTON BERLE, *Roastmaster*	ROCKY GRAZIANO
(Who else?)	BARRY GRAY
MANNY AZENBERG	PAT HENRY
ABRAHAM D. BEAME	TONY MARTIN
MICHAEL BENNETT	WALTER MATTHAU
VICTOR BORGE	DONALD O'CONNOR
EDDIE BRACKEN	TONY ROBERTS
JACK CARTER	CLIFF ROBERTSON
PADDY CHAYEFSKY	JACK WESTON
MYRON COHEN	WILLIAM B. WILLIAMS
VINCENT GARDENIA	EARL WILSON
ROBERT GOULET	HENNY YOUNGMAN

Neil Simon is truly one of the nice guys—and the Friars love nice guys. They want them to finish last, but they are welcome to have the last laugh should the occasion arise. When you have Berle on your dais, though, don't expect miracles. Simon, in his long and illustrious literary career, enjoyed both a free lunch and a Dinner from the Friars. But twenty years later, he finally had the last laugh, by telling me, "I'm really not a Friar, embarrassingly enough to say. I know you invite me to everything, but I'm not a joiner. I don't go to anything. I don't go to clubs. I've been Roasted and I've been Toasted by the Friars. That was wonderful, but I stopped doing those things." Well, just don't spread that around, Neil, because the Friars are going to leave your name on their roster—they need some legit show biz guys for promotional purposes.

It could have been a scene taken from one of his plays, or maybe Simon just figured he'd vie for a little sympathy; in any case, his ploy of entering the Americana's Imperial Ballroom in a wheelchair changed nothing. The fact that he had been released from Lenox Hill Hospital just for this event, only to return later, was proof that he wanted that Friar membership whether he'll cop to it or not. Simon had been in the hospital for observation for an ailment relating to kidney stones, and he attended the event with his wheels oiled and his colostomy bag in check.

If the truth be told, the Friars are fully aware of the psychological ramifications of being one of their "guests of honor," and with that in mind, the light they shine at the end of that long and painful tunnel is a free ride the rest of the way. Once honored, be it via a Roast or a Dinner, the man or woman of the hour becomes an honorary lifetime member (and they don't even have to be ninety-nine!) There really should be some added incentive though, if you get Berle as the emcee. "This man we honor today," he announced at Simon's Roast, "has been my friend for over thirty years. And I was his for the first two weeks."

Looking around the room, Berle apologized. "Some big names were supposed to be here tonight. You didn't think that this pile of shit was the dais? It looks like the Jewish *Gong Show*. I need this lunch like Zsa Zsa Gabor needs a twat widener." But he did explain George Burns' absence, "He's having trouble with his pacemaker. Every time he farts, the garage door opens."

Pat Henry said, "Neil is a New Yorker. In fact, when he dies he wants to be cremated and thrown in someone's face." Victor Borge put things in perspective for anyone else who lost track of all the puns flying around the room, "I can't complain about this lunch because I didn't understand most of it." Speaking of not understanding, Henny Youngman is a Roast phenomenon. No matter who the guest of honor was—it could have been Satan himself—Henny would do his act. "Two guys meet, one says, 'What's the latest dope on Wall Street?' He says, 'My son.' . . . My wife lost all her credit cards. I'm not gonna report it; the guy who found it spends less than she does. . . . I like New York better than California; you get paid here three hours earlier." Neil really didn't have to check himself out of the hospital for Henny, that's for sure.

Jack Carter, whose virgin ears apparently had had enough— "I haven't heard such filth since Redd Foxx did a eulogy at his mother-in-law's funeral"—closed many of these Roasts. The rule of thumb may not have been broadcast, "save the best for last," but your ego certainly got a boost if you were asked to close. As opposed to Simon's ego, which nobody really gave a fiddler's fart about. "Red Buttons, who said to Nipsey Russell, 'Fuck Neil Simon, we'll call it 'The Shoeshine Boys,'" never got to be in one of his plays! I don't know why I'm thrilled to be here. I've never worked for this putz, I'm not a member of the Friars and this is the hotel where my wife caught me with a cunt." Jack was sweet enough, though, to not leave Berle out of the loop, "Milton, you lousy cocksucker—and I've had him, he is a lousy cocksucker!" Happy, Milton?

Unlike other Roast guests of honor, Simon had his own personal Roast material, "I'm up in Lenox Hill Hospital and they let me come out for a few hours. The doctors don't know what it is, but I can describe the pain to you. It's as if the Incredible Hulk was shaking hands with your cock for six hours! I don't mind telling you that right this moment I am peeing into a little bag attached to the right side of my leg. It's just another piss spot on this dais. I feel like I have been peeing luggage." All right, Neil, enough with the pee prose already! "I've always wanted to just come to one of these things, so to be the guest of honor has to be one of the best things that can ever happen to anybody. It's the best medicine I've had."

NORM CROSBY ROAST – 1979

(Norman, can you hear me?)

MILTON BERLE, *Roastmaster*	BOB FITZSIMMONS
MEL ALLEN	VINCENT GARDENIA
ABRAHAM D. BEAME	GEORGE JESSEL
AL BERNIE	JOHN LINDSAY
BERNIE BRILLSTEIN	ROBERT MERRILL
RED BUTTONS	CAL RAMSEY
JACK CAFFERTY	WILLIS REED
DICK CAPRI	CHUCK SCARBOROUGH
GUS CHRISTY	HENNY YOUNGMAN
FRANK FIELD	

The Roasts closed out the decade with a salute, albeit a middle-fingered one, to Norm Crosby. It was hysterically funny, not that he heard any of it. Known for being hard-of-hearing, Norm is one of those people who can take it as well as he can dish it out. This particular afternoon, he had to take it. It also seems fitting that Milton Berle should be the Roastmaster here, seeing as he was the first Roastmaster in 1949.

The jokes speak for themselves, so here's a sampling. Oh, and Norm, if you're reading this, you're probably seeing for the first time what was said, so don't get mad all over again—just enjoy.

Milton Berle: "It's a goddamn inconvenience to be here today, but I'd like a moment of silence for the security guard here at the Sheraton who said to Willis Reed when he came in here today, 'Where you going, boy?' . . . Norm has never said anything bad about me, although he did call my wife Ruth 'a yenta, a pain in the ass, and a bad hump,' but fuck her, that's her problem. . . . Look at this fabulous dais the Friars have assembled. Christ, if a bomb ever hit here today, who'd give a shit? . . . I've looked forward to this luncheon with all the anticipation of changing Bella Abzug's Tampax. . . . Norm Crosby got his beer commercials by kissing Anheuser's bush. . . . A lot of people wonder how Norm became deaf. He was going down on Charo right after she ate a Mexican dinner. . . . When we were in the VIP room, Norm told me that he found a new way to fuck. I said, 'No shit?' He said, 'Well, a little.' . . . At the age of ten, Norm was fucking his nanny, not his nurse. Nanny was a goat he kept in the backyard."

George Jessel: "The last girl I fucked was Betsy Ross. . . . I want to pay my respects to Norman Crosby and I only wish that his father, Bing, had left him a little money."

Al Bernie: "Don't try to talk behind Norm's back. He has a hearing aid up his ass, too. . . . Norm is the type of fellow who would eat Sara Lee and then have a piece of cake."

Gus Christy: "Norm can't hear, he can't talk, and if he keeps jerking off, he's gonna go blind. . . . I fully intended to buy Norm a year's supply of rubbers, but they wouldn't sell me just one."

Dick Capri: "Milton, if they put a blond wig on your cock, you could pass for Paul Williams. . . . My grandma and grandpa both have wooden legs. When they fuck, they start a fire. . . . Norm loves to eat pussy, and since he got his hearing aid, it's the only chance he gets to read lips."

Henny Youngman: "They have a new Polish jigsaw puzzle— one piece. . . . Norm is the Helen Keller of comedians. . . . He's the luckiest comedian in the world, he can't hear his own jokes." Wait a minute? Youngman finally Roasts the guest of honor, and it falls on deaf ears!

Red Buttons: "I've been rehearsing this routine for the last three weeks in front of my dog. So when I'm done, don't applaud; just run up here and lick my balls. . . . Abe Beame, who when he was introduced to Willis Reed, shook his cock hello, never got a luncheon. . . . Dracula's girlfriend, who said to Dracula, 'Are you sure this is a blow job?' never got a luncheon. . . . Casanova, who said, 'I want to be buried with my cat, I can't live without pussy,' never got a luncheon. . . . Bigfoot, who said, 'It's true, I've got a small cock,' never got a luncheon. . . . I was jerking off the other day to a picture of Jesse Jackson hugging Yassir Arafat, that's it." Huh?

It must have been one long afternoon for Norm, because he kept referring to his luncheon Roast as a Dinner; maybe it was just wishful thinking on his part. Since he didn't actually hear any of the bad things people said about him, he figured they were giving testimonials. He left the audience with a joke: "The Friars have always had a very special place in my heart. They give a lot of money from these Dinners to charity. In fact, Friars' money was instrumental in an operation at Mount Sinai, where they took a valve from a turtle's heart and inserted it into a human being. It was successful, and three weeks ago, the guy left the hospital. I'm happy to say that today he reached the parking lot." I think you've heard enough.

MIKE TODD TESTIMONIAL DINNER – 1958

(He never got a dinner)

"Due to the sudden death of our beloved member, Mike Todd, the Friars' testimonial dinner in his honor which was to take place at the Waldorf Astoria is canceled," read the small newspaper blurb. It was the Friars' formal announcement acknowledging the tragedy. It is one of the saddest chapters in the New York Friars Club's history. Todd, the master showman who died in a plane crash in New Mexico, was to have been the Friars Man of the Year for his outstanding achievements that year. "The night of March 23rd will see an out-pouring of celebrities from every field of endeavor to pay homage to not only a top theatrical showman and personality, but to a man who is a great humanitarian," read the Club's invitation to the sold-out event.

The Friars' executive director at the time, Carl Timin, was quoted in the press as saying, "We first got word of it Saturday morning. A member called and told me, 'Mike has crashed.' I was annoyed. I told him, 'Cut it out, I don't have time for gags.' Some gag! A little while later we got another call that Joe E. Lewis had been aboard the plane with him. We immediately put in a call to Joe in Florida. Thank God he was all right. He hadn't even heard about Mike; he'd been asleep." Todd's young bride of just over a year, Elizabeth Taylor, was also not on that plane, owing to a cold that had prevented her from joining him on the trip. Alan King remembers, "I was sitting in a little study in my house and I was writing my speech for that night, and I had the radio on and it said that Mike Todd's plane had crashed. Christ, it crashed on the way to his Testimonial Dinner. It was devastating." Programs for the event were immediately put under lock and key, lest someone jump on the morbid collector's item bandwagon. (I found the key but don't bug the Friars because, at this point, who cares?) The journal holds chilling reminders of a man who was truly larger than life, amidst accolades from Berle, Durante, Berlin, Tucker, Rodgers and Hammerstein, and other prominent show business types. One newspaper reporter at the time noted, "Airlines' standard ads, through no fault of their own, suddenly became almost like 'sick jokes' too eerie to describe." For the journal, Joe E. Lewis penned, "Around Mike Todd in 80 Seconds" as homage to his hit film *Around the World in 80 Days*. "There's very little I can say about Mike that hasn't already leaked out," wrote Lewis. "Mike always had what it takes to become a success—rich friends. In a comparatively short time he worked his way up from a newsboy to Elizabeth Taylor. Mostly I admire Mike Todd because he never forgot his friends. He'll not only give you the shirt off his back, he'll leave the cuff links in it. Well, I've been drinking to Mike all night and I think I'd better stop; his success is slowly going to my head."

The Friars were indeed devastated by the tragedy, but they are also indeed true show business troopers—the show must go on. They may have canceled the Dinner, but they still had a full house of ticket sales to contend with. "We had a meeting immediately," says event producer Buddy Arnold. "A committee sat down and said 'we have to cancel, but we don't want to give the money back. What we'll do is two months from now, people will use the same tickets but we will not honor anybody, and call it a Friars Frolic, like they used to do years ago.' And we did that, honoring nobody specific, honoring the Friars Club with big stars."

The Frolic showcased the talents of Jack E. Leonard, who was to have served as Toastmaster at the Todd Dinner, Jack Barry, Lou Holtz, Joey Adams, Johnny Mathis, and Joey

Bishop. Red Buttons played in a parody of *This Is Your Life*, which included Robert Alda. Pat Boone performed in a quiz show skit. Why do I find it funny that holy-roller Boone had any connection whatsoever to do with the Friars—must have been another case of a press agent working overtime for an up-and-comer. Bob Hope spoke briefly, one of his comments being, "Somewhere on some lonely frontier, Elvis Presley is defending us." Walter Cronkite also spoke at the affair.

The reason for the Frolic certainly wasn't a good one, but the event itself proved the resilience of the Friars. They learned over the years to make the best of their worst situations, and ultimately enjoy huge laughs in everything they do.

DINAH SHORE TESTIMONIAL DINNER – 1960

(Nuthin' could be finer!)

PHIL SILVERS, *Toastmaster*	BUDDY HOWE
BUDDY ARNOLD	ALAN KING
LUCILLE BALL	JACK E. LEONARD
POLLY BERGEN	JOHNNY MATHIS
JOEY BISHOP	ETHEL MERMAN
RED BUTTONS	GENERAL DAVID SARNOFF
ART CARNEY	ROBERT SARNOFF
JEAN CARROLL	JULE STYNE
JOHNNY CARSON	DAVID TEBET
DICK VAN DYKE	RICHARD TUCKER
CHARLTON HESTON	

With the sexual revolution of the '60s, the Friars apparently thought they had to do the "woman thing" again, just so they could get some good press. They opted for squeaky-clean Dinah Shore—which, if you think about it, is pretty funny considering the reputation of who was throwing the bash. All accounts of the event, as well as comments made during the evening, indicate that this was the first time in the history of the Friars that a woman was given a Testimonial Dinner. Oh, how quickly they forget. True, Sophie Tucker was a Roast, but Nellie Revell, in her day, was no slouch, folks.

Being a Testimonial Dinner, the tenor of the evening was far less ribald than their increasingly popular Roasts. And the guest of honor being a woman made them tread even lighter. That's not to say that they could completely hold their tongues, as evidenced by their parody of "Ain't Nothing Like a Dame" from *South Pacific* sung by a male chorus in monks' robes (oh, now there's a surprise):

Since the Friars Club was founded, we've had many big affairs,
For Jack Benny and Ed Sullivan and some other dignitaries,
Georgie Jessel and Steve Allen, Jerry Lewis, Milton Berle
But now what do we got, we got a girl!

We're supposed to rap the guest of honor but we refuse to,
It's so frustrating when a Friar cannot use the kind of words he's used to
We got nothing but a dame, Dinah gives us no scope,
If we had Skelton here or Hope, we could say that they both push dope

If we just had Perry Como we could say that he's a pig
We could even spread a rumor Joe E. Lewis doesn't drink
We could louse up Frank Sinatra by suggesting he's a fag,
But now what do we got, Eddie Fisher in drag

Did you keep the damn "Dame" tune in your head? Otherwise, it just doesn't work. "Anything ribald tonight you just heard," announced Master of Ceremonies Phil Silvers, "we thought we'd camouflage it with a song, but this is as far as we go . . . unfortunately." Phil and the Friars had a busy week; he and Alan King had also helped hang a sign on a lamppost in Times Square designating it "Friars Square" for a day. Can you imagine Disney allowing a Friars Square there today—they'd probably prefer the prostitutes and drug dealers to that!

Silvers seemed lost with the format of honoring someone sincerely, "What can you say about this broad? The only thing I can think of is she's been pregnant twice and that was legitimate." No fun there. Not to mention, Silvers may have also felt slighted since he wasn't the first choice for the emcee spot. "The role of Toastmaster is new to me and it's because of an emergency—for two reasons. Our beloved Abbot Joe E. Lewis was felled by a rancid Alka-Seltzer pill in Pittsburgh, and George Jessel is busy tonight in Butte, Montana, at a dinner explaining what a Ben-Gurion is." (Well, what is a Ben-Gurion?) He finally shared what exactly his role as Prior entailed—and, surprisingly, it was more than just being able to entertain his grandchildren with silly tongue twisters like: Friars Prior Phil finds funny puns for flaky Friars Frolics. "I have been the Prior for the last five years, and I don't know what it means. One of my duties is, in our Monastery, in our main hall at the Club, there's a large bell, and if the Lambs Club decides to attack, I have to ring that bell." Does Tom Dillon, the current Shepherd of the Lambs, know about this? (Shepherd? Oy!) But, more importantly, does Sally Jessy Raphael, the current Friars' Prior, know about this? And can she say the tongue twister five times fast? Another job task of Silvers': "If an iceberg is seen in the vicinity of 55th Street and Madison, I have to make sure our cards don't get wet."

The Friars figured if Dinah didn't bring enough class with her, they had a backup plan: the distinguished tenor of the Metropolitan Opera Company, Richard Tucker. But since Dinah did bring her class with her, they got two for the price of one. Tucker sang *Mattinata* by Leon Cavallo. The only reason I knew what the heck he sang is because the Club's maitre d' is Italian (otherwise, you would have read *Matilda* by Lenny Kravitz, 'cause that's what it certainly sounded like to me).

While introducing NBC President David Sarnoff, Silvers inadvertently called him the "jock" of Gibraltar instead of the "rock." Believe it or not, the audience tittered and Silvers blushed, commenting that one of the reporters would write, "It was a wonderful evening, but Phil Silvers said a dirty word." He then went on to say, "This is no Freudian slip because this activity has left the man I'm gonna introduce." Interesting that these guys said things a hundred times worse at their stag events, and then they bend over backwards to behave at these Testimonials where women are present. He said jock, for heaven's sake! Sarnoff was a businessman by trade, but there's something about getting up in front of the Friars that literally makes everybody a comedian, which explains, "I was told by the Toastmaster that I had only one minute to say everything I know about Dinah. And considering that her husband is here tonight and my wife, that may have been a wise limitation." Did I say all comedians had to be funny? Besides, what do you expect from a jock?

Comedian Jean Carroll had an in with the Friars, being married to Buddy Howe, who served as dean of the Friars Club from 1964 to 1981. Another in was that she was a pretty funny stand-up comic, "My kid, she's one of those teenagers that give you ulcers if you let them. She became a beatnik and at first I don't like beatniks, but I don't want to oppose it. I don't even want to hit her because she hits back. I'll tell you the truth, I've accepted it. I don't mind the sneakers and the sloppy jeans and the sweaters down to the crotch, but why the beard?"

"Ladies and gentlemen, this is a memorable evening for me," announced Art Carney. "I have so many people to thank. The producer, the director, scenic designer, all those who took part, but most of all, the chef who turned out one of the finest Shore dinners I've ever had. There's a play on words there if you look for it." And while you're playing with words, try this one by Silvers, "Tonight our Man of the Year is a woman. A woman who has perhaps the largest fan club in America. I'm sure you've all heard of Diners' Club." Makes you sorta miss the Roasts, don't it?

The always-limber Dick Van Dyke, fresh from his turn in *Bye Bye Birdie*, was a special treat. Johnny Mathis sang a great rendition of *Witchcraft*, which was well worth the $75 ticket, a price that they complained seemed exorbitant. "But it does give us extra money for charity and it keeps a lot of the Friars out of here," reasoned Silvers. Speaking of out of here . . .

JOE E. LEWIS TESTIMONIAL DINNER – 1962

(Bottoms up!)

MILTON BERLE, *Toastmaster*   TINA LOUISE
JACK CARTER   TONY MARTIN
CHUBBY CHECKER   THE MCGUIRE SISTERS
MYRON COHEN   BARBARA RUSH
JACK DEMPSEY   NIPSEY RUSSELL
JOE DiMAGGIO   BLOSSOM SEELEY
EYDIE GORME   FORREST TUCKER
KENNETH KEATING   EARL WILSON
STEVE LAWRENCE   JULIE WILSON

Joe E. Lewis, as Alan King has said, was one of the most loveable guys around. Since he was hanging around the Club's bar day in and day out, the Friars figured it was time to get him out—so they held a Dinner for him at the Waldorf-Astoria. Milton Berle kept his act clean as Master of Ceremonies, "Lots of luck on your new arrival, Eydie, and I hope it's a boy. I hope you invite me to the bris. A bris, Senator Keating, is a medical function my people turned into a catered affair." Berle can't fool me. No matter how you slice it, he is far too preoccupied with penises for a man his age.

Jack Carter did a riff on the government, "Imagine a whole cabinet made up of all Friars, with Milton as President. I can see Sophie Tucker in Labor, it's all within the realm of possibility. Imagine if Jack Benny was Secretary of Treasury, 'Well, for God's sake, I think we ought to get some money back from the farkakte French government. At least we ought to get a lump sum, like Brigitte Bardot.' And I can see beloved Joe E. Lewis as Secretary of Interior. If there's any interior left in the secretary." But it was, after all, a Testimonial. "So now, I drink a toast to you, Joe E. Lewis. [Imitating Lewis—whatever the hell that would sound like] 'Here's to Eve, the mother of our race. Who wore a fig leaf in just the right place. Here's to Adam, the father of us all. Who was Joey on the spot when the leaves began to fall.'"

Singer Tony Martin, who sang a parody in Joe E.'s honor, suggested, "Why don't we team up. I think the world's ready for another Martin and Lewis." Berle put things in perspective about Tony, though, and explained why he has no respect for him, "Of course, he can't be bright. Any guy who has a beautiful girl like Cyd Charisse sitting at home and comes here to honor a drunk."

Nipsey Russel got over his fears of performing at the Club's event, "This is my first appearance at a gala affair for the Friars, and I was a little bit disturbed when I saw the gentlemen donning the hoods." You just knew those stupid monks' robes would get them in trouble one day, "To all the white people that are using Man Tan, I want you to know that I'm using a bleaching cream called Yellow Fellow. If you're nice enough to brown down, the least I can do is meet you halfway." He also showed his allegiance to the president, "I admire John Fitzgerald Kennedy. Any man who can spend thirty days vacationing in Paris and then convince 180 million people that he hurt his back planting a tree."

You have to hand it to the Friars; they were always timely with their musical talent. Chubby Checker was the hottest thing going, with "The Twist," and there he was teaching the entire ballroom how to swivel—it's a blessing in disguise that Forrest was the Tucker on the dais this time and not Sophie Tucker.

Joe E. was touched when he received his award at the end of the night—not sober, but touched. "I got to carry another load home, huh? If I thought you were gonna eulogize me this much, I'd have done the decent thing and died first. Words fail me. I don't know whether to throw funny lines or to say something serious. But deep down in my heart at this moment, this is my gift. I see a lot of friends, new friends, and that's my life story. And this is my epitaph. I don't want a monument. All I want is your continued friendship, goodwill, and a few winners, too, you know. May the good Lord take a liking to all of us, but not too soon. Show me a room that has relative humidity, and I'll show you a bunch of sweaty relatives." Are the tears flowing yet? And, after that, the audience screamed, "More, more!" He said, "I'm filled up here, no, I can't." And he didn't. But he was still loveable.

JOHNNY CARSON TESTIMONIAL DINNER – 1965

(He kept things flowing)

JOEY BISHOP, *Toastmaster*	BUDDY HACKETT
MARTY ALLEN	BUDDY HOWE
WOODY ALLEN	ALAN KING
MILTON BERLE	ED MCMAHON *(sort of)*
CHAMPAGNE BUCKET	ETHEL MERMAN
RED BUTTONS *(you never know)*	JULIET PROWSE
JACK CARTER *(maybe)*	STEVE ROSSI
NORM CROSBY *(possibly)*	SOUPY SALES *(probably not)*
BILLY DANIELS	DICK SHAWN
EYDIE GORME	MAYOR ROBERT WAGNER

Johnny Carson is considered one of the best of the Roasting and Toasting Friars. His wit, adept ad-libs, and quips put him in a class unto himself. One of the more amazing aspects of his appearances at these Friarly events was that his act was generally clean—he could be saucy and still be sweet, unsavory without being insipid and spicy without being lewd. That's not to say he didn't curse like the best of the boys; he simply used his supply of ribald verbiage sparingly. Being good at dishing out while taking it, he also made the perfect guest of honor—he loved a good joke, even if the punch line was directed dead center of his own self-esteem. Carson was honored four times by the Friars: a Roast in 1962 and two Dinners, in 1965 and in 1979, not to mention a televised Roast in 1968 as well.

Okay, time to set the record straight on the Friars Club's televised events. When Comedy Central aired the Drew Carey Roast in 1998, it was announced that it was the first-ever televised Roast in the history of the Friars. That's not true exactly, but it's not a lie either. Bear with me, and I'll give you the timeline lowdown. In 1958, Ed Sullivan allowed himself to be the guest of honor at a televised Roast that aired during his Sunday night time slot on CBS. The sponsor was Kodak, which spared no expense in plugging their cameras at the proceedings. On the dais were Joe E. Lewis, Walter Cronkite, Jack Carter, Jack E. Leonard, Joey Bishop, Morey Amsterdam, Phil Silvers, and some others. The comedians were scripted and, needless to say, it was clean—very clean, too clean. It was not the best advertising for a Friars' Roast, that's for sure. Not only were the guys scripted, but they looked and sounded like they were scripted. Apparently Amsterdam and Leonard were hired to "heckle" from their places on the dais. If only these two geniuses of heckling were allowed to do their own material, they would have come off funny instead of just plain annoying. In a word, it was a disaster.

It's a pretty good call that the Sullivan Roast kept the Friars off television for the next few years. But let's face it, what's the point of putting a Roast on TV if you can't curse? (Can I just say, once and for all, that the Dean Martin Roasts were *not* the Friars Club Roasts.) Next up on TV was Johnny Carson in 1968. It was an episode of *Kraft Music Hall* and Alan King was the emcee. Finally, this one was a hit, so Kraft did four more: Milton Berle and Jack Benny in 1969, Don Rickles in 1970, and Jerry Lewis in 1971. In spite of the fact that these, too, were scripted, they were winners. "They were all scripted, that was the beauty of it," says writer Marty Farrell, "because we wanted to do them with full control." So you had lines like these at the Rickles TV Roast: "I'm here to say something nice about Don Rickles, and for *that* you need an actor"—George C. Scott; "Don's family moved a great deal when he was young, and never told him where"—Alan King. The scripting, however, didn't seem to hinder the comics this time. Although by the Lewis Roast, interest or maybe just ratings waned. "That was the least successful of the Roasts. I always believe that there must be a certain amount of love between the people that are Roasting and the honoree, and I don't think that existed with Jerry," says Farrell. Oh my. As for Drew's Roast, you'll see. But it was different, so they're still not liars.

Heeere's Johnny! Joey Bishop was the Toastmaster for Johnny's Dinner. Looking around the dais, he noted, "If Carson weren't here, we could have done this whole thing in Yiddish." Buddy Hackett, who was to be closing the show, at one point yelled out to Bishop, "Why can't I follow somebody dull—like you!" Ethel Merman sang a medley of her hits, but that's not an act you want to follow either. Famous sidekick Ed McMahon said, "Carson has the average man's breakfast—a whiskey sour and a kumquat."

The most riveting of tales from this event has literally become the stuff from which urban myths are made. There are so many versions of this story that it makes one wonder if alligators really are living in the sewers of Manhattan. "You know the night Johnny Carson had to go the bathroom real bad, sitting on the dais?" Friars bad boy Hackett coyly asked in an interview for a documentary about the Friars. "He said, 'I gotta go to the bathroom.' I just took the champagne bucket and put it under the dais table, and he peed and filled up the bucket."

That's funny, because to hear Jack Carter talk about it, "The Roast where Carson peed, he was sitting next to me. I gave him the bucket. He was sitting there like this, 'Jesus Christ, I gotta go to the toilet.' I took a champagne bucket off the table, I put it under and said, 'Here, go ahead.' Buddy Hackett said, 'Right now, as I'm standing here, Carson's pissing on my leg.' Which is a stock joke, but Carson was really peeing. Nobody knew but me."

Oh, is that so? "I remember," muses Norm Crosby, "Carson was Roastmaster for Sammy Davis, and he was wonderful. He was peeing on Ed McMahon. He was sitting there on the dais. He couldn't get up to go to the bathroom and Ed was standing up and he was saying, 'Johnny is my dear friend, and I've always enjoyed working with him; and I've always respected his ability; and I've always known that he was the boss; and I did what he asked me to do; and as a matter of fact right now he's peeing on my leg.' And he was. Oh my God, it was hilarious. I was on the dais." Yeah, but was Johnny?

"One of the funniest, most outrageous things that happened out here was Johnny Carson, who peed," says Red Buttons. "He just didn't leave the dais. They brought him a bowl and he was hidden and he peed sitting there, into this round bowl at one of the affairs. In California." Calif . . . ?

Ed McMahon pleads the fifth, although he does admit, "I wasn't on the dais, as I recall I was in the audience. I used to kid around, if he sneezed in the valley and I was in downtown Beverly Hills, I'd say 'God bless you.' I mean, we just felt each other and with a look I just knew something was going to happen, before he had to use the champagne bucket."

According to Soupy Sales, "I had my own Roast in '65 and it was great, except that I had to go to the bathroom. I was peeing in a pitcher underneath the table because I couldn't leave and Marty Allen and Joe E. Lewis were sitting next to me. I couldn't leave because it was about me. I was sitting right next to the podium and I asked Marty Allen to hand me a pitcher and he said 'All right.'"

All I have to say is, don't drink the champagne at a Friars Club event.

BARBRA STREISAND TESTIMONIAL DINNER – 1969

(Musical memories)

DANNY THOMAS, *Toastmaster*	JOE E. LEWIS
HAROLD ARLEN	ETHEL MERMAN
GENE BAYLOS	DAVID MERRICK
SAMMY CAHN	ROBERT MERRILL
JEAN CARROLL	DON RICKLES
CY COLEMAN	RICHARD RODGERS
MARTY ERLICHMAN	HAROLD ROME
EYDIE GORME	PHIL SILVERS
JERRY HERMAN	RAY STARK
PAT HENRY	JULE STYNE
BUDDY HOWE	ED SULLIVAN
LEO JAFFE	WILLIAM B. WILLIAMS
GEORGE JESSEL	ROBERT D. WOOD
BURTON LANE	RICHARD ZANUCK
STEVE LAWRENCE	

It was probably a wise move on the part of the Friars to have a courteous Testimonial for Barbra Streisand as opposed to a rowdy Roast—if only to showcase the music, of course. (What else would there be to fear?) While she drew a record crowd of 135,000 to her free concert in Central Park a season earlier, the Friars certainly couldn't complain about the record numbers at their own private happening at the Waldorf-Astoria. They are a picky bunch, though. In spite of the likes of Steve & Eydie, Ethel Merman, David Merrick, and their own legends of comedy—Rickles, Jessel, and Silvers—the Friars were cranky that a charity event on the West Coast caused many of the celebs in the L.A. area to bail out on them. Namely, Jack Benny, who was originally slated to have been the Toastmaster. But Danny Thomas seemed to fill Benny's shoes quite well, at least according to *Variety:* "'Thomas is impressed with the beauties of the English language, and he embellishes and poeticizes and puts flowers where most Toastmasters wouldn't. He said he wasn't going to be funny in this role as it's not his bag. His sole bid for outright laughs was a routine of the fiery Sicilian passions of his wife. However, he provided a note of class and color to the chair'." Sounds like Danny just used too many big words for the Friars to handle.

Barbra seemed to share the bill with the music of those composers whose music and lyrics helped put her on the map of superstardom. Harold Arlen, Richard Rodgers, and Jule Styne were among the musical geniuses who performed parodies of their famous tunes just for their favorite gal.

Admittedly, you may have to have a working knowledge of these hits to find some semblance of a tune, but their lyrics are superb, so either stick with it, or go get a pretzel, then come back and jump to the next event.

Harold Arlen, *Come Rain or Come Shine*:

> I'm gonna love you, like nobody's loved you, come rain or come Stark
> My Brooklyn princess, who eats her cheese blintzes above Central Park
> Travels with her Jason to the chic Paris salons
> Then gets a new face on that is not quite British but beautifully Yiddish
> She overcame me, with clothes cockamamie from Bergdorf's & Klein's

She broke all records, including my records, but not Jule Styne's
Her days will always be sunny with trunks full of taxable money
But I'm with you, Brunnhilda, I'm with you rain or shine

Jule Styne, *Time After Time:*

Time after time, I tell myself that I'm so lucky to be Jule Styne
When things seemed so dark, I walked up to Ray Stark
And I said, please meet a friend of mine (Barbra Streisand, Ray Stark,
Ray Stark, Barbra Streisand)
Miss Streisand sang and I played
He said she looks just like my maid
Just you do your job and I'll do mine
Which just goes to show, how much producers know
He said Belle Barth would be divine
You all know the switch
The maid she made him rich
For which he hates Jule Styne

Richard Rodgers, *The Sweetest Sounds*

The sweetest sounds she's ever made are still inside her head
The best reviews she's ever had are waiting to be read
Notes that issue from her throat, will still be lovely things
And the world will know its happiest times when wondrous
    Barbra sings
Whenever Barbra, our Barbra sings.

Oh, those *People* and their *Memories!* I just didn't want to be
left out.

Needless to say, Don Rickles had much to say about the
guest of honor. You just needed a Yiddish dictionary to understand what the yentzen he's talking about, "Ladies and gentlemen, my dear friends, Danny Thomas, all of you, I'm so fed up
with this farkakte affair you can't believe it. This Jewish girl, her
mother a year ago was in Rockaway holding on to the ropes.
Barbra, I say this publicly, I never liked you! Mother, God bless
you. The mother, Barbra's mother's sitting here, gesund, with
naches, is that the mother? Give her a nice hand. God bless you,
darling. Your daughter's a dummy, mom, I'll tell you that right

now. You got a dummy daughter that made it, and everyone is shmeichel her now." But he's no dummy, he made a proper exit, "And so to you, mom, to you Barbra, gesund, may God bless you. It is an honor to be on your dais, it is an honor to be here tonight."

As for Barbra herself, "This was an incredible evening," she wrote in liner notes years later for one of her CD compilations, "the highlight of which was a tribute by seven American composers. To get a sense of what that meant to me, just think about the sweep of those seven careers: Harold Arlen, Richard Rodgers, Jule Styne, Harold Rome, Cy Coleman, Jerry Herman, and Burton Lane have given us some of America's most beautiful, moving, and enduring popular music. For them to sing me their songs, with special lyrics written by Sammy Cahn (Richard Rodgers wrote his own), was an unforgettable honor." For the Friars to give a tribute to Streisand—well, that was pretty unforgettable, too. What they did seem to forget, however, was to keep a record of the night so they wouldn't have to rely on her own CD liner notes for the memories.

CAROL BURNETT TESTIMONIAL
DINNER – 1973

(You sure it's not a Roast?)

DICK CAVETT, *Toastmaster*	SYLVIA MILES
RICHARD CHAMBERLAIN	GARRY MOORE
RHONDA FLEMING	JIM NABORS
STU GILLIAM	FREDDIE ROMAN
JOE HAMILTON	DICK SHAWN
HARRY HERSHFIELD	JULE STYNE
BUDDY HOWE	ED SULLIVAN
HARVEY KORMAN	BOBBY VAN
PEGGY LEE	BEN VEREEN
HAL LINDEN	LYLE WAGGONER
LORNA LUFT	BARBARA WALTERS
WALTER MATTHAU	WILLIAM B. WILLIAMS

The most amazing thing happened at Carol Burnett's Testimonial Dinner—Hal Linden actually made the Friars' Song bearable! He did what no man or woman had done before: he breathed some life into that creaky old tune. Admittedly, the song was well past middle age, but it was still younger than George Burns and he was still ticking. Linden gave it more of an upbeat flavor, and it almost came off sounding like an Irish ditty. He invited the audience to sing along, but as usual with that song, the request fell on deaf ears.

Dick Cavett was the Toastmaster, but right from his introduction he was labeled "Roastmaster" so it was anybody's guess how the night would go. He had no problem switching hats if it was, indeed, a Roast, "You can actually measure Carol's stature just by looking at this dais. Obviously, every big star was out of town. This is a Roast, isn't it? Carol is not the first woman to be honored by the Friars by any means. Actually, the first one was a belly dancer. They didn't call it a Roast, it was a shake and bake." Cavett seemed to have a handle on the Friars' history better than most, "I'm not a Friar, and I don't know how this Club got started. The only Friar I know much about, in college I had to read about the Friar in Chaucer's *Canterbury Tales*, who was rotten, drank too much, ate too much, told vile stories, seduced girls—maybe I do know how this Club got started. Was anyone else going to do Chaucer jokes?" He got off Chaucer, only to get back to Roasting Carol, "I'm trying to remember the facts about Carol because the bio that CBS sent over was not helpful. The first two facts on it were *Once Upon A Mattress* and "has three children," and even Jacqueline Susann knows that isn't possible. If you think these remarks have no particular continuity, wait until Ed Sullivan gets up here."

Talk about psychic! Ed did get up there and proceeded to lull the audience into a stupor, "Carol Burnett was born in Dallas, Texas, the Lone Star State, which produced, as you know, two presidents, Dwight Eisenhower and Lyndon Johnson, as well as Debbie Reynolds, Mary Martin, Mrs. Bing Crosby, Joan Crawford, Jimmy Dean, Josh Logan, Cyd Charisse, King Vidor, B.J. Thomas. . . . " This is all very interesting, Ed, but is there a punch line? There wasn't.

Harry Hershfield, who appeared at so many Roasts since the dawn of man, was now eighty-eight and was thrilled to finally be invited to attend "a quality party like this." He then proceeded to tell a joke about a rapist. I'll spare you the joke, but the punch line was, "So one woman called up the other and says, 'Mrs. Gottlieb, a raper is going through the building.' She said, 'I gave already.'" That's quality for you.

Walter Matthau had starred in *Pete 'N Tillie* with Burnett and was an unexpected guest, "I was surprised Walter was there. I wasn't told, so that was a thrill for me. When he walked in and sat down on the dais, I was very touched by that." What didn't touch her were Matthau's kind remarks, "I'll go anyplace they're having a party for Carol Burnett. I don't really think she's a great star, she's talented to a degree. She was very restrained in the picture. Her television show, she's quite funny, she's not really a great star like Clark Gable or Greta Garbo. But because she is so sweet and so nice and such a beautiful girl. . . . " "*Bullshit!*" Burnett yelled out. A nonplussed Matthau retorted, "That's a Russian word. It means 'thank you' in Russian."

"Carol didn't want me to tell this," said Cavett, who threw out several tidbits throughout the evening. "But she flew in today and she was ill on the flight here and spent most of her time in the restroom on the plane. Actually, she didn't but I said that because I wanted the chance to say, 'she went from the flying can into the Friars.' This is a pun that I worked on all night."

Dick Shawn is one of those performers who keeps you guessing as to what stunt he may pull, but he was relatively normal this evening. "I worked with Carol Burnett on a show on Broadway and I can't say that I really *know* Carol Burnett, but I know her. We did the show *Fade In, Fade Out*, and it did." He then sang a parody of "Silent Night" as the orchestra played *Also Spracht Zarathustra* (you know, the theme to *2001: A Space Odyssey*), "I hope I didn't offend anyone. Listen, if I did that that way ten years ago, in Las Vegas, it would have been considered sacrilegious, but today it's just bad taste." Remember I said "relatively" normal.

"My first dinner that I ever performed at was the Carol Burnett Dinner," remembers Freddie Roman, "and I was a nervous wreck. It was a star-studded dais. It was out of this world, and I was about the sixth or seventh speaker and I was the new kid on the block." But the new kid pulled it off, "I know my being here has to be one of Carol's great thrills. I mean, for her to find out that Freddie Roman was going to be on her dais tonight is like finding out that Truman Capote is hanging out with your son. I'll never forget the first time I met Carol. It was during the salad, and as long as I've known her she hasn't changed. Carol is one of the funniest ladies on TV, although Paul Lynde does come close." Freddie also answered the question on everyone's mind, "Listening to Ed Sullivan was a thrill. I thought it was a Dinner for Texas!"

Stu Gilliam definitely was under the impression this event was a Roast, "I am an authority on ugly. Now, a lot of you are sitting there saying, 'Is he actually going to call Carol ugly?' I am, friends, and I think that in this instance we should look at our values because beauty is such a fleeting thing. Beauty is only skin deep; ugly is to the bone. I can sympathize with Mr. Joe Hamilton, because it is a problem courting an ugly chick. Let's face it, fellas, we've all done a little charity work." Cavett may not remember a whole lot from almost thirty years ago, but this moment was crystal clear, "Each time he repeated the phrase it seemed to get farther and farther away from him, and in the end I think he played to total silence. It was one of the most embarrassing things I've ever witnessed at a party in a room with people with tuxedos. Ill-advised." Carol's memory chose the diplomacy route, "I remember that there were a few little zingers or barbs that I thought weren't very funny, I can't tell you what they were. I remember that that did occur."

Harvey Korman answered the question of what it was like to work with Carol, "The best way I can answer that, and I'll ask you to bear with me, is someone once asked Terry Thomas—you know the funny English actor with his teeth parted in the middle— 'What was it like working with Red Skelton?' and I have the same answer. Terry said, 'Well, it's rather like farting in a windstorm.'"

Ben Vereen was red-hot, starring in *Pippin* on Broadway that year, and the Friars got him to perform *Corner of the Sky*. A real class act. Boring, but classy.

When Buddy Howe presented Carol with her award (they may have been up to watches that year), Carol said, "I would like to refuse this on the grounds of the inhuman behavior that the gentiles are given at the Stage Delicatessen." She also reiterated Matthau's thoughts, "I'll go anywhere anybody will give me a party." But for her formal acceptance speech, to hear Carol tell it today, it would seem she had inherited the Friars' genes that Victor Herbert and Irving Berlin had coursing through their self-esteems, "I don't like getting up in front of my peers and trying to be funny or performing; it's a very odd thing. I'm much less nervous in front of regular folks. It frightens me less than getting up in front of a room full of show business pros. It terrifies me. So I thought, 'Oh gosh, this is such an honor and I'm so thrilled to be a part of this, but oh, what am I gonna do?' I remember Dinah, when she was honored, I think she sang, so I talked to Ken and Mitzi Walsh, who are professional material writers, and they said, 'Why don't you get up and sing'?

"I had this lovely Bob Mackey gown on and I was fully made up—eyelashes, the whole nine yards. So I got up and I said, 'I'm so, so touched by this evening. I really don't have a speech, but I do have my song. So I started, 'I'm so glad we had this time together,' and the audience applauded. Then I sang, 'And tonight I'll pull my ears for the Friars,' and they applauded. Then I went into, 'And I'd also like to thank the waiters, for the de da,' so it got sillier and sillier. I was just staying on, singing about the busboys, singing about the ladies' room attendant, singing about the airline that flew us in, the pilot, the flight attendant, that I liked the food on the plane, and singing about the salad, and on and on. They didn't quite, I'm sure, know how I was going to finish. I'm sure they thought I'd have a cute punch line and get off. So Harvey finally said, 'Oh, shut up!' and hit me with this pie. We brought it in when we came in for dinner in a brown paper bag, and Harvey guarded it throughout the entire meal. Nobody expected it to happen to a woman because I was gowned and coiffed and it was funnier happening to a woman, I believe, than it would be to happen to a guy in a tux. It got me off with a laugh." Well, Carol, we expect nothing less!

FRANK SINATRA TESTIMONIAL DINNER – 1976

(Nobody move!)

HOWARD COSELL /	ROBERT MERRILL
ED MCMAHON, *Toastmasters*	JAN MURRAY
SPIRO AGNEW	DON RICKLES
ABRAHAM D. BEAME	JILLY RIZZO
MILTON BERLE	STEVE ROSS
GOVERNOR HUGH CAREY	FRANK SINATRA, JR.
JOHN DENVER	DAVID TEBET
CARY GRANT	SARAH VAUGHAN
PAT HENRY	JOHN WAYNE
GEORGE JESSEL	JERRY WEINTRAUB
JOHN W. KLUGE	WILLIAM B. WILLIAMS
JERRY LEWIS	

"I'll tell you why we're all up here tonight, and I'll tell you it in one word—*fear!*" If Milton Berle's comment doesn't clue you in that the guest of honor was Frank Sinatra, then you haven't sat through enough A&E biographies of ol' blue eyes. It was an auspicious occasion, and not because former vice president Spiro Agnew was on the dais. Leave it to the Friars to invite the least-invited person at that time on their dais. But Frank literally was the Friars' Chairman of the Board, still settling into his new position as Abbot. Finally, the Friars had an Abbot who came with his own ring to kiss.

Needless to say, Sinatra's Dinner dared to be different right from the start. "Frank, being Mr. Sinatra," explains Ed McMahon, "invited me to be the Toastmaster and then forgot and invited Howard Cosell to be the Toastmaster. So it wound up being the both of us." Cosell worked the first half of the event, leaving McMahon to clean up with the heavyweight closers.

"Because the king of entertainment has deigned to honor us with his presence, however briefly," announced Cosell, "as you look at him now, an antique relic of yesteryear, clinging grimly to the memories of the past and living off the blissful nostalgia of elderly people at every arena where he appears." And this was just the beginning.

By the time McMahon took over halfway through the proceedings, the audience was either thrilled to have learned new words from Cosell or thrilled that they didn't have to hear from him for the rest of the night. Guess what category McMahon fit into? "As you know, Cosell could expound, he was very loquacious, had a great use of the language. He introduced the guy who had the rustic cabin where Sinatra used to be a waiter and later singer, and he introduced him like he was Cecil B. DeMille; 'And this little cabin, and he saw the light, and he was the magic' and he went on and on and on. So by the time I got up there after Cosell had milked every introduction dry, I said, 'It's such a pity that in Howard Cosell's great knowledge of the lexicon, he never learned the word 'brevity.'"

Speaking of brevity, or lack thereof, "I've never seen such a crowd. I would've said mob, but you know how sensitive he is," blasted Berle, giving a string of stinging comments to anyone within earshot. "Howard, I'd like to shake your hand, but I see you're busy. . . . Everybody picks on Cosell. He is a man that has been maligned, abused, insulted, spit on, and deservedly so. . . . Governor Carey, it's a great pleasure to be up here with you. I don't know why everybody picks on him, he hasn't done anything. . . . I got so much gas in me, I'm followed by Arabs." It's all about image. Care to read more? "Why are we honoring this man tonight, this aging Jerry Vale. . . . George Burns was supposed to be here tonight, something came up and he was very proud. . . . I'm very glad George Jessel's here, I think. Looks like he died ten years ago. . . . This Paul Anka of the menopause set." But one thing about Berle, he never lost sight of the venue he was playing, this was not a Roast; so it was important to talk about Frank the humanitarian. "It was this man who built the Eisenhower Memorial Hospital in Palm Beach and put all his friends in it."

Please memorize this joke of Berle's; it's just a fun little bit that will give you hours of pleasure as you read through this book: "Laugh it up, Governor. I laugh when you speak." Trust me, it may not do much for you now, but it will kick in up the road.

Frank Sinatra, Jr., sang "My Favorite Things," which one would think for any kid of Frank's everything better be his favorite. George Jessel asked Sinatra how old his son was, and when he said "Twenty-nine," Jessel said, "I've got underwear older than that!" These images that they keep conjuring up are just not healthy.

Robert Merrill, of Metropolitan Opera fame, said, "Walter Goldstein [the Friars Club's Executive Director] handed me this piece of paper when I walked in the door tonight and said, 'Sammy Cahn wrote this lovely tribute to Frank and *do it!*' I don't even know it. I don't even know the piano player. But I took one look at Jilly Rizzo, and I'm gonna do it." Oh, to be in a room full of Frank and his friends, Jilly, etc. The song Merrill sang was a parody of "My Way." Jan Murray also learned his "you'll do it Frank's way" lessons, "He has such a quaint way of sending invitations. I mean, last Sunday a guy drove up to my house in a cement truck and asked me for my shoe size. Ten minutes later, I had plane tickets."

The Friars may not always have class, but they certainly know where to get some when they need it, which is why they invited Cary Grant on occasion. "It's a curious thing with me. I come to these things, and I get up and the moment I get up on my feet, I cease to function. I don't function very well lying down either. I, uh, have a dread of making an ass of myself in front of you." Or maybe he just owed some money to a certain someone who was seated on the dais.

Pat Henry was feeling brave that night, "Frank, this isn't your kind of audience, there's a lot of people here with necks. . . . I'll tell you how big Frank is, he wears a cross and nobody's on it. . . . Frank was very sick and one by one we were allowed to go into his room and visit. We'd kiss his ring. I don't mind, but he usually had it in his back pocket. Now he's getting old; he's getting weird. He's starting to move that ring around a lot. I don't like that."

"This is a song that Frank wrote, and it'll tell you a little bit more about why his songwriting career lasted so briefly," said John Denver, who then broke into a song that began, "Saturday night in Toledo, Ohio. . . . " I wonder if you still got in trouble with Frank if you were mean, but right?

"I cannot thank all of you enough for tonight," said Sinatra after he was presented with his watch. "I will not be able to thank you enough for the rest of my life. Put me down for a favor, each and every one of you." Rumor has it that Jimmy Hoffa is the only one who tried cashing in on that.

DAVID BRINKLEY, WALTER CRONKITE, AND HOWARD K. SMITH TESTIMONIAL DINNER – 1978

(The Marx Brothers were busy that night!)

JOHNNY CARSON, *Toastmaster*	JIM JENSEN
LAUREN BACALL	HENRY KISSINGER
BILL BEUTEL	PENNY MARSHALL
JACK CAFFERTY	ROBERT MERRILL
JOHN CHANCELLOR	ROB REINER
KIRK DOUGLAS	BURT REYNOLDS
FRANK FIELD	CHUCK SCARBOROUGH
JOEL GREY	DINAH SHORE
BUDDY HOWE	MIKE WALLACE
JACOB JAVITZ	WILLIAM B. WILLIAMS

I had every intention of leaving this portion blank. I mean, it's a Testimonial Dinner for three newsmen, for God's sake! But take a look at that dais—okay, skip a name or two, but if they managed to get Lauren Bacall, Penny Marshall, Rob Reiner, and Burt Reynolds—not to mention Carson—to show up, they can't be total slouches in the "fun" department. And Johnny is always funny, "To be a guest of honor at a Friars' Dinner, the Friars set a very high standard. One, you must own a suit. Two, you must be free on a Friday night. And that's about it." The sad part is, he was dead serious.

"My only hope is that there is no earth-shattering news that breaks tonight during dinner, because if the roof caved in on this ballroom, Captain Kangaroo would be doing the news later tonight." Here's a Friar tidbit—Bob Keeshan, AKA Captain

Kangaroo, was a Friar. Just in case you thought it was only for old has-beens. "Half of this dais has reported some of the most dismaying, horrendous news in world history, and the other half of the dais has caused it," observed Johnny. You have to admit, when he's on a roll, don't interrupt. "Howard Cosell was originally supposed to be here tonight, but Howard is busy having himself cloned, so he will have someone to talk to. . . . Barbara Walters was supposed to be here, but she is busy working on her next special, an exclusive interview with Jesus Christ and Charo. . . . A lot of people wonder where Walter got his catchphrase that he signs off with on the news every night. That goes back to his lovely wife, Betsy. She came up with that on their wedding night, when she said to Walter, 'That's the way it is.'" Walter Cronkite and sex jokes—there's something you don't read every day.

John Chancellor was pretty funny for a man who makes a living from ruining people's days, "With all of these great speakers, I feel like a long-tailed cat in a room full of rocking chairs. I want to tell you what it's like to be the junior member of a partnership. Brinkley gets to give news on the secretary of state; I get the Son of Sam. He gets to cover Henry Kissinger's wedding; I get Henry Winkler's wedding." Sour grapes are always so much sweeter when dispensed at a Friars Club event, don't you think?

Dinah Shore sang "Three Guys in a Newsroom" to the tune of "Three Coins in the Fountain," which must have put the crowd in a fun, silly mood. Stephanie Mills, fresh from *The Wiz*, bopped through "Ease on Down the Road," which must have put the crowd in a foot-stomping mood. Robert Merrill sang "Figaro." I'll leave it up to you to figure out the crowd's mood at that point.

Laugh-a-minute Mike Wallace played stand-up comic for a minute or two, "Cronkite is a lousy loser at tennis and a genuinely second-rate sailor." Raise your hand if you got that, and raise both of them if you also found it funny. But don't base his comedic talents on one joke alone, "Smith is the only man I know who is simultaneously a friend of Richard Nixon and Alger Hiss. Most Americans get their news from these three men—no wonder the country is in the shape it's in." Now you see why I considered having just a blank page for this section.

Burt Reynolds was on such a roll at the end of the '70s and was a huge catch for any dais, "I thought it would be safe to follow Mike Wallace, because I knew he wouldn't be funny"; he was also amazingly astute. "I really don't know these three men. I did have a chance encounter once with Howard K. Smith—we both answered the same singles ad in a magazine."

Carson was the master because of his timing with certain ad-libs, such as this one: "When Dave Tebet was putting together this Dinner he said to me, 'Johnny, you will be the only one on the dais doing funny material or comedy,' and I want to thank him for keeping his promise."

Kirk Douglas spoke, "I can't tell you what a privilege it is to be spending hard-earned money on a Dinner honoring three men who have brought bad news into my house for the last twenty-five years." Wait? They made Kirk pay? You know, Kirk Douglas had a Testimonial Dinner in 1977, and Gregory Peck was the Toastmaster. How cool is that? Not to mention the dais had the likes of Burt Lancaster, George C. Scott, George Segal, and Lily Tomlin. But here you sit reading about a Dinner for three evening news anchors, and you probably heard of only one or two of them—that's funny, right?

If Henry Kissinger ever considered giving up the political life, the Improv has a slot waiting for him, "President Carter gave a fireside chat wearing a sweater, making him the first president ever to begin his term by pulling the wool over his own eyes. I inspired that unusual, rhythmic way that Brinkley talks."

For anyone who may not realize it, Walter Cronkite is actually a funny man. At a Roast once, he just walked up to the podium and simply said, "Fuck you," and sat down again. He kept it clean during his Man of the Year acceptance speech, but just as witty, "I want to ensure my wife and the IRS that I am neither dead nor retiring. I was a little late, I did my show tonight, but I know that a lot of you have been here since the bar opened at seven, so you would have missed my evening news—so I'll read it to you." And he did! "I've been inspired by Johnny," continued Cronkite, "Now, I'm going to have a guest anchor on Mondays and Fridays, and I'm going to play Vegas once a month." He could probably pull that off, too.

Well, there you have it—the end of another funny Friars' era. They rock 'n' rolled through the '50s, grooved through the '60s and sought to make the '70s stand for something more daring than just being known as *The Brady Bunch* decade. The bad boys had grown up, only it was Peter Pan who was leading the Rat Pack right into a whole new epoch. They sold their salacious souls in exchange for bawdy laughter and never looked back. Which may explain their tendency to hold on to old jokes tighter than programs of old Roasts and Dinners.

Looking ahead toward their golden years, the Friars' cast may change a bit, for obvious reasons (not everyone can live to a hundred, unless you've played God in a movie, of course), but their legacy certainly lingers. And funny like nobody's business!

CHAPTER 4

1980s—DEVILISH DINNERS AND ROWDY ROASTS

Tough guys and tempestuous gals

TESTIMONIAL DINNERS

1980	Dr. Henry A. Kissinger	1984	Dean Martin
1981	Burt Reynolds	1985	Milton Berle
1981	Buddy Hackett	1987	Red Buttons
1982	Cary Grant	1988	Barbara Sinatra
1983	Elizabeth Taylor	1989	Alan King

CELEBRITY ROASTS

1982	Dick Shawn	1986	Jerry Lewis
1983	Sid Caesar	1987	Rich Little
1985	Phyllis Diller	1989	Bruce Willis

One by one they come and go. A bunch of decrepit relics of yesteryear, each clinging to the same tawdry lines of the past worth nothing.
—Howard Cosell, at the Jerry Lewis Roast, 1986

Milton had a tough childhood. He was abandoned by wolves and raised by his parents.
—Jan Murray, at yet another Milton Berle Dinner, 1985

By the time 1980 reared its regal head around the uninspiring '70s (let us not forget that was the decade that Chevrolet gave us the Vega), the New York Friars Club was seventy-six years old—and most of the jokes were older than that. No longer the new kid on the block, the Friars Club now ruled the show biz kingdom with their tart tongues and biting wits. They were poised and ready to take on the tough guys of Hollywood. Those elite few whose commanding presence intimidated many were indeed the perfect fodder for the Friars' very special badge of honor.

While two separate entities of riotous Roasts versus sophisticated Dinners continued to exist, the ever-closing gap between the two did not go unnoticed. *Variety* noted in an article covering the Friars Testimonial Dinner in honor of Alan King in 1989, "The line of demarcation between the formal Friars dinners and the raunchy stag luncheons is continuing to narrow. Some predict ultimate erosion." Then again, maybe Alan just brought out the worst in people.

DR. HENRY KISSINGER
TESTIMONIAL DINNER – 1980

(Accent on the testimony)

KIRK DOUGLAS, *Toastmaster*	MATTHEW, MARK, LUKE & JOHN
WILLIAM F. BUCKLEY	ROGER MOORE
JEAN CARROLL	PETER NERO
BARRY DILLER	GREGORY PECK
EPHRAIM EVRON	LOU RAWLS
ASHRAF A. GHORBAL	BARBARA SINATRA
BOB HOPE	FRANK SINATRA
BUDDY HOWE	DAVID TEBET
LEO JAFFE	ROBERT F. WAGNER
JACOB JAVITS	MIKE WALLACE
NANCY KISSINGER	BARBARA WALTERS
JOHN W. KLUGE	WILLIAM B. WILLIAMS

Apparently someone thought that perhaps the Friars weren't taking themselves seriously enough, and when those thoughts occur, visions of Dr. Henry Kissinger dance in people's heads. While it is true that the Dinners are resplendent in class and sophistication, perfect for honoring one of the nation's foremost politicos, the Friars will forever embody the spirit of the phrase, You can dress them up, but you can't take them out. Certainly not to the Waldorf-Astoria Hotel. "With all his wondrous achievements," announced Toastmaster Kirk Douglas, "what I admire most about him is that he has been appointed to the Nobel Sperm Bank. The mind boggles to think that in another generation any woman can go to any sperm bank in America and order a Henry Kissinger with an American accent." That's wrong on so many levels. Douglas had begun the evening with, "Dearly beloved, we are gathered here tonight to honor a man who has flown more air miles than Jonathan Livingston Seagull; has tasted more ethnic dishes than a New York politician; and who has awakened in more Hilton Hotels than Zsa Zsa Gabor. A man who speaks with an accent but never with forked tongue." Anyone remember *Jonathan Livingston Seagull*? Those Friars were always so topical.

If Kissinger, the man, was Toasted this particular evening, his haughty personality was Roasted. Here's what Barbara Walters had to say this night, "Everything pompous that you could possibly want to say about him he says about himself first. This past Tuesday I heard Shimon Perez, the leader of the opposition party in Israel, toast Henry Kissinger at a small dinner by recalling when he first met the then Secretary of State, 'Shall we call you Mr. Secretary or do you prefer Dr. Kissinger?' And with great modesty Henry Kissinger answered, 'How about simply, Your Excellency.'"

While in 1980 Kissinger was married to Nancy, Walters recalled a time when he was one of the sexiest single men alive. She had interviewed him for the *Today* show in 1970. "Our producer said, 'Make sure you tell people who he is.' So I spent fifteen out of the twenty-minute interview telling people who Henry Kissinger was, and assuring them that in spite of the accent he was *our* national security advisor. At the end of the interview, I said of this new bachelor around Washington who was beginning to stir some attention, 'Dr. Kissinger, how do you feel now when people are beginning to call you a swinger?' And he said, 'I love it now, because when I bore people they think it's their fault.'" So when you read about Kissinger again at Barbara Walters' Dinner in 1994 and start nodding off, it will be all your own fault.

Ashraf Ghorbal was the ambassador from Egypt who probably has his own sitcom over there now. The short-statured politician complained that he had to stand between Gregory Peck and Barbara Sinatra during the "Star Spangled Banner," and Peck told him to "stand up." He was going to bring a motion up to the UN, "When national anthems are played, I feel short people should stand and tall people kneel." Ephraim Evron, the ambassador to Israel, apparently has a competing sitcom, addressing the crowd thusly as he approached the podium, "Your royal highness, ladies and gentlemen. If there was one thing we learned very quickly when Dr. Kissinger arrived in Israel, it was his modesty." (I love that word "thusly," by the way.)

William F. Buckley must have given the guest of honor ego lessons, "Henry Kissinger was toying with the idea of running for the senate, always assuming that Jack Javits elected to retire. He confided this rumination to me, soliciting my advice, which is much more valuable than my support."

Bob Hope is one of those legends in his own time and he isn't represented enough at these events, although the Friars did have a Dinner for him in 1953. Can you feel a digression coming on? It'll only take a minute, I swear, and I promise to throw in a politico so you won't lose the feel of Henry's bash—how's that? So at Hope's Dinner in 1953, George Jessel was the Toastmaster and in attendance was Vice President Alben W. Barkley. Just out of curiosity, how many of you Americans knew that Mr. Barkley was the VP in 1953? "Jesse Block phoned me to come to the Hope Dinner and say a few things," said Fred Allen, "while Jessel's on the phone, there's Berle, the Abbot of the Friars, on TV doing my jokes! Swell timing these Friars have; Monsignor Fulton Sheen is doing so well on TV that his sponsor, Admiral, is planning to put out a new set, specially for the clergy. It will have stained glass tubes."

Berle was at Hope's Dinner, of course, "I'm happy Hope's not opposite me on TV. I have enough trouble with Fulton Sheen." To which Jessel responded, "You've now heard file No. 9." So basically Berle has always recycled jokes, is that the deal? Hope, for his part, had this to say—and this is one of the reasons why this little digression fits so perfectly, "No man could be so great as these fellows said I was. But they finally convinced me." Such modesty won't be seen again until, say, 1980.

Hope also added about Berle, "He's great and I love him on television. He's Mr. TV. At least he was until Tallulah got on." Wasn't that a nice look back?

In 1980 Hope put the Kissinger evening in perspective by pointing out, "I haven't had a night like this since Howard Cosell invited me to his reading of the *Encyclopedia Britannica*." It was the Friars Club meets *Masterpiece Theater*—with a Teutonic flair. He continued with a little celebrity gossip, "Fred Astaire was at the Kentucky Derby today, and he's going to marry jockey Robyn Smith. He's going for the long ride. I think it's a marvelous thing, I think it's brave of Fred to marry someone carrying a whip. And I can't wait for the wedding with Gene Autry singing, 'We're back in the saddle again.'" He moved on to religion, "The Israeli Ambassador, I know they don't have kosher food here but the Waldorf did the next best thing, they had Sammy Davis bless the whole bit."

Hope did spend some time talking about the Friars, "This is a great organization, they do this every year, it's a charitable organization. All these wonderful members gather every day to discuss the fate of less fortunate poor people—their gin opponents. It's not generally known, but Robert Taylor, Georgie Jessel, and myself started the L.A. chapter of the Friars in 1938. It was Jessel's idea; he needed a place to hide out from paternity suits. I was the original Abbot of the L.A. Friars. I really was; it's a very responsible position, it's true. Very responsible, about as important as dialogue director on *Deep Throat*, and I enjoyed it." He ended, appropriately, on politics, "Ronald Reagan. I can't wait to see an actor in the White House, won't that be great? With Max Factor as head of the state department. I can see the president sending over Don Rickles as ambassador to Iran. He'd walk in to the Ayatollah and say, 'Look, Kakamanie, you need a new flea collar.'"

Frank Sinatra was filming *The First Deadly Sin* during this time (his first film after a ten-year absence), so he arrived late to the Dinner. Lucky for him, his wife, Barbara, had saved a seat for him on the dais, not that he took it. Rumor has it that he opted to stand backstage because he didn't want to share the dais with Barbara Walters. Maybe she made him cry once

Elizabeth Taylor explains to Dinah Shore and Frank Sinatra her philosophy of diplomatic relations with Cold War countries—or maybe it was how she got the flower to stay in her hair all night.

Red Buttons breaks up Steve Allen and Dick Shawn.

Phyllis Diller and Buddy Hackett get even—Friars style!

Phyllis Diller as Claude Rains, or is it Dr. Smith from *Lost In Space*?

Milton Berle with Bruce Willis, who was wondering why he ever agreed to this.

Madeline Kahn, Burt Reynolds, and Dinah Shore know a better Dinner is going on "right over there."

Buddy Hackett gets applause from Sid Caesar—why?

Frank Sinatra, Shirley MacLaine, and Dean Martin, who is wondering where the hell he is!

Kirk Douglas and his chin join Barbara Walters, Henry Kissinger, and Mike Wallace.

Milton Berle, Jack L. Green, Red Buttons, Lucille Ball, and Steve Allen all make fun of Red because they had Dinners before he did.

Below left: Buddy Hackett and Alan King play "Any Joke You Can Tell I Can Tell Funnier." Below right: Tony Curtis asks David Tebet, "Are you sure I'm invited to the Cary Grant Dinner?"

Pat Cooper, Jack L. Green, Dick Capri, Buddy Hackett, Henny Youngman, Jerry Lewis, and Norm Crosby—put them all together they spell F-U-N-N-Y.

David Tebet, William B. Williams, Barbara Sinatra, Frank Sinatra, Barbara Grant, and George Barrie wonder what in heaven's name Cary Grant is supposed to do with that really ugly Friars Award.

or forced him to admit that he would like to come back as a fern in the next life. In any case, it's just a rumor. I wouldn't give it a second thought. After addressing Kissinger as "Dr. Strangelove," he apologized for his tardiness and said, "Henry, I owe you another apology. I was asked to sing your theme song tonight but, unfortunately, I don't know the words to 'Heil to the Chief,' otherwise I would have done that. Too often these affairs wind up as a contest as to who is the funniest or the most eloquent. So far, while I was waiting backstage, neither of those things did I hear. Since I am neither, I'll say what I have to say the best way I know how and get back to my movie set and a bottle of Jack Daniels. You're a hell of a man, Henry, and there's only one thing between you and I we can't decide—who is more humble, you or me." Oh, I say once a man has had his Jack Daniels, he's beyond humble.

The guest of honor may not be known for his comedic skills but he certainly rose to the occasion, stating, "I would like to thank all of those who have spoken so eloquently on my behalf. You have said nothing, which any rational man could disagree. And you have omitted much that my office would have been glad to supply to you. I will cherish what you have said nearly as long as I will quote it, as classic examples of Anglo-Saxon understatement. There has been some comment here about my ego, which I frankly rather resent. My wife Nancy does not agree with it. Neither does my dog Tyler. Nor do my staff assistants, Matthew, Mark, Luke, and John."

Kissinger also needed to set things straight with dais guest Mike Wallace, "Before I go any further, let me clear up the unpleasantness that has been mentioned here regarding the program *60 Minutes*. I'm quoted as saying they were going to do a hatchet job and that I was threatening to sue them. They claim I was seeking editorial control. It is all a terrible misunderstanding. *60 Minutes* is doing a program called "The Shah–Kissinger Connection" that I cannot accept. Anything that gives me second billing is a hatchet job. As for the editing, all I asked for is that they must use complete sentences. They said they would allow me up to fourteen minutes. That did it right there. I don't have any sentences that go less than fifteen minutes."

In spite of the fact that some members afterward complained that the Dinner was "too political and serious," they should look at the bright side, who would have guessed that this evening would have as many laughs as it did? Although the fact that it took place a mere six years after the Nixon debacle didn't heal at least one Friar's political wounds. One member fervently refused to attend the proceedings as a spectator, owing to his anger at anything associated with the former disgraced president. Maybe he spent the evening with Howard Cosell and that exciting encyclopedia of his.

BURT REYNOLDS TESTIMONIAL DINNER – 1981

(Everybody but his hair was there)

JOHNNY CARSON, *Toastmaster*
RICHARD ANDERSON
ELIZABETH ASHLEY
ABRAHAM D. BEAME
ROBBY BENSON
DYAN CANNON
BERT CONVY
HOWARD COSELL
LARRY CSONKA
DOM DE LUISE
PHIL DONAHUE
DOUGLAS FAIRBANKS, JR.
NORMAN FELL
MADELINE KAHN

ED MCMAHON
REVEREND JESS MOODY
WILLIE NELSON
JOE PESCI
GARY PUDNEY
JERRY REED
CHARLES NELSON REILLY
ROBERT W. SHAPIRO
DINAH SHORE
DAVID STEINBERG
MARLO THOMAS
ROBERT URICH
BARBARA WALTERS
PAUL WILLIAMS

When Burt Reynolds was feted in 1981, the paparazzi were out in full force to see if his ex-flame Sally Field would show up— well, an ex did show, but not the one everyone "really likes." It was the one everyone really loved: Dinah Shore. She commented, "When the history of this particular age is recorded, it will be in the books that Burt Reynolds has done more for little old ladies in tennis shoes than anyone." She then lifted her evening gown to reveal a pair of sneakers, to which Burt yelled out, "I don't know about little old ladies, but you knock my socks off."

Johnny Carson was the Master of Ceremonies, who may have been told it was a Roast, "We are gathered here tonight for one purpose, to watch Burt Reynolds give the finest acting performance of his career—being humble, generous, warm, loving, charitable. And to become the world's No. 1 box office star without possessing any of those qualities is quite an achievement."

The Dinner sold out both balcony levels of the Waldorf-Astoria Hotel's Grand Ballroom, which goes to show the star power Burt commanded in those early '80s. If only Sally had come, they would have literally been hanging from the crystal chandeliers.

Speaking of hanging from light fixtures, live-wire Willie Nelson was a featured performer at the Dinner. Guess he didn't get the memo about its being a black-tie affair, or maybe he just couldn't find his black bandanna, since he opted for his usual regalia of jeans, T-shirt, and red bandanna around his neck. It's a wonder he made it to the stage at all, seeing as he and his band were quite content to pass the time in their Waldorf-Astoria suite. Then again, it's a hell of a lot easier to toke joints in the privacy of expensive hotel rooms than on an open dais with ladies in sequined gowns and sneakers. When Willie and his crew were buzzed (as in called) to come down to the Ballroom to perform, they weren't exactly rushing to the gig, being happily buzzed (as in stoned) and all.

Eventually, though, he found his way to the Ballroom to croak out "Mona Lisa" and "Georgia on My Mind." Being a music legend he was a big hit. Probably a result of the huge hit he took right before he went on.

How fitting that the dessert of the evening should include chocolate Charlotte Russe lined with lady fingers—Burt was, after all, a major sex symbol, being the first nude male centerfold in *Cosmopolitan* in 1972. Then again, songwriter Paul Williams had an interesting line in a parody of "The Rainbow Connection," which talked about Burt being short, macho, and not really needing women, "I think he sleeps with Hal." Some audience members found the line inappropriate and poorly timed, as nasty rumors had apparently been circulating about Burt and his *Smokey and the Bandit* director friend Hal Needam. Maybe Williams figured it was safe "Roast" territory since Hal had just gotten engaged to be married the day before. Then again, Burt's speech did include the line, "There's no such thing as gay rights, it's just human rights." Alrighty then.

Madeline Kahn didn't mince words during her tribute, "I want to talk about Burt—it'll just take a minute." She also sang her own personal song, which had the lines, "It's surely not his brain that twirls my skirt / I love him 'cause he's just Burt." If not for nothin', Burt certainly did have more women praising him on this dais than any guest of honor before him. Elizabeth Ashley offered this one up, "I may be the only woman on the dais who has not known Burt in the biblical sense." At which point Marlo Thomas, seated next to hubby Phil Donahue, stood up from her chair protesting the accusation. Madeline Kahn waved her hand as if to say, "Ditto!" Ashley just purred, "But we all lie, don't we?"

Carson was there to step in as defense for anyone who took jabs at Burt's acting abilities, "Some critics put down Burt, saying he lacks range and depth. But I ask you this, 'Could Lord Olivier jump a ravine in a Chevy pickup?' I'm talkin' art. So Burt, this is your night. Unfortunately, it's Robert Redford's year and you have many years to look forward to not winning an Oscar." Carson also noted, "A lot of people have compared Burt to Cary Grant, but I don't think Cary would go to a posh French restaurant and ask to see the Gatorade list."

Sounds like Burt feels the same way everybody else does about his acting, "I'll probably never win an Oscar, so I'll do my speech now. I may not be Brando or Pacino, but dammit, I show up! I'd like to thank all the little people, but I don't associate with them anymore." It was also a night of revelations: "That's right, the eyes might go first. Only in my case, the hair went first. Some of it is in the drawer upstairs." Then his humble side showed through, "I invited everyone here tonight that I love. I sat listening, and I kept thinking, 'What a great guy!'" Then he praised his dais, "My days as a leading man are numbered, so I started a breeding program and out of that came Robert Urich, who is part me and part Shetland pony. I was especially touched by Robby Benson being here, because he just passed through puberty a minute ago. And Johnny Carson. Everybody says Johnny is a hard guy to get to know—so I stopped trying." Long around midnight, he got pithy, or maybe that's pitiful or perhaps just plain pathetic, "I'll make you proud of me. I've got something real good in me and it's going to pop out one day and all those people out there will be surprised, except you here tonight." And damned if he wasn't right! Almost twenty years later he popped—he's like a clairvoyant.

BUDDY HACKETT TESTIMONIAL DINNER – 1981

(Give this man a Roast!)

JAN MURRAY, *Toastmaster*	SCOTT RECORD
KAYE BALLARD	FREDDIE ROMAN
GENE BAYLOS	GEORGE SEGAL
RABBI WILLIAM BERKOWITZ	DICK SHAWN
MILTON BERLE	TOM SNYDER
CAB CALLOWAY	PAUL SORVINO
BILLY DANIELS	RUSTY STAUB
GREG EVIGAN	JULE STYNE
FRANK FIELD	MISS UNIVERSE (IRENE SAEZ)
BOB FOSSE	MISS USA (KIM SEELBREDE)
SANDY HACKETT	JACKIE VERNON
JOE KELLMAN	JACK WESTON
HAL LINDEN	HENNY YOUNGMAN
TONY MARTIN	

Jan Murray was the emcee for the Buddy Hackett Dinner, which apparently boasted such big names as Joe Kellman. Okay, while the Friars Club may be one of the premier entertainment organizations in the world, it doesn't negate the fact that the Joe Kellmans of the world will be invited to speak at their events. In this particular instance, Joe, the owner of a glass manufacturing company and a close personal friend of

Buddy's, was given his fifteen minutes of Friar fame. When he closed after a very long and somewhat tedious routine, he told the audience that it would be his last performance—the entire ballroom broke into applause. Even Milton Berle said, "Now there is one act even I'll never steal!"

Murray announced, "Just one news item. They hijacked a bus of Japanese tourists today, but thank God, they got over two hundred pictures of the hijacker." Ba-da-boom! Looking over the dais, the witty emcee proclaimed, "Do you realize that if a bomb dropped here tonight, the funniest guy in America would be Ernest Borgnine?" So that's where they got the ludicrous idea to Roast Borgnine in 1988—don't panic, though, you won't be reading about it here. (Well, we can't do them all!)

Murray read a telegram, which brought tears to Buddy's eyes, "I had planned to be with you on this happy occasion, but I had a previous engagement to speak in Tripoli at a dinner honoring Khadafi. Love, Don Rickles." Hackett yelled out, "He wasn't even invited!" Nothing personal to the dais, but Murray announced, "A special thanks to Walter Goldstein, who drove the entire dais over from the unemployment office." Walter was the Club's executive director at the time and I guess he had a car. Unless he used Gene Baylos' car, which Murray talked about in his intro of the comic, "Gene Baylos is a real success story. In 1962 he couldn't afford a 1962 car, and now he lives in one." We're not sure what Baylos said about the guest of honor, but he did joke, "I'd like to tell you what three different nationalities say when they are making love. The Italian woman says, 'Mamma Mia.' The French girl says, 'Ooh la la.' And the Jewish girl says, 'Max, the ceiling needs to be painted.'" Berle actually had a few international jokes as well, "Jewish foreplay is three hours of begging. Italian foreplay: 'Marie I'm home.'"

Hal Linden provided musical memories for Hackett, singing his own special version of "My Way," complete with a near-perfect Hackett imitation. It noted Buddy's use of risqué language—"Words he never learned from Jerry Falwell"—and led into such lyrics as "That crooked smile / that precious wit / the man has style / so full of . . . wisdom"—well, it was squeaky clean Linden doing the singing. What the hell were you expecting him to rhyme with wit? Guess the techies offstage thought the music would sound sweeter if the lights were dimmed, regardless of Hal's need for a script, prompting him to yell, "Don't turn the lights down, I'm reading this!" Or perhaps he was just scared to be in the dark with all those Friars, known for their quick wits and even quicker hands. Being a Dinner and all, there was more music and it was really good music. Cab Calloway performed "Come On, Get Happy," which people did whenever they heard him sing—he was so great at Friars' events (and other events, too, I'd imagine). Billy Daniels, another legend at these Friar affairs, sang "Mack the Knife," so Buddy had the music to remember if he didn't care for the comedy.

Kaye Ballard also sang; I'm just not sure what it was, but she did say, "Buddy really has got class, he is the only comic who has not appeared in a Mel Brooks movie." Dance legend Bob Fosse pirouetted his way to the podium—or maybe he just played with his bowler hat and contorted his way up—to honor Buddy. He read a review of a play the guest of honor had starred in, *I Had a Ball* (no, it wasn't an account of what went on after the Lucille Ball Roast in 1961). Fosse read, "Hackett isn't human exactly, more like a baked potato out for a short stroll." Isn't that better than half-baked?

"The people of Beverly Hills are a very fancy people," said Freddie Roman. "In Beverly Hills, when a lady gives birth, she breaks Perrier." And what about Freddie's family values? "Buddy's family is here tonight. My parents couldn't be here because they are in Ft. Lauderdale. Bell and Harry Kirschenbaum. When I went into show business my whole family changed their name to Kirschenbaum." I hear the same thing happened to M. Night Shyamalan—he's the director of *The Sixth Sense*. After Freddie finished, Murray said, "Imagine being that funny and still work clean, that son of a bitch. Those were some of the funniest lines Milton Berle will do at the next Roast." No need to go back and reread the lines he's talking about, they've been omitted—I don't want Berle stealing material from this book.

The very talented George Segal was there, "Buddy's my

neighbor, that's how I know him. I'm in the acting profession, which as we know, is much higher than the saloon business. He taught me how to get drunk—at 11 o'clock in the morning." Then George broke out his banjo and that's when I hit the fast forward button on my Walkman.

Henny Youngman actually mentioned the guest of honor's name, "Buddy was always heavy. I took him out to dinner once and he ate sixty dollars' worth of food. Then he asked me, 'What do you think I ought to wash this down with?' I said, 'Lake Erie.' I'm glad to see Milton here tonight. Milton was supposed to get a vasectomy, but the doctor said, 'Let sleeping dogs lay.' I'm so tired. Last night I had a terrible nightmare. I dreamt that Bo Derek and my wife had a fight over me and my wife won.'" But he did use Buddy's name.

Berle, of course, threw caution to the wind and opted for his Roast material. The night ran a tad long and since he closed the show, he had a lot of time to sit and record the other comics. "My suit's out of style from waiting to go on," he announced. But he did bring endearing words from the wee ones, "Yesterday when I was leaving my house in Beverly Hills, my five-year-old grandson asked me, 'Where you going, Grandpa?' and I said, 'I'm going to New York. The Friars are honoring Buddy Hackett,' and the kid said, 'Give that shithead hell.'" So he did. "We are here to honor this little man with a rubber face, or is he a little rubber with a man's face?" And there's always room to taunt those that can't speak for themselves, "My dear friend George Burns was going to be here tonight, but last week he got an erection and now he's waiting for the crazy glue to set in." Other comics discuss Berle's anatomy; Berle opts for the ninety-and-over set. He shouted to Henny Youngman, "If there is a fire here tonight, we leave alphabetically!"

Hackett was deeply touched by the accolades, "A lot of people came here tonight and made it wonderful for me—and none of them are on the dais." Now is that nice, to insult Joe Kellman that way?

CARY GRANT TESTIMONIAL DINNER—1982

(Cheers and tears)

FRANK SINATRA, *Toastmaster*	MYRNA LOY
MUHAMMAD ALI	DINA MERRILL
GEORGE BARRIE	JOE NAMATH
TONY BENNETT	RYAN O'NEAL
JACQUELINE BISSET	GREGORY PECK
TOM BROKAW	JILLY RIZZO
GEORGE BURNS	HARRY REASONER
RED BUTTONS	CLIFF ROBERTSON
CHARLIE CALLAS	IRENE MAYER SELZNICK
SAMMY CAHN	SIDNEY SHELDON
GOVERNOR HUGH CAREY	JENNIFER JONES
CY COLEMAN	BARBARA SINATRA
HOWARD COSELL	GEORGE STEINBRENNER
MARVIN DAVIS	GEORGE STEVENS, JR.
FARRAH FAWCETT	JULE STYNE
ALEXANDER GODUNOV	DAVID TEBET
BENNY GOODMAN	JACK VALENTI
BARBARA GRANT	JOE WILLIAMS
JACK L. GREEN	MADAME SYLVIA WU
RALPH LAUREN	
PEGGY LEE	OH, AND TONY CURTIS TOO!
RICH LITTLE	

When Cary Grant was honored with a Dinner in 1982, the Chairman of the Board himself, Frank Sinatra, served as emcee. David Tebet, a tough-talking, no-nonsense former NBC talent executive (he's the man who discovered Johnny Carson) was producer of the Friars Dinners for almost twenty years before stepping down in 1994. Grant was one friend Tebet managed to keep, considering his track record with other pals, "Practically every year I've lost at least one or two friends on every show. At the Cary Grant show, I had four friends of mine and they came and asked me, 'Am I invited to the Cary Grant affair?' I would say, 'I can only send invitations to the people he has requested to be on the dais. Why don't you call Cary?' One time later I came into the Club and they were there, and they snubbed me—they wouldn't talk to me. True story. This happened to me quite a few times." From what we've heard some of these guys say about each other at these events, is that such a bad thing, David?

While Tony Curtis was certainly on Grant's "A" list, he apparently wasn't going to take any chances. He incessantly called the Club to confirm both his invite and then his RSVP. The calls became an amusing, if not welcome, routine for Friars Club Executive Director Jean Pierre Trebot. Today, such behavior has a clinical label: obsessive compulsiveness. In the early eighties it had one as well: really annoying.

Though Grant may have been a tough guy in movies, in later years he was quite a different sort. "Cary Grant was a very good friend of mine," says Tebet, "and I went to his house and he was very reluctant to do it. He was very afraid of being in front of an audience. I mean really afraid. Scared to death if he's on stage. One of the nicest men you could ever meet. I told him the only thing he had to do was get up and say 'Thank you' to the New York Friars. So he said he would do it, and it was a fabulous show."

Maybe Cary's trepidation had something to do with this Jack Carter memory, "I remember one terrible event and it hurt me because I idolized Cary Grant. He loved to come to Roasts. He loved to laugh and be with the guys. Finally, he got up enough nerve to get up and Roast. And it was a big Roast at the Beverly Hilton or the Century Plaza." Okay, so it's a California Roast story; I never said they didn't have them—this is the only one I was told about. "Berle was the Toastmaster and he had warned everybody, don't pick on Cary Grant, no cheap shots, be thrilled he's here. Cary Grant gets up, and he tried a little joke, and they chuckled at it. And he tried another one, and it was very lightweight, cute. He tried to do it a little humor, you know. Somebody should have given him better jokes; he did about two. When he sat down the next comic got up and he looks at Cary and he says, 'Cary, next time come prepared.' And the crowd winced, groaned. Cary Grant got up and walked off the dais and never ever came back to a Friars' Roast again. And we lit into the comic after that, 'what a cheap shot, to take at

Cary Grant, none of us would mention it,' that always upset me." So maybe Cary had good reason to avoid another mortifying Friar moment.

Someone who was conspicuously absent from that fabulous show, by the way, was Milton Berle. He felt snubbed at not being invited to participate in the evening and left the Club for almost two years. The official reason given for not inviting him was that he was really a "Roastmaster" and not a "Toastmaster." But rumor has it that some people were afraid that he would say something that would embarrass Grant or Sinatra, who was the Abbot at the time. In an interview he gave at the Monastery upon his return, Berle said, "I felt very slighted being the Club's Abbot Emeritus and not being included in other things. I guess there was a new regime here. And some of the people were a little disrespectful to me. Now, I don't think I'm that special, but as Abbot Emeritus I could have been treated differently." The Friars refused to accept Berle's resignation—he is, after all, the man who saved them from obscurity. They also sent him a petition with seven hundred signatures on it, asking him to return to the fold. So fear not, soon enough you'll be reading, "Laugh it up, I laugh when you act!"

Trebot is always amazed at star powers like Cary Grant who can't honor a simple request such as, "May we have a current photo for the cover of the accompanying Souvenir Journal?" After six decades in show business, in a career that brought him to superstardom, the only photo Grant could present to the Club was a picture of himself—at the age of six! Necessity turned the Journal cover into one of the most unique ever in the history of the Club—it prominently features the photo with Grant's autograph, Archie Leach, the name he was known by at the time the picture was taken.

For other Friar staff members working on the Dinner, Cary Grant became the stuff from which memories are made. When Trebot's assistant, Dale Roth, went to Grant's Waldorf-Astoria Hotel suite to go over notes with him, he kindly invited her to dine with him in his room when they were through. Flustered, Ms. Roth declined, admitting that she had to get back to the Club to type up the dinner menus for the main dining room's evening fare. For God's sake, woman, what the hell were you thinking? Today, Dale laughs, saying, "I thought I would be fired if I took him up on his offer." How many people would kill to put on their unemployment application under Reason for Termination: "Had dinner with Cary Grant in his hotel suite."

At the Dinner, Red Buttons got on a roll and there was no turning back: "Ladies and gentlemen, we are privileged to be here tonight to honor Cary Grant, a man who's not only a friend to me, he's a perfect stranger. Cary is a good man. A man with a heart. A man who spends three hours a week in hospitals teaching nervous people how to eat Jell-O. A man who once took Ray Charles to a Marcel Marceau concert. Cary Grant is always there. At a Joan Crawford child-slapping contest in Selma, Alabama—he was there. In Harlem, at a symposium of Puerto Rican doctors who write out all of their prescriptions in spray paint—he was there. In the South Bronx, on a sightseeing bus tour for nostalgic German tourists who miss World War II—he was there. That's why this man is getting a dinner because some of the biggest people in the world never got a dinner. Adam, who said in the garden of Eden, 'I've got more ribs, you got more broads?'—never got a dinner. Moses, who yelled when the Red Sea parted, 'What the hell was that? I was just going in for a dip'—never got a dinner. Noah's wife, who said to Noah, 'Don't let the elephants watch the rabbits'—never got a dinner. Amelia Earhart, who said, 'Stop looking for me and see if you can find my luggage'—never got a dinner. Jack the Ripper's mother, who said to Jack, 'How come I never see you with the same girl twice?'—never got a dinner. Jimmy Carter, who said to Pope John, 'Next time bring the missus'—never got a dinner."

While the likes of Buttons, George Burns, and Charlie Callas kept the comedy flowing, Peggy Lee and Joe Williams kept the audience enraptured with their tunes. (After Williams did his stint, crooner Sinatra crowed, "Showoff!") But it was Grant who brought the audience and the dais to their feet, if not to tears, with his touching thank you. Rather than stand at the podium, he had requested a wing-backed chair, placed in the center of the stage, so he could be comfortable. Taking Tebet's advice to heart, even those few words of thanks were uttered through choked-back tears and watery eyes. Perhaps the audience was more moved at seeing this great man, toward the end of his career and his life, touched by the accolades that were so lovingly presented. Can we now please get back to some nonsappy stuff?

ELIZABETH TAYLOR TESTIMONIAL DINNER – 1983

(Who's afraid of Joan Rivers?)

DINAH SHORE, *Toastmaster*	ROBERT KLEIN
ELIZABETH ASHLEY	ROBERT LANSING
GEORGE BARRIE	JANET LEE
ABRAHAM D. BEAME	GINA LOLLOBRIGIDA
JACQUELINE BISSET	VICTOR GONZALEZ LUNA
ELLEN BURSTYN	*(Elizabeth's escort)*
RED BUTTONS	ROD McKUEN
SAMMY CAHN	ROBERT MERRILL
LEN CARIOU	ROGER MOORE
JOHN CULLUM	MARGARET O'BRIEN
FRANK SINATRA	BROOKE SHIELDS
ELLA FITZGERALD	MAUREEN STAPLETON
MARTHA GRAHAM	GEORGE STEVENS, JR.
ALEXANDER GODUNOV	CHERYL TIEGS
BUDDY HACKETT	CICELY TYSON
RUBY KEELER	BEN VEREEN

The Friars Club Testimonial Dinner for Elizabeth Taylor must have been bittersweet for her—an honor, to be sure, but one can't help wonder if thoughts of Mike Todd and his untimely demise en route to his Friars' Dinner weren't lurking somewhere in her mind. If appearances are to speak for themselves, however, she seemed to enjoy the event—the tardiness of the guest of honor and ire of the Abbot notwithstanding. When it was time for the show to start, Ms. Taylor was nowhere to be found. Then again, a lady on her special evening is entitled to be fashionably late—perhaps just not when Frank Sinatra is the date she is holding up. Sinatra, as the head of the Friars, was a stickler for Friarly events starting and ending on time. Twenty minutes later, after various assistants and aides had been summoned to fan out throughout the Waldorf, Ms. Taylor emerged from a bathroom—as resplendent and breathtakingly beautiful as befits a lady-in-waiting (or is that a waiting lady?). Only Elizabeth could incur the Sinatra wrath and live to tell about it! If you are looking to read the reason for the delay, no one is talking, which is a wise move considering the individuals involved. Still in all, what the hell was she up to?

Dinah Shore was the Mistress of Ceremonies and, as far as we can tell, was the first woman to have this revered position. Then again, isn't every woman who does something for the Friars the "first" woman *ever* to do it. But if you don't believe me, just ask Dinah, "If I'm a little nervous tonight, it's because it's the first time a woman has ever been asked to perform this particular function at the Friars." She probably said that at her own dinner, too; maybe she learned it from Nellie Revel. This was during the time when Taylor and Joan Rivers were feuding, so this being a Dinner in Liz's honor didn't bode well for Joan, and Dinah fired the first shots, "Dave Tebet told me that the gold tables are $10,000 and the platinum tables are $7,500, and the silver tables are $5,000. Now, if there are any of you here who would like to see Joan Rivers and her husband, you can go over on Lexington Avenue for the Formica table." Taylor then asked, "Is Joan Rivers here?" When Dinah told her she wasn't, Taylor shot back, "Joan Rivers, if you're here, eat your heart out."

Rod McKuen jumped on the Rivers bandwagon as well, "I was a little upset about a few remarks made earlier about Joan Rivers. Few of you probably realize that about a year ago, she was gang-banged by the New York critics, and nobody wants a pick of the litter." My, that was some catty little group up there on that dais.

Robert Klein kept things breezy though, which can come in handy when people are being maligned and Abbots are still fuming over late guests of honor, "Unfortunately, I have never worked with Miss Taylor. We just met prior to the Dinner. When she was busy doing *Cat on a Hot Tin Roof*, I was working in 8 millimeter, for my dad, nothing risqué. I feel my accomplishments pale before our honoree. I was on *What's My Line?* near the end of its tenure and it was so pathetic, I was the mystery guest and they didn't get me, and they took off their blindfolds and they still didn't get me." And today?

There's a certain image that springs to mind when Roger Moore's name is mentioned—but this isn't it, "I was told by Dave Tebet that I had two minutes, which gives you time to go to the bathroom—that's if you don't lift the seat. Why am I here? I know why I'm here. My name is Burton, James Burton. I just had the old man's fantasy. I've been sitting, playing knees with Brooke Shields, with my wife sitting on my left. I wish I'd gone to the bathroom." Taylor told him, "There's still time," to which Moore said, "What do you think I'm doing here?" and then launched into the flavor of the evening. "Joan Rivers is the depressed areas' Don Rickles, only not quite as pretty. The largest thing in America is Joan Rivers' tongue, but we are not here tonight to praise Joan Rivers, rather to bury her." Sounds like Joan wasn't the only one dying this evening.

Not that Red Buttons was introducing this legend when he made this joke, but it could serve as one for here, "Ella Fitzgerald, not only a giant star, but a civil rights leader. A woman who almost died one day when she wouldn't pick the cotton out of an aspirin bottle. God bless you, Ella." At least Ella Fitzgerald kept the class intact. She sang "Night and Day," and the audience hoped she'd sing it all night long. But then the night got back to that quirky track it had been traveling, when Buddy Hackett took over as engineer, "You might be interested in what happened to Joan Rivers last night—a peeping Tom threw up on her window. Before I go into the guest of honor and the guests of the evening, I have a few words left over from the Dick Shawn stag Roast: two Jews were on a bus . . . oh, you're not allowed to do carryovers? Any man in the universe who has never fantasized about our guest of honor is either a fag or an agent. I have tried to pattern my life and career after her. When she converted to Judaism, I did the same."

Owing to Taylor's humanitarian endeavors, Buttons joked,

"Elizabeth Taylor is right now building a halfway house for girls that don't want to go all the way."

Frank Sinatra presented Taylor with her Friars Club Oscar and as he approached the podium the orchestra played, "New York, New York." "Don't ever play that song again! I had enough of "My Way," which was a pain in the ass and I don't want this one to become a pain in the ass." Oh my, if only he had shared that with the rest of the world. "I was honored to be a part of this evening here, and I'm also honored to think that the bars don't close until 4 o'clock in New York—beautiful idea." Berle has his penis and Frank had his Jack Daniels—you got a problem wit dat, bubbe? "It is my pleasure now to give Miss Elizabeth Taylor what every member of the Friars wants to give her." Hackett yelled out, "Can I be first?" Elizabeth said, "Shut up and sit down," which gave him his answer, but Sinatra told him, "No. We're gonna draw straws." You just know what a lesson in futility that turned out to be.

"This is a gift from the Friars organization to our lovely lady of the evening." Liz just shrieked, "Whaaaat?" (Actually, she had been shrieking like that all night.) "You are a lady and you belong to the evening and to every month and every year of our lives. I just made that up and I thought it was pretty goddamn nice to say that. I coulda said something kinda like he said, but I'm not gonna do that." When he handed Elizabeth her gold Piaget watch with diamonds, Sinatra was reading from a prepared speech. "And it says here pee-ah-jay, like I don't know French. Like I'm a schmuck. Like I don't know how to say Piaget. If Dave Tebet wrote that there's gonna be a fistfight in the lobby." He then put the watch on Taylor—well, he tried to put the watch on her, after a few minutes he yelled for Dinah and Liz said dryly, "Never mind."

Elizabeth was quite honored, in spite of the fact that she, too, couldn't get it straight about just how many women had been honored, "I just want to say thank you for that. To be the fourth woman, I think is just wonderful." Four, six, ten—what's the difference at this point? It's not like anyone was keeping count—obviously. "I really don't quite know how to express my thanks, to thank you for all of this. The jewelry, that I can dig."

Dig? And the '60s were when? "Now I hope there's nobody in the house with heart trouble, because I think it would be a wonderful idea if the next Abbot is a female. But not me, I'm a flake." Apparently the Abbot was the one with the heart trouble, as Sinatra yelled out, "It's a boy's club!" Little did he know such a phrase would be extinct a mere five years later. As for Taylor's being a flake—ah, never mind.

DEAN MARTIN TESTIMONIAL DINNER – 1984

(Shouldn't someone tell him he was there?)

FRANK SINATRA, *Toastmaster*	SUSAN LUCCI
LUCILLE BALL	SHIRLEY MACLAINE
ABRAHAM D. BEAME	ROBERT MERRILL
MILTON BERLE	GARY MORTON
RED BUTTONS	JOE PISCOPO
SAMMY CAHN	ROBERT SARNOFF
ANN CARLYLE	DICK SHAWN
DICK CAVETT	BROOKE SHIELDS
SAMMY DAVIS, JR.	BARBARA SINATRA
ANGIE DICKINSON	DAVID TEBET
RUTH GORDON	DIONNE WARWICK
GARSON KANIN	WILLIAM B. WILLIAMS
SUGAR RAY LEONARD	STEVE WYNN

There was so much hoopla going on in the audience of the Dean Martin Testimonial Dinner that radio personality and Friars Club Dean at the time, William B. Williams, sounded ever so distraught trying to get the mob's attention, yelling, "Put down the shrimp salad!" Seeing as Marie Antoinette was not on the dais, one can assume the order wasn't to "let them eat cake," so it must have meant that the show was about to begin.

Poor Dean Martin. Forever labeled the least-sober member of the Rat Pack, he continued to be attacked thusly during his Friars' fete. His pal Frank Sinatra was the Toastmaster, which seemed a more appropriate title than ever in light of Frank's assessment, "We are paying tribute to a man who doesn't even know he's here. One of the rarest of men: a wit, singer, raconteur, and a drunk. In his constant state of illusion, he is perpetually in Disneyland." This, spoken by the man who wed twenty-one-year-old Mia Farrow when he was fifty.

But Dino is all smiles in the pictures, so perhaps he didn't mind the slander one bit. Or maybe he just didn't hear it, as Shirley MacLaine, the only unofficial-official female rat-packer, pointed out to the crowd, "I could pour my heart out to Dino, confident that in the morning he wouldn't remember a thing." But the alleged out-of-it-Martin jumped on Shirley's *Out on a Limb* escapades, "I don't think either one of her oars is touching the water. Every week Shirley calls me, but she calls from places that have no area codes."

Not that this should come as any surprise, but as you have come to learn, nothing is sacred at Friar events. With that in mind, consider Red Buttons' comments, "Dean has a very dear friend, Jerry Lewis, who is now hot in France. But years ago, so was Joan of Arc."

Dick Cavett thought this Dinner was the perfect opportunity to make some entertainment history, "The world is full of people who brought great historical meetings off. I brought Joe Piscopo to meet Frank Sinatra, thanks to the Friars. We were back there in the room you go into before you go on stage, and there's a reception line. It always has three people in it you don't recognize and the rest you do. I said, 'C'mon, Joe,' and he said, 'I don't know. I've never met Sinatra, but I've done him on *Saturday Night Live* any number of times.' So we go down the line and we get to Mr. Sinatra and I said, 'Mr. S., this is Joe Piscopo,' and Sinatra reached out to say hello to Joe and did in fact say that and moved quickly to the next person in line. After we got out of the line, Joe said, 'Whew. I think that was a little chilly. I think he knew of me all too well.' That appears to be the last they spoke." In spite of the Arctic reception, however, Piscopo actually performed that night and after Sinatra introduced him he said, "To be introduced by Frank Sinatra, I'm petrified. May I call you Frank?" Can you guess what Frank said? "You can call me sir!" As if he didn't already have a handle on how his night was going with Frank, Piscopo then sang "Ol' Man River," imitating Sinatra.

But if you're going to be doling out "whews," then Cavett fared better with Sinatra himself, "I remember quickly lettering a joke and I thought it would be funny to hand it down to Sinatra. He was a row and a half in front of me, so on a five-by-eight card I wrote, 'If Berle bombs, I have twenty minutes ready. You were great in *Suddenly.*' I thought, 'Oh God, what have I done, I'm gonna have to hide behind Piscopo.' He starts to read it and my heart stopped, and he looks back at me and gives me the million-dollar grin. Every bit of charisma the world has is crammed into that moment, and it just chilled me delightfully, through and through. It was the opposite of what Piscopo got."

Lucille Ball was an honorary Friar, owing to her being given her own Roast in 1961—you can just bet she thought she was the first woman Roasted. She said of that event (well, she didn't say it here at Dean's event, but when the hell else am I going to be able to quote Lucy?): "Johnny Carson was the emcee and the committee told him that ladies as well as gentlemen would be in the audience and please do not say anything off-color. So Johnny said, 'Ladies and gentlemen, what a thrill it is to present Miss Lucille Testicle,' good ol' Johnny!" What she did say at Dean's Dinner was, "I've done some private research into his personal activities. Dean gave up six nights of his valuable time to tutor George Burns in a refresher course on sex. . . . He just made a grant to Johns Hopkins University for the research and development of a new liver."

If you want things put into perspective, then invite Dick Shawn to speak, "One of the good things about a Tribute and not a Roast, where you attack someone, is that everything this evening can be said again at his funeral." He obviously never attended a memorial at the Friars Club. "I did a tribute to Milton Berle to mark his seventy years in show business. That's incredible, when you consider that Yugoslavia is only forty-eight years old. I also did a tribute for Sammy Davis, Jr., and fifty was his lucky number—fifty years in show business, fifty of the most important people in show business on his dais, the man makes $50,000 a night—but he's only fifty inches tall. . . .

There isn't a man in this room that at one time didn't say, 'I wish I had what these three guys had' [Sinatra, Martin, Davis], except for their livers." Was that said at their funerals?

The Martin Dinner was an important milestone for the Friars family—Milton Berle returned to a Friars' dais. It's not nice to fool with Mother Nature—or Mr. Television! (Aren't they one and the same?) In spite of Milton's previous dais snubs, he was back and in fine funny form despite the ulcers he caused for David Tebet, who produced the evening. "Milton would go on for twenty minutes," says Tebet, "so we wrote the speakers and said to keep to about three minutes because there was a lot of people and if anybody runs over, people will start walking out. Berle got a telegram from Sinatra and myself, asking him would he please keep to ten minutes. Comedians are an unusual breed, and Berle came back with his usual prompt answer, 'I take bows that last longer than ten minutes!'

"The night of the dinner, he got up. He looked at Sinatra. He looked at me. And he did twenty-three minutes!" laughed Tebet. When Berle took center stage he taunted those that dared to put a time limit on his material, "I'm not going to stay on long—if you believe that, you'll also believe that there is going to be a Liberace junior!" He proceeded to give a list of the world's thinnest books, among them was one on famous Jewish astronauts and "10,000 Years of Irish Cooking." About Sinatra he said, "He walks with kings and plays with queens—as long as they're dealt by hand." For the guest of honor, he said, "Waiting for Dino to stop drinking is like leaving the porch light on for Jimmy Hoffa." Eventually he finished and inevitably got the last laugh—literally!

"This is one of the highlights of my career," said Martin, "but not *the* greatest highlight. The greatest highlight of my career was when I talked back to Frank. For the last year Frank and I have been doing shows together and having a lot of fun, but all of a sudden he thinks we're a team. I said to him, 'I once was part of a team, and I didn't like it then and I don't think I'm gonna like it now.'" He then sang "Mr. Wonderful, that's me. . . ." Who can argue with that!

MILTON BERLE TESTIMONIAL DINNER – 1985

(Again!)

HAL KANTOR, *Toastmaster*
JOEY ADAMS
LUCILLE BALL
ABRAHAM D. BEAME
TOM BOSLEY
RED BUTTONS
DICK CAVETT
HOWARD COSELL
NORM CROSBY
SAMMY DAVIS, JR.

GEORGIA ENGEL
LARRY GERSHMAN
DON KING
JAN MURRAY
AL RYLANDER
DICK SHAWN
JACKIE VERNON
ABE VIGODA
HENNY YOUNGMAN

Milton Berle was Roasted by the Friars in 1953, 1959, 1967, and 1974. He was honored with Testimonial Dinners twice—first in 1963, and again in 1985. Either he was the funniest human to have ever walked the face of the earth, or he was blackmailing the Friars big time. Jan Murray did not let the Berle marathon go unnoticed, "I can't tell you how choked up I am to be honoring Milton Berle for the 297th time in my career!" He also let it be known that "last week, I appeared at a snack in his honor."

Hal Kantor flew in from California to officiate as Master of Ceremonies. Noting that Berle was also the president of the California Friars, Kantor said, "Milton Berle is so prized by his membership that he is the first president they've ever had to insure against crucifixion." You can be damn sure in the event that ever happens, Berle would demand the Friars throw him a Last Supper!

Surprisingly enough, or maybe owing to the fact that it was a Dinner and not a Roast, Lucille Ball had nothing but kind words for Milton and his wife, Ruth, prompting Kantor to quip, "Thanks, Lucille. Sincerity at a Friars' affair is about as rare as virginity at Malibu High School." Maybe she held back the jokes because she was afraid she'd be hearing them at the next Friars' event—spoken by Berle.

Kantor had so many witty comments throughout the evening, so I'll just throw them haphazardly around the way he did: "Milton is a man I've admired for years—none of them recently." The musical portion of the evening was supplied by Sammy Davis, Jr., who sang "Candy Man." Signature song or not, who was he kidding—serenading one of the toughest and brashest guys in comedy history with a song dripping in enough sweetness to put the entire cast of *Annie* into diabetic shock? This is, after all, a Dinner for the man who slapped a tongue down on the table in front of Maurice Chevalier!

Here's a shock—Dick Cavett managed to insert a Berle-penis joke, "Milton has the most famous organ this side of Radio City, but there are women here tonight so we won't talk about that." Then again, isn't that the audience that would want to talk about it? The Friars definitely suffer from penis envy when it comes to Berle—and that's no joke.

For eons, Berle and Henny Youngman had a routine, and to actually have been able to witness these two geniuses of comedy perform it is akin to having watched George and Gracie on the vaudeville circuit. Henny would be up at the podium telling his legendary one-liners, and Berle would get up and yell, "You're too close to the microphone, back up!" Cut to Henny backing up. Again, Berle would yell as he went running up to the podium (these men had such energy on the dais), "Still too close, back up further!" Finally Henny—who at this point may as well phone in his jokes—says, "How far do you want me to go?" Berle's comeback, "Do you have a car?" gets them every time. So many of these jokes and routines became Friar staples and no matter how many times members of the Friars Club attended an event, and no matter how many times they heard the same jokes or saw the same stunts, riotous laughter erupted every time. It is sort of like watching reruns, only the stars actually age with each viewing.

"Milton made his film debut in silent movies at the age of five in Lon Chaney's classic drama, *The Hunchback of Notre Dame.* Every morning, about 5:30, Milton was brought to the studio, where he curled into a fetal position and was strapped to Lon Chaney's back. It was then that Milton established his reputation as one of Hollywood's greatest humps." A Kantor quip.

"When it was announced that there was going to be a Dinner at the Friars for Milton Berle," said Joey Adams, "everyone fought to be on the dais. Those who won aren't here." But Dick Shawn noted one of the losers (of the fight to be on the dais, not in life) grew up to be mayor of New York City, "I want to thank the Friars for bringing together some of the great comic minds to honor Milton Berle—people like Abe Beame."

Not to totally change the subject (because I'm not; it's about Abe Beame), but he was mayor from 1974 to 1977, stands about five foot two, and has graced pretty much every dais since Victor Herbert's—or something like that. Along with being a former statesman he is also the Chairman of the Friars Foundation, so he's no slouch. Every introduction the Friars makes brings attention to his height: "The former mayor of New York City who is going back into politics—Mayor Giuliani has hired him as his own personal Mini-Me"—Jerry Stiller Roast, 1999; "He is the former mayor of New York, but what you may not know is since then he has found part-time work as a Beanie Baby"— Drew Carey Roast, 1998; "Yet another former mayor who has gone into television; he just signed on to be a Muppet"—Danny Aiello Roast, 1997. Inevitably, he's also always asked to stand up—in spite of the fact that he already is standing. His reaction? He's pretty cool with it, but then again, we're not sure he actually hears what's being said. Where were we, oh, Berle Dinner, right. . . .

"We are here tonight to sing his praises and tout his virtues and tell whatever other lies we can think of. It's not the duty of a Master of Ceremonies to bore his audience, but to introduce others who will." Guess who that was?

Dinner or no Dinner, Red Buttons is there, "Milton Berle is a wonderful man. A man who believes you should close Radio City but keep the Rockettes open." While this is the last formal tribute the Friars gave to Berle, this is surely not the last you'll hear of him at Friars' events. Berle is a show business staple and definitely the backbone of the Friars—even he will tell you that, which he did at the end of the night. "I think it was Walter Winchell who said that the greatest love affair since Romeo and Juliet is Milton Berle and Show Business, and he was right!" Except, of course, for the love affair between Milton Berle and Milton Berle.

RED BUTTONS TESTIMONIAL DINNER – 1987

(Finally, he got a dinner! Now shut up already!)

STEVE ALLEN, *Toastmaster*	NORM CROSBY
DANNY AIELLO	EDDIE FISHER
CAROL ALT	BUDDY HACKETT
LUCILLE BALL	KITTY KALLEN
GENE BAYLOS	GARSON KANIN
MARTIN BAUM	PEGGY LEE
JOSIE BELL	JACKIE MASON
MILTON BERLE	DARREN MCGAVIN
VIVIAN BLAINE	JAYNE MEADOWS
JOE BUSHKIN	GARY MORTON
LEN CARIOU	JAMES NEDERLANDER
KITTY CARLISLE HART	ANTHONY QUINN
JOSEPH CATES	FREDDIE ROMAN
CY COLEMAN	BROOKE SHIELDS
HOWARD COSELL	RUSTY STAUB

Youngman had his one-liners; Benny had his violin; Burns had his Gracie; Berle had everyone else's jokes; and Buttons had no Dinner. Red Buttons can give you a litany of others who never had Dinners: "Abraham, who when God told him to circumcise himself said, 'Why not? It's no skin off my nose,' never got a Dinner. Jim and Tammy Bakker, the Children of a Lesser God, they never got a Dinner. Lee Iacocca, who said to Dolly Parton, 'Why do you need air bags?' never got a Dinner. Stevie Wonder's mother, who said to Stevie, 'I warned you,' never got a Dinner. Julius Caesar, who said to his wife, 'No way are we naming that baby Sid,' never got a Dinner"—but on May 16, 1987, he had to take himself out of some of the funniest punch lines since "Take my wife, please." Thanks to the Friars, Buttons finally got his Dinner—at the Waldorf-Astoria.

Although, to hear Buttons tell it, he almost didn't get this Dinner either, "Well, there was a little bit of a scandal connected with my Roast [sic]. This is what got back to me from people at the Friars who were there. It seemed that Davey Tebet was against me being the guest of honor and they told me that he walked out of the meeting and said, 'I don't want any part of this.' I forget who he wanted that year. Maybe he didn't think I was big enough or it would be a successful event. When I was offered the Roast [sic], of course, I accepted it." Maybe Tebet's problem was that Red kept calling it a Roast. He was a bit of a stickler for that detail—Tebet may have ruled the roost but not the Roasts; the Dinners were his domain.

Steve Allen was the Master of Ceremonies at the long-awaited event and Buddy Hackett summed up the star-power that was seated on the dais, "There's not really a lot of celebrities here tonight. I wanted to go to the Cary Grant Dinner, but they wouldn't even sell me a ticket." To make sure Red wouldn't add to his act "never had a Roast," Hackett gave him one of those as well, "Red, you are the Man of the Year and you just got picked by a flip of the coin. If it had been heads, it would have been Bella Abzug. Then they wouldn't have had to have rented this place, they would have held the Dinner in her ass."

While Norm Crosby never quite got the hang of the English language, he did manage to put things in perspective, "It's great to sit up here in a pubic place with all of these people who are not ashamed to sit up here and admit that they are not working tonight." By the way, Norm's use of the word "pubic" is perfectly acceptable at a Friars Dinner, as opposed to a Roast, where it would be considered much too tame.

Milton Berle, fresh from his own dinner the year before (and you can bet Tebet didn't produce that one, either), closed the show, "I flew 3,000 miles to honor a yutz who lives a block and a half from me." If anyone knows his audience, though, Berle does as he easily shifts from Roast mode to Dinner mode with nary a blue word to be found, "I am the Abbot Emeritus of the New York Friars Club. That's nothing to applaud—that's like doing the choreography for the *Joe Franklin Show*. Sinatra couldn't make it. He's in Rome at the Sistine Chapel posing for a wall. Sinatra did give me a present to give to Red; it's his favorite Jewish good luck charm—a rabbi's foot." Then again, as with all things Friarly, give Berle something borrowed (jokes, perhaps?) and he'll give you something blue, "The men on this dais all look like they screwed Eleanor Roosevelt—recently. George Burns: having sex at his age is like shooting pool with a rope." Just what we need—another Kodak moment to picture.

"My wonderful friends," Red announced, "I joined the Friars forty-one years ago while still in uniform. I was a bellhop at the Astor Hotel—little humor, Steve, just throwing it in—I watched the Friars go from a loft at the Edison Hotel to the handsome edifice on 55th Street. A great deal due to the dedication and driving force of our Abbot Emeritus Milton Berle." See? People can be nice. "God bless you, Milton. Beautiful man. A man who once went to an orgy and stole the grapes." Nice only goes so far at the Friars. But this was an interesting testament by Red, "God bless you, Milton. And publicly tonight I may never get another chance to do it, thanks for writing 'Sam, you made the pants too long.' You launched my career. He did, Milton wrote the parody." Who knew?

After accusing Allen of sending artificial flowers to an artificial heart recipient, and telling the crowd, "To my buddy, Hackett, who may talk out of the side of this mouth, but everything he says comes straight from the other side of his mouth," Buttons gave us his list of I-was-there's—"In Williamsburg, Brooklyn, at an over-forty singles club for Hasidic midgets who believe that Danny De Vito is the real Messiah, I was there! In Pittsburgh, at a small cocktail party for premature ejaculators, I was there. I left early, but I was there!"

If anyone was more deserving of a Dinner, it was Buttons—if only to shut him up about never having had one. But mostly to validate what the Friars had known all along—that guys named after a primary color have more fun.

BARBARA SINATRA TESTIMONIAL DINNER – 1988

(Pretty in pink—sort of)

LEE IACOCCA, *Toastmaster*
LUCILLE BALL
ABRAHAM D. BEAME
SAMMY CAHN
TITA CAHN
JOANNA CARSON
ALTOVISE DAVIS
SAMMY DAVIS, JR.
ANGIE DICKINSON
TOM DREESEN
ARLENE FRANCIS
BARBARA GRANT
JACK L. GREEN
KITTY CARLISLE HART
LEO JAFFE
BEVERLY JOHNSON
KIRK KERKORIAN
ALAN KING
JEANETTE KING
DR. HENRY A. KISSINGER
NANCY KISSINGER

JERRY LEWIS
DEAN MARTIN
ROBERT MARX
DINA MERRILL
ROGER MOORE
LUISA MOORE
GARY MORTON
GREGORY PECK
DON RICKLES
ROBERT W. SARNOFF
BROOKE SHIELDS
DINAH SHORE
FRANK SINATRA
JULE STYNE
DAVID W. TEBET
CHERYL TIEGS
DONALD TRUMP
IVANA TRUMP
ROBERT WAGNER
DIONNE WARWICK

Why have a dinner for Frank Sinatra when his wife is standing by? Hence the Friars Testimonial Dinner in honor of Barbara Marx Sinatra. To say that Mrs. Blue Eyes was a vision this evening would be an understatement. The Grand Ballroom of the Waldorf-Astoria Hotel was abuzz over the slinky pink ensemble that the shapely guest of honor had donned for her salute. Or maybe it was the pooffy organza wrap adorned with huge pink dahlias that had them all mesmerized. Then again, the elegant watch the Friars presented to Mrs. S. seemed overshadowed by the dangle earrings, bracelet, and rings that she wore on her own accord—so it's anyone's call, but no one denies that Barbara was indeed the belle of her own ball.

Barbara was chosen as the Friars' Woman of the Year owing to her philanthropic ventures with regard to children. She was specifically singled out for her work with the Barbara Sinatra Children's Center at Rancho Mirage, California, an organization that gives aid to abused children. Don't forget, people, the Friars humbly admit that they do have that charitable side. As emcee, producer David Tebet chose Lee Iacocca. Why? Perhaps Tebet knew the wacky side of the Chrysler Corporation's CEO, "I knew that Lee Iacocca was a good friend of the Sinatras, so I wrote him a letter," says Tebet of his brainstorm. "I was told by his PR man that this date was a week before a board meeting and he never goes anywhere or does anything then because there is nothing more important than the board meeting. So he finally called me and he said, 'You sure I'll have a good time?' and I said, 'The best time of your life.' I'll never forget when he said, 'Yes.'" So much for know-it-all PR men. The choice must have worked, as Iacocca "proved to be a witty and charming Toastmaster with an excellent sense of timing and ability to ad-lib," or so said *Variety*.

When Tebet called Barbara with the news that he had secured Iacocca, he had to track her down in a hotel in Monaco—we're talking Mrs. Frank Sinatra here, let us not forget that. "Someone at the hotel said, 'Barbara is taking a shower,'" remembers Tebet, "and I said, 'No! You tell her the news that I have. She'll come out of the shower.'" Wonder if even Frank could muster that courage. "And sure enough, she put on her robe and I said I've got some great news for you and she started screaming on the phone." But maybe it was for a towel?

"Frank ordered me to be here tonight, that's why I'm here," said Iacocca. The big guns were out in full force for this extravaganza, from the Gregory Pecks and the Henry Kissingers to Lewis and Martin and Ball and Rickles. Sammy Davis, Jr., sang "You're Nobody Till Somebody Loves You" and Dionne Warwick warbled "That's What Friends Are For." After Dinah Shore's rendition of "Georgia on My Mind" Iacocca commented, "You can't watch Dinah if you're diabetic"—yea, well, try listening to Sammy Davis, Jr., sing "Candy Man"; that'll get the insulin going.

Alan King loves to foster that controversy, "Milton Berle is not here; he's still pissed off about the Cary Grant Dinner." Even today I bet Berle is pissed off about that Dinner—now if only he can remember who Cary Grant was.

There were some words of affection for Iacocca from Tom Dreesen, "I've never met a man who makes seven figures and still drives an American car." I bet Lee wept after that. Dreesen also said, "I have been the opening act for Frank Sinatra for five years, and that's why I can relate to Barbara Sinatra. I know what it's like to get that call in the middle of the night saying, 'Mr. Sinatra wants you to perform this evening.'"

Barbara's hubby paid tribute to her in his special way, describing her as his "Roommate, my confidante, and who also is beautiful and does fine laundry." Laundry? Barbara Sinatra? Perhaps someone should have started a charity for her. Then again, it could have been Jack Daniels talking. The loving wife suggested that she would have liked to reciprocate with how fine her husband is, but he threatened to break her kneecaps if she did. Oh my, tenderness abounds in the Sinatra household.

The busy Toastmaster may or may not have had a successful board meeting, but according to Tebet, "It was a great evening and Iacocca said he had the best time of his life, hands down!" Enough about Iacocca—what about Barbara's kneecaps?

ALAN KING TESTIMONIAL DINNER – 1989

(Memories of me, me, me!)

GOD, *Toastmaster*	ANJELICA HUSTON
JOEY ADAMS	ELLIOT KASTNER
LAUREN BACALL	ETHEL KENNEDY
SAMMY CAHN	JOSEPH KENNEDY
BILLY CRYSTAL	SIDNEY LUMET
BILLY ECKSTINE	PAUL MAZURSKY
ROCKY GRAZIANO	ROBERT MERRILL
BUDDY HACKETT	ANNA MOFFO
KITTY CARLISLE HART	JOHN NEWCOMBE
LENA HORNE	ANTHONY NEWLEY

Joy Philbin	Claire Trevor
Regis Philbin	Jack Valenti
Tony Randall	Gwen Verdon
Robert Sarnoff	Lou Weiss
Gary Smith	Elie Wiesel
Rusty Staub	Joe Williams
Gloria Steinem	Irwin Winkle
Peter Stone	Henry Winkler
David Tebet	

When Alan King was honored with a Dinner in 1989, he tossed out tradition and acted as his own Master of Ceremonies, "Why should I let the other speakers grab laughs and applause while I sit around like an idiot?" Interesting point. Of course, this did leave him open for a jab or two, such as this one from Jack Valenti, the head of the Motion Picture Arts & Sciences, "I think it's remarkable that King has achieved the status whereby he could probably write his own birth certificate, preside at his bar mitzvah, and probably preside at his own funeral."

King took the ribbing in stride, jumping on the bashing bandwagon himself during the Dinner, "I'd like to welcome each and every one of you to the most complete ego trip of all time," he announced to the SRO audience. "One does not accept an honor like this without truly believing he deserves this—everything else is bullshit." After remarking, "I'd like to explain the reason for my emceeing my own dinner—nobody else wanted to do it. I talked to my contemporaries and they said if it was a Roast we would have been there, but as a Tribute we feel in all good conscience we can't show up," Buddy Hackett yelled from his sideline place on the dais, "You mean it's not a Roast?" To which Alan responded, "It's so nice that Sir John Gielgud showed up to grace our evening." At this rate that Friars' age-old question of "What's the difference between a Roast and a Dinner?" will never be resolved—not that they care.

Buddy Hackett doesn't need to stand at the podium to do his act; he tends to just shout things out from his place at the dais as these events progress. Of course, it's usually to say how they're not progressing, "I'd like to get on before the pacemakers shut off—especially mine!" But it's not time for him yet, so you'll have to be patient, too.

This was not Alan's first time being honored by the Friars. Let us not forget his Roast in 1961 and a Dinner in 1971. "Johnny Carson got sick on me, so at the last minute I got David Frost to emcee; he was very good. That first Dinner, in '71, on top of everyone else I had seven presidential candidates. I had all the Kennedy sisters, Ted was there. John Lindsay was thinking about running for president. There was Coretta King." Actually, just to name-drop a bit more here—that first Dinner was pretty impressive for its dais guests: John Glenn, Lena Horne, Jack Benny, Veronica Lake, George Plimpton, Ethel Kennedy; it was an astounding group. Proceeds from the Dinner went to benefit the Robert F. Kennedy Foundation and the Martin Luther King, Jr. Foundation. So don't let Alan fool you; there's a heart that's mighty large buried under those cigar ashes.

"Redd Foxx was dirty at that Dinner—we never had that before. By today's standards, it was nothing. I wasn't shocked, but I was embarrassed for everyone," explains King. "So the second one, I said to Jean Pierre, 'I'll be my own Toastmaster. Nobody knows these people better than me.' I had the Benny Goodman orchestra, and we closed with Billy Eckstine and Joe Williams. Lena came up and they sang the blues for about fifteen minutes and tore the place apart."

In between, of course, there was the comedy, "It is show time!" announced the Master of Ceremonies. "You know how many arms I twisted and how many asses I kissed to get this group here tonight?" He mentioned that he was a lot older than the last time he was honored, "The only place hair grows now is in my nose and my ears. Just where I need it. I go to the barber now to hear. Nothing works anymore. I took better care of my car than I did my body. I am sick and tired of bran!" As he should be.

"I have been given four minutes to give my tribute to Alan, which is considerably more than I need," said the always persnickety Tony Randall. "It's a thrilling evening, above all because I'm situated between two legends. On my right, Lena

Horne, and on my left, Claire Trevor, who never stopped smoking for one moment. Alan, I was particularly impressed the way you set the tone for the evening with the hemorrhoid and armpit jokes. The rest of us don't have to strive for the class you spoke about. I'm here because of Dave Tebet, of course, who sent me this note that I should like to share with you: 'Dear Tony, thanks for accepting, it's been tough.'"

Hackett finally got his chance. "Alan is my fifth closest friend. He used to be seventh, but two guys went to the chair. He did ask me not to say, you know, to work on the edge, like I do on the *Tonight Show* and not use the language which flows from me freely like mother's milk or cat shit. I owe Freddie Roman a favor 'cause I have a very ugly cousin and I asked him to have sex with my ugly cousin and he did it. And I said to my ugly cousin, 'How was it, Arnold?'" Then he told the following joke and, well, so much for working clean. "Ethel Kennedy is here tonight, God bless you darlin'. I was lucky enough to be her guest at Hyannis and lived in the house. And me and Alan went up there together and Mr. Blackwell reviewed us. If you're here tonight, Mr. Blackwell, you're number one on the dead list, asshole. He wrote, 'Alan King's tuxedo was impeccable. The line of accent from the heel to the toe on his trousers was three-quarter length. He had a slim blue thread where the pocket kerchief should be, a remarkable innovation. A gambler-type vest of another color. Mr. Hackett's tuxedo looked like he fucked a penguin and it blew up." Well, he did say he thought it was a Roast.

Billy Crystal gave his touching remarks, "I'm the only one up here who hasn't had open heart surgery. Thank you, Buddy, it was a joy to watch you work. You are to taste what Exxon is to the Alaskan coastline. The man that did Alan's bris did his nose. Did you know that? Same guy. Alan King did the Ed Sullivan show ninety-three times, which is more than anyone in the history of television. Live shows, which is more times than Ed was on live, actually. And it wasn't that he was better than anyone else, but he had pictures of Ed in a motel with Señor Wences' hand. Alan is more than a comedian; he's a social climber."

You have to give Alan credit—he did know how to make an exit, "When you've been a saloon comic for forty-six years and a Friar for forty-three years, this is about as good as it gets, and I'm very grateful. I promised Dave Tebet that if he would allow me to emcee this, there'd be no tears." He lied, of course, but he was able to bring on that incredible finale he mentioned with Joe Williams, Billy Eckstine, and Lena Horne—say, maybe he is God!

DICK SHAWN ROAST – 1982

(Sometimes you just want to shower after a Roast)

BUDDY HACKETT, Roastmaster	GEORGE KIRBY
STEVE ALLEN	FREDDIE ROMAN
GENE BAYLOS	JOEY TRAVOLTA
RED BUTTONS	JACKIE VERNON
DICK CAPRI	HENNY YOUNGMAN

Seeing as Dick was known around the Monastery for his unorthodox antics, it stands to reason that his time on the ego-chopping block would be particularly lewd and crude. His Roasters took great pains to make sure Dick felt right at home, and when you have Buddy Hackett as Roastmaster, then consider it done. "Dick is a peculiar kind of guy. He's different from the rest of the comedians. Years ago in Las Vegas me and him and Joey Bishop was fucking the same girl. Me and Joey got the clap; Dick got diabetes. He's very unusual."

"Dick Shawn doesn't have much of a sex life," opined Dick Capri, "His idea of a threesome is jerking off with two hands." Capri also shared this gem, "Dick is dating a woman that's so old she had to have her cunt lifted." Oh, stop cringing, you were warned at the top that this wasn't going to be pretty!

Jackie Vernon shared, "Dick likes to masturbate in the movies. If you don't believe me, call TWA." Red Buttons actually uses this joke in his explanation, or possibly defense, of how the Friars Roasts were dirty for the sake of being funny as opposed to just dirty for the sake of being smutty, "You see, there's a difference between vulgarity and wit. Some of those Roasts had some of the best wit you've ever heard. It was just wonderful stuff. It just wasn't fuck, fuck, fuck, and all the words and all that. I mean, that's kids' stuff; it's boring and wasn't that. We tried to put a spin on it. I'll give you a for-instance. They Roasted Marty Allen and I said about Marty Allen, I said, 'He likes to jerk off in the movies,' and I said, 'If you don't believe me, ask anybody on TWA.' You understand what I'm saying? That's the spin, that's the twist. But that's wit. There's a difference between saying that and, 'He likes to sit in movies and take his cock out and whatnot'—you understand what I'm saying? There's the difference. It's the best example I could give you." It's also a great example of how these jokes are told and used by everyone else under the sun. I won't even mention the fact that Marty Allen was Roasted in 1965—good Lord, Jackie!

Freddie Roman, who has the cleanest act in the Catskills, certainly knows how to play to any audience—and at this Roast, the audience got this: "Buddy is the only guy I know who can go to the bathroom to take a shit and get arrested for dumping toxic waste." A little bathroom humor with your lunch, sir? And that was just for the Roastmaster. For the guest of honor Freddie offered, "Dick Shawn is such a prick, he once took Sammy Davis, Jr. to an Ella Fitzgerald concert just to see if Ella's voice could shatter Sammy's eye." And it wouldn't be a Roast if there wasn't a penis joke thrown into the mix: "Dick's cock is so small and pointy, he once tried to put it in a girl's mouth, she turned her head and he pierced her ear and validated her parking ticket at the same time."

Henny Youngman launched into his own agenda, "Last time I was at the Friars, they had a fresh seafood dinner—the catch of the day was hepatitis. There's a new show on the coast, it's called *That's Incredible*—next week they're putting on a Puerto Rican family with only one kid." But don't assume that Henny didn't offer a Roast-like zinger when push came to shove, "Dick recently went to the old ladies' home and did a benefit for himself. He fucked Helen Hayes."

Steve Allen, who has also served as Abbot of the California Friars, has been around a Friars' dais or two and has his own observations about these events. "If I had to make a choice, I would choose being a host. Not that there's any more glory to it—I'd really rather be home—but because you get eight or nine chances to hit one over the fence. Whereas, if you're only on for four minutes, it's your chance for the night. You might have an off night and people think he wasn't very funny today. You can't just get up and make jokes about the Hollywood Freeway— well, you can, a lot of people do, but I can't."

At Shawn's Roast, Allen practiced what he preached, "It was great to see Henny Youngman go from comedy to incoherence in thirty seconds." But he isn't one to dwell on any one person too long, so he moved on, "I'm very honored to take part in any public event connected with the Friars because I don't know of any other organization that does such an effective job of providing a point of connection between show business and organized crime." He was just kidding, of course. Right, Steve? Steve? For Shawn he quipped, "Dick has been known as an up-and-coming comedian for thirty-five years that I know of personally. And he is still up, but he's not coming as frequently. Dick is quite old. He's the second white man to make love to Sophie Tucker." You know you're in trouble when they start pulling out the Sophie Tucker jokes.

Other than certain branches of government, how many organizations can boast they've had ex-cons as guest speakers? Which explains George Kirby's riotous moment at the podium. He had just come off a three-and-a-half-year prison sentence for drug trafficking, "A lot of guys get up here and say, 'I'm very glad to be here,' and you don't know if they're lying. But with me, you know it's true." This one line even beat out the penis and pussy jokes for most laughs—and nothing ever beats out penis and pussy jokes! George explained, "I'm proud to be a member of the Friars Club, so proud, that when I was doing time, I kept up my dues." He may have said things about Dick, too, but who cares when you've got a prison theme going.

Joey Travolta is a double-threat in show business—he's John Travolta's brother and was married to Dick Shawn's daughter. Whatever the hell a "double-threat" really means, it makes for a good segue. His opening statement, "I'm fucking your daughter!"

is something every daddy wants to hear in front of two thousand people. Travolta then read a poem paying homage to his father-in-law: "The stage is set now to honor the man / He's a genius in comedy, so I ask you to stand / For a toast in his order / We love you, Dick Shawn / And I'm still fucking your daughter." Lest you think the iambic pentameter works better when you hear those sweet words spoken as opposed to reading them, guess again. Bad poetry is bad poetry, no matter how you slice it.

Red Buttons didn't miss a beat, "Joey, I fucked Dick Shawn's daughter, too. As a matter of fact, it was *after* you married her!" Dick was pretty lucky this time around, though, seeing as Red chose to list those who "never had a dinner." Among them, "Mae West, who was fed through a cock in the intensive care unit." This is a pretty good place to stop with Red. Although there was no stopping Shawn, "Thank you for the information, Joey. I suspected you were fucking my daughter. The reason I didn't feel too bad is because I got her at twelve." When you read what Dick did at the Jerry Lewis Roast, you'll understand that this man has no boundaries—on any level.

Shawn also questioned the Friars' choice of guest of honor. "Why would they pick me?" he asked. "Because they are running out of Jews!" And that includes Sammy Davis, Jr., who was Roasted in '64.

"The memory of this Roast to Dick will stay with him forever, like a bad case of herpes," said Dick Capri. If he only knew that just reading about it could make one feel the same way. Now run to the doctor, get some penicillin, and keep on reading.

SID CAESAR ROAST – 1983

(Your Roast of Roasts!)

BUDDY HACKETT, *Roastmaster*	SAMMY CAHN
ERNIE ANASTOS	DICK CAPRI
GENE BARRY	LEN CARIOU
GEORGE BARRIE	CHARLES "HONEY" COLES
ABRAHAM D. BEAME	NORM CROSBY
BILL BEUTEL	JIM DALE

ERROL DANTE	DICK SHAWN
JACK L. GREEN	JULE STYNE
ROGER GRIMSBY	BILLY TAYLOR
ED HERLIHY	JACKIE VERNON
JOHN JOHNSON	ABE VIGODA
JAN MURRAY	WILLIAM B. WILLIAMS
WILLARD SCOTT	

Of the myriad words out there to convey the essence of a Roast—obscene, smutty, ribald, lewd, etc.—the Friars have opted for the more genteel description of "blue language" to describe their vicious verbal attacks on the guests of honor. They must know they're fooling no one, because no matter how you mask the descriptions, any seven-year-old will tell you that a dirty word is a dirty word. In the days when women were cut a little language slack, even by the Friars, the Club took great pains to ensure that females were free and clear of the vulgar onslaught. At the Sid Caesar Roast, the Club's officers seemed to take particular heed of any women who were present when the stag show began. That interest would eventually add the word "ironic" to their ever-growing list of dirty words. William B. Williams spotted a woman in the audience during his introductions of the nonspeakers on the dais: "Miss. This may seem like an imposition, but can you get out!" He seemed to have an easier time having the woman escorted off the premises than the waiters—who were also persona non grata at such events, "Waiters, I don't know how to tell you this, but fuck off! If you're waiting for a tip, you've come to the wrong Club!" Whatever happened to the more genteel, albeit wimpy, "Would you mind leaving?" Then again, Milton Berle used to shout, "Immigration!" which usually did the trick—so much for manners.

Buddy Hackett was the Roastmaster, who also seemed to be on non-Friar alert. Identifying a lone waiter on the floor, Hackett intoned, "If that guy doesn't get out, I want two guys to hold him up and I'll fuck him in the ass! But then we'll never get rid of him." Again, in a telling display of irony (keep reading, all this irony will come together and you'll laugh and laugh),

Hackett said, "It's fitting that I'm the Roastmaster because I know Sid Caesar better than anyone here—except for his wife, Florence, who is made up to be one of these guys tonight. I don't know which one, but we got one of those detectors coming in from the airport. It doesn't seek out metal, but it's a pussy detector and as they pass through, if it rings, then we know that Sid lost another filling."

An interesting note here. At every event, be it a Dinner or a Roast, "The Star Spangled Banner" would be sung by a prominent singing personality. There is nothing more incongruous than listening to opera greats Richard Tucker or Robert Merrill belt out a beautiful rendition of the national anthem, followed by, "Okay, you cocksuckers! You're in for one piss-ass event here, that's for fuckin' sure." Only the Friars would carry their patriotism in their hearts while their tongues sound like they're shooting a scene from *The Exorcist.*

Dick Capri took a safe approach to Roasting—attack those not on the dais, "I went to Elizabeth Taylor and Eddie Fisher's wedding and at the end of the ceremony, I didn't have a glass to break, so I stepped on Sammy Davis' eye." There's nothing like a glass-eye joke to keep the Friars in hysterics—remember it the next time you have to make a wedding toast.

Hackett's son Sandy, who is also a comedian, said at the Roast, "I told my dad that I was nervous being here on the dais with all these guys who are twenty, twenty-five, thirty years my senior and he said, 'That's all right, just pray for a hard-on and you'll be able to sell it to one of them.'" To which the elder Hackett chimed in, "If you could just save that hard-on until we get back to LA and lend it to me. It doesn't mean anything to me, but your mother will be so appreciative."

Jan Murray told the crowd that Sid Caesar "has been in a coma for thirty years. Right now as I'm standing here talking to you, he's pissing on my shoes. Sid had a tough childhood; even Sid's parents hated him. Up until he was six years old, his mother was still trying to have an abortion." Just in case you need another masturbation joke fix, Murray had this to say: "Just before the luncheon, I went into the mens' room and Jackie Vernon was sitting on the toilet looking at a magazine and jerking off—and he wasn't even embarrassed. He even showed me the picture he was looking at—it was a platter of cold cuts."

Dick Shawn, who knows a thing or two about zany stunts, philosophized, "Sickness and weakness are two different things. Sickness is when Sid Caesar takes Mel Brooks and hangs him out of a twenty-story window and lets him dangle. Sid's weakness is that he didn't let him go!"

For Norm Crosby, Caesar didn't even have to be in the room for him to spew forth his absurdities, "God made pubic hair curly so it wouldn't take your eye off. God gave Adam a woman and an apple, and the putz ate the apple. We should all have faith, the people in our business, who knows better about faith than comedians? One of the first stand-up comedians in biblical days was Shecky of Nazareth, who was the cruise director on Noah's Ark. After forty days and forty nights, he went to Noah with tears in his eyes and said, 'I've had bad audiences, but *they're* animals!'"

After all this, Caesar said, "When men fly three thousand miles just to tell a few jokes about you, that's love." It's also insane.

As for that irony, keep reading.

PHYLLIS DILLER – 1983

(Busted!)

PHYLLIS DILLER ROAST – 1985

(Let the punishment fit the crime!)

BUDDY HACKETT, *Toastmaster*	ROGER GRIMSBY
ABRAHAM D. BEAME	ROBERT MERRILL
SAMMY CAHN	PAUL RIGBY
DICK CAPRI	TONY ROMA
JACK CARTER	FREDDIE ROMAN
ERROL DANTE	MARVIN SCOTT
PERRY DILLER	ROLLAND SMITH
HUGH DOWNS	MILTON SUCHIN
NORMAN FELL	JACKIE VERNON
FRANK FIELD	JACK WESTON
WAYLON FLOWERS & MADAME	WILLIAM B. WILLIAMS

One of the more hilarious jokes ever played out at a Friars' event took place off of the dais. In 1983, you remember, women were still verboten at Roasts and "stag" was the order of the day. Phyllis Diller changed all that with a wig, a mustache, and a three-piece suit. Well, let's face it, she never was a clotheshorse. Phyllis explains, "I had a beau who was a Friar, Howard Rose, and he kept wanting to take me to one of those Roasts dressed as a man. He just thought it would be a big fun thing to do, and the more I thought about it the more it appealed to me. I was not trying to move mountains or make a statement of any kind. It wasn't women's lib; it was me, the jokester, willing to do anything for a gag. Anyway, it must have taken me a year to assemble the suit that fit me and the shoes. The shirt I had to buy in the boy's department to get one to fit my neck. I had a special wig made and a mustache and eyebrows. Everyone said I looked like Claude Rains!

"So finally the day came and in order to make it work, Howard bought an entire table for ten people—which meant no one ever really got close to me. Close enough to realize that I was a fake. Sid Caesar was being Roasted, and it was a marvelous show. The fact that all the people at the table knew me and were in on the joke, it worked. I was very nervous because, you realize that being dressed as a man, I couldn't go into any john. I couldn't go into the mens' room for obvious reasons and I couldn't go into the ladies' room because there would have been screams.

"It was the funniest and dirtiest thing I've ever heard in my life. The funny part of it was that this was when, at the Friars' luncheons, they even disbarred the waiters from the room and locked all of the doors!" Can I just say, "Here we go again!" As with all milestones involving women, labeling Phyllis as being the first female to crash a Roast may be a bit premature. If one were to sift through what little archives are left in the attic of the Friars—or maybe this one was found under the stairs—one would come across a clipping from the *Star* dated June 1977, with the headline, "Our girl (with the mustache) crashes Tom Jones' all-male show." It seems Gail Bryce, a writer for that paper, got all gussied up in her tailor-made suit, hair, and mustache and snuck into the Roast for Tom Jones. In the article, Gail said, "I felt like Judas at the Last Supper. One by one, actors, comics, and singers stepped up to tell jokes that got dirtier and dirtier. In my opinion, women haven't been missing much." She had a sticky moment or two, though, "I was a disaster as a dinner companion. I coughed out 'George' during the introductions, pointed to my throat, and then forked through the chicken remembering to take bigger bites than usual." Gail also had that bathroom problem to contend with, "Here was the moment of truth, mens' or ladies'. I picked the moment carefully and used the empty mens'." Walter Goldstein, the executive director at the time, is quoted as saying to her later, "You're the first woman to get away with it." Yeah, yeah, like we've never heard that before.

While Phyllis' incident may have thrown the Friars into a bit of a tailspin at the time, they bounced back in their typical bawdy fashion—punishment by Roasting! They put Diller in the hot seat in 1985 with Buddy Hackett at the helm, "Usually when we have an affair like this, they always pick on the guest of honor: 'He's got a big dick.' And they talk about his dick, how big his dick is, or he's got a little, bitty dick. His dick is so small they always talk about how small his dick is. That a fly tried to fuck it or something like that, you know. But today, gentlemen, we have a dickless luncheon."

How come after every Roast people talk about how hysterical Dick Capri was, yet nobody knows who he is? Just wondering. "I did a lot of homework on Miss Diller, and she's highly educated, refined, and quite a gourmet. Phyllis knows the correct wine that goes with a blow job. That's why whenever she's in New York, she always eats at Tavern on the Groin. It's not true that she once fucked Buddy Hackett and instead of coming, he left. And it's not true that her orifice is so large it has its own area code." They really do say that about Dick, though, being hysterical.

But if you want the opposite of the reaction Dick got, they had a Phyllis Diller impersonator—maybe it was Jim Bailey. Maybe it wasn't, but let's just say the room was pretty quiet during these, um, jokes, "I used to work as a lampshade in a whorehouse, I couldn't get one of the better jobs. . . . We have far too many kids. See, in my day, we didn't have the pill—it was either trick or treat." There were about a hundred more of these. Just a sampling to show that not every act at a Roast is a good one.

Jack Carter gave a rundown of the previous women honored; just go with it, it's less stressful that way. "What a historic evening in the Friars' history. On only three occasions have women ever been honored or been allowed into the hallowed hall of the Friars. That was Sophie Motherfucker, as we called her, because she hated all comedians. Then, of course, there was Lucille Testicles, and Phyllis Dildo, who strangely enough are the only three ladies in show business that were never fucked by Georgie Jessel." Sounds like the ladies lucked out on that one. But on with the Roast. "I love this adorable woman. This talented and oversexed woman, this woman has a diaphragm that works on voice command. Here's a woman whose sex life went from Vaseline to Polygrip. She's had a face-lift, a tit-lift, an ass-lift, a chin-lift. She finally went to her doctor and said, 'What about my sagging vagina?' He said, 'That'll take a forklift.'"

If they thought they were getting even, they had another thing coming, as the feisty dame not only took it, but shot it right back at them, "Thank you, thank you, thank you. I can't tell you what a thrill it is to be Man of the Year. And I also feel that I'm at a terrible disadvantage, I feel like Linda Lovelace with lockjaw. Without Buddy Hackett, this would be just another Roast—with him, it's just another Roast. But I kowtow to him because he's so terribly rich."

Diller must have taken notes during the Caesar Roast she slipped into two years earlier because she just kept shooting at the boys with both barrels, "I can't tell you how it feels to be at your Roast and Bob Hope can't show but Dick Capri can. Jack Carter has the disposition of an old Hoover vacuum cleaner—it sucks. We invited today my old college buddy, Hugh Downs, to give this place a little class—it didn't work. Hugh is about as exciting as vapor lock. I'll tell you what Hugh is like. He has a little black book, so beside Joan Collins' name he wrote, 'Has good posture and likes to bowl.' And Freddie Roman, my God, I'm about as tight with him as Ronald Reagan is with the Pointer Sisters."

If anything came out of Phyllis' antics, it was that the boys started to look at each other sorta funny. They never quite knew if the guy they were seated next to was really a guy or a girl— or just really funny looking.

JERRY LEWIS ROAST – 1986

(France should be so lucky)

BUDDY HACKETT, *Toastmaster*
WALTER ANDERSON
SAMMY CAHN
DICK CAPRI
PAT COOPER
HOWARD COSELL
NORM CROSBY
HUGH DOWNS
BOB FITZSIMMONS
BOB FOSSE
ROCKY GRAZIANO
JACK L. GREEN

DARREN MCGAVIN
BUTCH LEWIS
ROBERT MERRILL
LEROY NEIMAN
JOE PISCOPO
FREDDIE ROMAN
ROBERT SAKS
CHUCK SCARBOROUGH
DICK SHAWN
FRED TRAVALENA
JERRY VALE

Roastmaster Buddy Hackett was still reeling from the scandal of the Caesar Roast, so he advised everyone in the audience of the still-stag Roast for Jerry Lewis, "Phyllis Diller sneaked in a few years ago and she dressed up like a man. So ever since then we've been doing this. Gentlemen, kindly reach over to the man next to you and if you don't feel a cock and balls, merely rise so we can have the broad taken out." Now you can see why these guys desperately needed to get women in there.

Lewis had been the guest of honor at a Friars' Testimonial Dinner with his partner, Dean Martin in 1955. Milton Berle emceed the Dinner and there were a dozen comics such as Jack Carter, Henny Youngman, Phil Silvers, Steve Allen, and Joey Adams on hand to roastly Toast them. Marilyn Monroe was even on this dais, sitting next to Eddie Fisher. John Rumsey was also there. Please don't tell me you've forgotten your history lessons from the previous chapters and don't know who this founding father is?

But that was a Dinner; this, according to Hackett, was a whole new ball game for Lewis, "Jerry said he's never been to a Roast. Well, how do you Roast a man who has done so much for humanity in this country? A Roast is where you pick a guy apart. You rip his nuts out. You destroy him. You put such shit on him, and he has to smile like he's having a good time. I went to him before and asked if he was a little nervous. I said, 'I don't want to really embarrass you, I just want to do my job. What are some of the things you would like me not to say?' and he told me. Do you know he jerked off in his mother's soup when he was eleven? His first piece of ass was his cousin Al?" There is no such thing as "off the record" at the Friars Club.

Pat Cooper brings a certain psychotic flavor to every Roast he attends, "What burns my ass is, they sent me a ticket to come from California to here and I was here all the while! I know Jerry's disappointed. They were supposed to have his first girlfriend here today, but they don't allow sheep in the room. . . . He does a great telethon where he always kisses Sammy Davis. He'll never get AIDS, he'll get spades. . . . I must be honest with you. Before I came up here I was very nervous, but my friend Norm Crosby said, 'You have a right to, you're not that talented.' That's why I love Norm; he never lies, he stutters a lot, but he never fuckin' lies."

Another Italian on the dais was Dick Capri (not that it matters what his heritage is, but I figure since he brought it up, then so can I). "We're here to Roast Jerry Lewis, which is different for us Italians because we usually don't Roast people, we ice them." Oh, I would never have crossed that line. "Jerry and I go back a long time; first time I met Jerry was in sunny California. I remember vividly, certain things you just don't forget. I remember he had a deep dark tan on his face; Nell Carter was sitting on it. He was pouring his soul out to me about all the dumb things he did in his life, all his disappointments, the bad investments. The last one was ridiculous; he invested in a chain of Jewish funeral homes called 'Jake-in-the-Box.' His biggest regret is that he didn't fuck Eleanor Roosevelt—twice." For Norm Crosby, the English language is a veritable sea of tongue-twisting translations honed only through his internal thesaurus, "There is a certain maggotism that Jerry Lewis has that a certain sanction, a crotchiality, that excretes from him that is so unusual, people respond to him. People of every ethnic, of every social level respond to him. I know he doesn't want to talk about the wonderful things he does, but I have been privileged to work with Jerry on the telethons. I answer the phones once in a while and people answer him that would never respond to anybody else. We got a contribution Labor Day from a synagogue in Harlem that caters only to black Jews, it's called Temple Beth You Is My Woman Now."

"I'll tell you, one of the funniest things I ever saw at any of the Roasts was Dick Shawn at a stag," recalls Red Buttons. "All the stuff was going on and they finally got to Dick Shawn. And he got to the mike and he threw up all over the mike. He just stuffed a lot of stuff in his mouth and everything else that nobody saw and just walked up and 'blecch.' Well, that was one moment I will never forget. I think it was a highlight moment. I went on the floor, we all did. We miss him a lot; Dick Shawn was brilliant." Think *Porky's* for the Geritol set. After the laughter died down, which took forever, Shawn said, "Seemed like the only thing to do." Talk about your understatements. "We are honoring Jerry Lewis, and we all know the French look at him as more than a comic, more than a humorist, but a way of life, a force to release the tensions in our lives. In America he's funny, but in France—Chaplin, revered. But we must also remember that it was the French who invented cocksucking and cunt lapping. The Greeks invented fucking in the ass and the Jews, finger fucking.

"Jerry is the first one to earn his living being, literally, crazy. He was the original crazy comic. The Abbot and Costellos were silly. Charlie Chaplin was not crazy, but Jerry showed us a side, at a time in America, where it was okay to be crazy and have the courage to do it. Pee Wee Herman today has taken that slack, crazy—I have no idea what I'm talking about right now but it's not important. The important thing is I finished the sentence. And in America if you can finish a sentence, you can get a job." Maybe Dick was justifying that he wasn't the only crazy performer in town, or that he was employable. When Buddy returned to the podium, he surveyed the mess and said, "Boy, can you imagine how good he would have been if he was feeling well? You know, this looks better than what was on my plate."

Robert Saks, who produced the Friars Roasts for ten years, was not a funny man. Not that there's anything wrong with that, but unfortunately, he thought otherwise and audiences cringed when he got up to introduce the Roastmaster each year. However, at the Lewis Roast, he said this, which was sort of funny: "Jerry Lewis is the man who drove Dean Martin to drink—and then pulled away before he came out of the liquor store." You won't read another joke from Bob again. I promise.

As with all honorees, Jerry received a Piaget Polo watch from the Friars, which they gave to him to pose with for photos before the Roast. Every time Jean Pierre Trebot would hand Jerry the watch to use in the pictures, Lewis literally threw it right back at him—Trebot thinks it's because he's French. At the end of the evening, Jack L. Green presented Jerry with his watch, officially. "Cheap piece of shit," he said. "I threw it again, didn't I?" And he did. What he didn't toss away, however, was a check in the amount of $10,000 to help fight muscular dystrophy. Again, they won't say it too loudly, but the Friars give elsewhere than at the office.

"To follow Dick Shawn is like walking into a room of diarrhea," said Lewis. "I want to thank Bob Saks and Jean Pierre, the two assholes that got me into this. They haven't stopped calling my office, telling me, 'You have the largest Friars luncheon we ever had.' I could not, in good conscience, understand what I did to motivate so many people that wanted to come and see me eat shit." Oh, I bet that if he thought real long and hard, he'd come up with a few reasons—all the honorees eventually do. "I have in my pocket prepared material. And I have to tell you that the one thing that I learned is that when you're on the spot you have to make edits. The edits you have to make are vital; you either go with what you had in mind, or you make an edit and jump to something else. You have to wait until you're standing in front of a lectern with vomit on it to make these decisions. Now, I cannot honestly tell you that my dad taught me in the young years how to work with vomit on a lectern." What? People don't vomit in France?

RICH LITTLE ROAST – 1987

(So much time, so little material)

NORM CROSBY, *Roastmaster*	ROBIN LEACH
RICHARD ANDERSON	BUTCH LEWIS
ARTHUR ASHE	E.G. MARSHALL
ABRAHAM D. BEAME	PAT MCCORMICK
HARRY BELAFONTE	ROBERT MERRILL
JACK CARTER	LEROY NEIMAN
PAT COOPER	SCOTT RECORD
PROFESSOR IRWIN COREY	PAUL RIGBY
HOWARD COSELL	FREDDIE ROMAN
ERROL DANTE	MARVIN SCOTT
MIKE DOUGLAS	PHIL SIMMS
CHAD EVERETT	ROLLAND G. SMITH
DR. FRANK FIELD	DICK SMOTHERS
EDDIE FISHER	TOM SMOTHERS
LOUIS GOSSETT, JR.	MICHAEL SPINKS
SHECKY GREENE	JACKIE VERNON
ROGER GRIMSBY	SLAPPY WHITE
MARVIN HAMLISCH	FLIP WILSON
SKITCH HENDERSON	CARL WOLFSON
JIM JENSEN	HENNY YOUNGMAN
ROBERT LANSING	

One would think that Rich Little's philosophy that imitation is the sincerest form of flattery would have made him a willing participant for the Friars' own misguided interpretation of affection. Then again, guests of honor may walk onto the dais of their own accord, but inevitably wind up being carted off bawling and cowering. Perhaps honoring Little with a Roast was the Friars' backhanded way of bringing attention to those suffering with multiple personality disorders. (Knowing them, their first choice could have been Sybil, who perhaps declined because she was busy with a dinner party for seventeen.)

"Rich Little is living proof of the ancient adage that imitation is the sincerest form of making a living when you have no talent of your own," announced Roastmaster Norm Crosby. What would a Roast be without a little penis envy, as Crosby so delicately illustrated, "In case anybody is worried about the size of this incredible dais, I want you to know the time allotted to each speaker depends on the size of his organ. Now, if you have a four-inch cock, you do four minutes, if you have five, you do five, a six-inch cock you do six. I'm delighted to announce that most of the dais guests will just bow." Still in all, it's interesting how many people in the ballroom of New York's Sheraton Centre that day checked their watches each time a speaker approached and departed the podium.

Mike Douglas, whose talk show became a showcase for so many Friars, isn't known as a comedian per se, but he did share, "I did my show for over twenty years, some 6,000 shows, and I owe an awful lot to Rich because he was very seldom on the show." Perhaps this would be a good place to reiterate: "Mike Douglas, whose talk show became a showcase for so many Friars, isn't known as a comedian per se."

Talk about an impressionist's worst nightmare: Howard Cosell was in attendance, "I'm here to honor a man who has made his entire living by mimicking me—the authentic talent." Chad Everett opened up for the crowd, "When we were doing *Medical Center*, Rich showed me his impression of a thermometer—every time I bent down, he stuck his head up my ass." Spoken like a true sex symbol of the '60s. Speaking of the '60s, the Smothers Brothers sang a little ditty just for Rich, "Oh Rich Little, oh Rich Little, FUCK YOU." They may have been ostracized from the networks, but an act like that is guaranteed a slot on the Friars' hit parade.

Robin Leach may be a very funny guy at a party for the rich and famous, but as any guest of honor will tell you, a Roast is no party. "It's a pleasure to be here to salute Emanuel Lewis." That's it, folks. That's Robin's joke. Get it? If you do, then please share it with the rest of the class.

"Why do Jewish guys die before their wives? They want to. . . . Berle was going to be here tonight, but he ran into a little trouble; he's having a charisma bypass. . . . And that's what I have to say about Rich Little." Just another anonymous Roast in the zany brain of Henny Youngman.

Slappy White felt a little lonely at the podium, "I can't stay on too long, the fucking white guys took up all the time. And why is my silverware chained to the table?" Milton Berle was not at this Roast, but I know you've grown accustomed to having his penis around, so I'm going to take him up on his offer. "We had Slappy White once, on a dais, this is an anecdote which you can lay in any place because it happened at the suggestive Roasts." How many chances will I get to use a Slappy White story, so here goes Milton's tale: "I started off by saying whatever I said, then I said, 'Lucky I got here on time. Because before the show I had to go in the bathroom in the toilet and take a leak and I nearly didn't make the dais. While I was standing in front of the urinal in came Slappy White and he rushed in and he took out his dick and he said, 'Oh my God, I just made it!' I looked at it and said, 'See if they can make one in white.' That's an anecdote." Thanks Milton, I owe you one.

Pat Cooper ranted on and on about his annoyance with the Friars for not inviting him to the Elizabeth Taylor and Roger Moore Dinners. Inviting him to Rich Little's Roast, however, wasn't exactly what he had in mind as restitution. Don't even get him started on the yo-yos that each dais member received— the one with the Friars' logo on it. Yo-yos?

Dare we go right to the penis joke in Jack Carter's act? "Rich's cock is so small, he once raped a broad and she never found out." Well, even Jack admitted there was slim pickings of topics by the time he closed the show, "The only subject left is finger-fucking Phyllis Diller." Feel free to go back to the penis joke to get that image out of your head, if you like. Or better yet, go play with your yo-yo.

Rich Little may be a man of few words, but his voice is a

veritable dictionary of personalities and they all showed their appreciation. His impressions of Cosell, Leach, George Burns, Ronald Reagan, Oliver North (how '80s!) and Johnny Carson went on so long, the audience started leaving. Apparently the lunch was quickly transforming itself into a midnight snack. Freddie Roman remembers Little's speech as the longest of any honoree. If one were to reflect on Little's penis size versus time spent at the podium—Berle, eat your heart out!

BRUCE WILLIS ROAST – 1989

(Laugh Hard!)

MILTON BERLE, *Toastmaster*	PAT McCORMICK
DANNY AIELLO	BOB MELVIN
ABRAHAM D. BEAME	ROBERT MERRILL
RICHARD BELZER	JIM MORRIS
ALAN BREGMAN	ROBERT MORTON
JAKE BLOOM	JAN MURRAY
DICK CAPRI	REGIS PHILBIN
JACK CARTER	MAURY POVICH
CHARLES "HONEY" COLES	SCOTT RECORD
PAT COOPER	SAL RICHARDS
HOWARD COSELL	ARNOLD RIFKIN
NORM CROSBY	GERALDO RIVERA
FRANK FIELD	FREDDIE ROMAN
JOE FRANKLIN	JOE ROTH
BOBCAT GOLDTHWAIT	MARVIN SCOTT
GILBERT GOTTFRIED	PAUL SHAFFER
WOODY HARRELSON	JOEL SILVER
PHIL HARTMAN	ROLLAND G. SMITH
DOM IRRERA	MICHAEL SPINKS
VICTOR A. KAUFMAN	STEWIE STONE
ROBERT KRAFT	BILL TUSH
ROBIN LEACH	JACK WESTON
BUTCH LEWIS	DAVID WILLIS—*the Dad*
RICH LITTLE	HENNY YOUNGMAN
JON LOVITZ	

Ask Jack Carter what his most memorable Roast was, and he will most likely mention the Bruce Willis Roast in 1989, "I almost didn't get on. It was almost four in the afternoon and Milton [ten points if you can figure out Milton who?] didn't put me on. It looked like he was not going to introduce me because he put on Pat Cooper and I said, 'I gotta follow Pat Cooper because I close the Roasts. I'm the closer.' And I see that he's now introducing busboys and thanking the hotel and the waiters. 'Let's hear it for the help.' I stood up and I ran over and I grabbed his cigar and I broke it in half and I said, 'Maybe that will get your attention! Remember me? I'm sitting over there. I've been here for seven hours. Do you think I'll get on, or are you going to introduce some more busboys?' I went crazy, and I'm funny when I'm angry."

Berle, on the other hand, is funny all the time. As Master of Ceremonies he couldn't have cared less that it was the first Roast where women were allowed to walk freely through the doors without having to don a pair of boxer shorts. "If the saying is true, you are what you eat, today we are honoring the biggest cunt in Hollywood. Ladies, that's for openers. Wait a minute, there is nothing wrong with saying the word cunt because if it wasn't made to be eaten, God wouldn't have created it in the form of a taco. It is no secret, for the first time we have ladies in our audience today. Welcome to you all. And don't any of you guys in the audience have any illusions about getting balled or laid, not a chance—they're all Jewish housewives."

They didn't really mind having women there; let's face it, a bisexual crowd meant more people would be laughing at their jokes. (I sort of stole that bisexual joke from Norm Crosby; now I feel like one of the guys!) But back to Berle, "Out in Beverly Hills I'm known as one of the great chefs, but this is the first time in my culinary career that I have ever Roasted a New Jersey asshole! In the past, the Friars Club has honored many great stars—such as Sinatra, Hope, Jack Benny, George Burns—but today we have sunk to a new fuckin' low! Laugh it up, Bruce. . . . I laugh when you act!" YES! "Some of you may be asking yourselves, 'Why are we honoring this man?' Because we ran out of fuckin' Jews! Waiting for Bruce to win an Oscar is like leaving the porch light on for Jimmy Hoffa!" Hmm? Dean Martin Dinner, 1984?

Supposedly Berle was there as the Roastmaster because Willis refused to let anyone else do the job. If he couldn't have the grand master of Roasts officiating, then there would be no Roast—just goes to show, be careful what you wish for, you may just get it (literally). Berle announced, "When I called Bruce at home and I made the offer to let the Friars Roast him, you should have heard the response, 'What! You mean me fly to New York, sit on that hot seat, and try to smile while a bunch of comic cocksuckers bury you in their bullshit? No! Fuck those assholes! And fuck you, Berle!' And then his wife said, 'Now would you like to speak to Bruce?'"

Comedian Stewie Stone put to rest any confusion the audience that day may have had regarding the teaming up of Berle and Willis, "Some of you may be wondering why Milton Berle would be the Roastmaster for Bruce Willis. I didn't think they had anything in common, but I did a lot of research and I found out they do have a lot in common—Milton Berle *has* the biggest prick in show business, and Bruce Willis *is* the biggest prick in show business." There will be a test at the end of this book on how many different words can be applied to describe Berle's . . . thing. And let Dick Capri give you a chance to start things off, "Today I had the opportunity to see Milton Berle's dick. After all these years, he showed it to me. It had some white stuff on it. I said, 'Milton what's that white stuff on your dick?' he said, 'It's Polident.' I said, 'What's Polident doing on your dick?' He said, 'Martha Raye just gave me a blow job.' We all know how well-endowed Milton is; in fact, when Milton was circumcised Gene Autry bought his foreskin and had a saddle made of it."

There were a couple of comics, though, that remembered that Bruce was the guest of honor as opposed to Berle's schlong. Norm Crosby had this to say about Bruce, "This is a bright man, knowledgeable man. He knows things, he knows why God gave us whiskey and marijuana—so that ugly people can get laid, too." Joe Roth had once shared an apartment with Bruce, and just wanted to set the record straight, "Not that Bruce is gay or nuttin'. I mean, he used to grab my cock a lot, but I figured he was just foolin' around. You was just foolin', weren't you, Bruce? And he never held it for more than two or three minutes anyway."

Jan Murray also must have been given a note that Willis was on the dais, "I confess I don't love Bruce Willis. I don't know Bruce Willis, which says something about my career. I just flew 3,000 miles to honor a total fuckin' stranger. Look at the difference in our careers. Meryl Streep and Cher are fighting with fists to see who's gonna be his next leading lady. Wanna hear my latest project? Ruth Buzzi and Kaye Ballard want me to go on the road with them as a three-man act." Then he tried a new angle, "Lot of talk today about Bruce's cock. When I prepared this, I said, I know what, I'm gonna talk about it, nobody will think of that . . . this thing that he's got has its own heart and lungs." He held off on saying anything about Milton's appendage—for, like, a minute, "What a thrill it is for me to stand between the two biggest pricks in show business."

Leave it to Howard Cosell to bring a little class to the afternoon, "Bruce, I don't know a fucking thing about you, I never wanted to." Well, that wasn't the classy part—that was just funny. This is the class: "The people who put together this program may be responsible for its permanent, terminal demise. It is endless. It is stupid. The redundancy of filthy garbage has even surpassed anything that Berle has contributed to his long and ignominious career in show business."

The afternoon just kept getting weirder and weirder for Jack Carter, "I tell you something funny that happened to me at the Bruce Willis Roast. Willis invited a lot of the Comedy Store comics, four or five, and he had this Bobcat Goldthwait, and he got up and as he got up, he threw a license plate at me. It was my license plate, which had been taken off my car. I thought it fell off years ago. He had stolen it, taken my plate. 'Here's your license plate!'" It didn't take Jack long to find out what Goldthwait was doing with it once he got to the podium, "Besides honoring Bruce, one of the main reasons that I came tonight was to make amends.

"I'd like to apologize to Mr. Jack Carter. 'Cause a year ago I was going to a Christmas party and Mr. Carter cut off my wife. We were pulling into a parking space, and he took the parking space. And Ann said, 'You took our space.' And I jumped out of the car and said, 'Excuse me, we were turning in there.' And he said, 'Well, it's mine now.' I'm not a really mature man, so um, Jack has a license plate that says 'Jack's Car,' so I stole his license plate. The police actually stopped me and I said, 'Jack Carter took my wife's parking spot.' And I said he was kinda acting like a dick, and he goes, 'Ah, keep it.' But um, I would like to make amends to Mr. Carter. This is his license plate. I'd actually like to just return it tonight. Thanks." Do you really think he said, "Excuse me"? Carter's take on the whole Roast is pretty clear, "None of those Comedy Store guys that he invited did any good, not one of them; they all died. We had to save it. They have no relation, they don't know how to work a Roast. You got to work a Roast, you gotta do special jokes, you gotta grab an audience. Very few of them have audience appeal."

Andy Rooney has audience appeal, only he wasn't there. But Rich Little was—for far longer than his allotted four minutes, it would seem—and gave an excellent assessment of the Friars Annual Celebrity Roast. One that would have made Andy proud, especially since it was done in his voice, "Do you ever wonder why people come to a Roast? It's ridiculous. Nobody ever remembers the jokes afterward. You can't repeat them to your wife, your kids maybe, but not your wife. And it's embarrassing, sitting around listening to last year's jokes. And why do people always make fun of Milton Berle's cock? They should feel sorry for him. Can't cross his legs. Can't survive a hard-on anymore, and he needs three hands to jerk off. And why do they have these Friars Roasts anyway? Why don't they just rerun last year's Roast? Nobody would notice the difference. The comics are the same, the food is always the same; as a matter of fact, it's the same food as last year. The jokes are the same and they don't even need them anyway. They should just bring out a cock and a cunt and a fuck and a hump and let the audience make their own fucking jokes, kind of like a salad bar." Truer words were never spoken.

Ready for your dose of Pat Cooper? "A man called Frank

Sinatra is choosing this cocksucker to play his life? What the fuck is going on? That's like asking Milton Berle's cock to play Cary Grant. I'm sitting here three fuckin' hours watching Rich Little do a pilot. I don't give a shit. I came here at eleven, all the Jews went on early. I don't like the fuckin' smell around here, it's all pussy." Say goodnight, Pat.

Carter, as we know, did indeed close the show, "They told me it was gonna be a stag and I'm surprised to see a few transvestites here in the audience. . . . Where's Gloria Allred? God bless her. What a fighter. She took this legal case seriously, she went right to the supreme cunt. . . . I needed this night and this introduction like Harry Helmsley needs a condom. . . . Milton's incredible, he's amazing, and you proved that at this stage of your career, Milton, you don't have to be funny anymore. . . . Big fucking deal, *Die Hard;* he saved a building. Three hours on top of a fucking skyscraper, doing shit. At least King Kong caught a plane and he fucked Fay Wray." How special that Willis' dad sat proudly on the dais to hear such accolades about his son.

If this Willis Roast seemed long to read, imagine living it? The afternoon ran so long that Richard Belzer, Woody Harrelson, and Gilbert Gottfried—who had all been invited there to speak—never got on. If they were as vocal as Carter, that damn thing would still be going on. What was odd, though, was the fact that Harrelson wore a hat throughout the entire afternoon and only Pat Cooper mentioned it, "Now let me tell you what's goin' on in this fucking area. A greatness of a fuckin' star, and there's a man sitting on this dais with a fuckin' hat on. Now what the fuck is that? Is he coming or going? What the fuck is he doing on this fuckin' dais? He's sitting there playing with his putz. I come here, I took a fuckin' shower, I think I wasted it."

Eventually Bruce got up to accept his honors, "This fucking Roast took so long, I thought I was doing a love scene with Cybill Shepherd. The only difference is, this Roast gave me a hard-on." He then presented Milton with a dildo—a rather large one, like really large! God love Berle if he compares to it. "Milton, I present you with the honorary *Die Hard* cock, 1989 model. People say he can snap a man's neck at twenty feet with his cock. I don't know about that, but he was on line at the bank one day, pulled a hard-on, and the lady in front of him thought it was a holdup. Milton Berle is to comedy what George Bush is to full contact karate." Now, wasn't this afternoon just priceless—in a sort of a sitz bath kind of way?

My God, did that decade fly by or what? Barring the Bruce Willis Roast, of course. The Friars had laid the groundwork for their notable entertainment legacy long before the '80s, but they continued to carve their own unique niche in show biz history. They could afford to embrace the old while fostering the new and not skip a beat on their sharp wits and fresh jokes. (Who am I kidding?)

They sought to honor the legends before they lost them forever. Sinatra, Grant, Martin, Burns, Youngman, even Berle were of an era perhaps not soon forgotten, but certainly one slated for the history books. The Friars Club, after all, is a fraternal organization and with that camaraderie also comes compassion. Well, as compassionate as Jan Murray's interpretation of the Friars' honors can get, "The Friars likes to take stars and make unknowns out of them." Hey, Burt Reynolds made a comeback!

If the Friars thought this decade had its fair share of noteworthy events, they would soon discover the next one would offer the reason pacemakers were invented.

CHAPTER 5

OH, THOSE NAUGHTY '90s:
MAKING WHOOPI—AND MORE!

Exiting the century with the laughs intact!

TESTIMONIAL DINNERS
1990   DIANA ROSS
1992   CLIVE DAVIS
1994   BARBARA WALTERS
1997   JOHN TRAVOLTA AND KELLY PRESTON

CELEBRITY ROASTS
1990   CHEVY CHASE
1991   RICHARD PRYOR
1992   BILLY CRYSTAL
1993   WHOOPI GOLDBERG
1995   STEVEN SEAGAL
1996   KELSEY GRAMMER
1998   DREW CAREY
1999   JERRY STILLER

This is the best, I just smoked a joint with Sir Anthony Hopkins.
—JEFFREY ROSS, at the John Travolta and Kelly Preston Dinner, 1997

*Last time I was here, everyone was about a fuckin' thousand years
old and Berle was talkin' about his cock!*
—BOBCAT GOLDTHWAIT, at the Whoopi Goldberg Roast, 1996

Those press agents from the turn of the twentieth century would
plotz today if they knew that their little chophouse gathering had
grown to become the hottest ticket in town. So many private
clubs died out in the eighties—what self-respecting mover and
shaker had time to join anything but a gym?—but the Friars survived, as did their gym. They proved that, in most instances,
music and laughter win out over kvetching and whining—all
right, forget you read that load of horseshit. They complain if
the dipping mustard for their pigs-in-a-blanket is too spicy—
so maybe it's just sheer dumb luck that made them survive. But

survive they did, right through the end of the millennium—and beyond.

Their Roast format has been copied so often that they considered renaming it a "Xerox." Then they realized that would overlap with the same label they were giving to Berle's jokes. Yes, he's still a presence in this final funny decade—you lucky stiffs, you. But so many of his cronies are not, because you see, not everything funny happens on the way to a Roast. Then again, not to totally change the subject, but Henny Youngman's funeral in 1998 was probably one of the funniest events the Friars ever saw. Even at his memorial, which was held at the Monastery a few months later, Alan King said, "I was such a hit at the funeral that they brought me back."

The bottom line in this final chapter of the final decade of the final century of the millennium (that was so Captain Kirk) is that the Friars had honed their comedy skills so finely that the mere mention of their name invokes laughter. Or, at any rate, a smile. Okay, make that a smirk. They wrote the book on fun: now see how they pull it off in their twilight years—but with a younger cast, sort of.

DIANA ROSS TESTIMONIAL DINNER – 1990

(Call me Miss Friar!)

BRYANT GUMBEL, *Toastmaster*	BOB MACKIE
NICK ASHFORD	ANNA MOFFO
ABRAHAM D. BEAME	JIM MORRIS
GEORGE BENSON	ARNE NAESS
SAMMY CAHN	LEROY NEIMAN
OSSIE DAVIS	JERRY ORBACH
SUZANNE DE PASSE	LEONTYNE PRICE
DAVID DINKINS	DR. LEE SALK
JOHN FRANKENHEIMER	ROBERT SARNOFF
JACK L. GREEN	MARVIN SCOTT
LIONEL HAMPTON	BROOKE SHIELDS
LAINIE KAZAN	VALERIE SIMPSON
SHERRY LANSING	DAVID TEBET
GRAHAM FERGUSON LEASY	AL TELLER
DR. BARBARA LEE	JOE WILLIAMS

I don't know what's funnier—the fact that the Friars had a Dinner for Diana Ross or that Diana Ross is a Friar? Do you think she hung out at the bar, slammin' back tequilas with Sinatra, Jessel, and Sarry Saranoff? The Dinner was class all the way—as a matter of fact, it was so classy people probably wondered what the hell it had to do with the Friars. The *Epistle*, which always throws such events in the most positive of lights, outdid itself with this one, "She is also an active wife, mother, daughter, sister and member of a loving family. Guiding the evening's course was NBC *Today* show's head man Bryant Gumbel, a witty and charming emcee who is one of the bright spots of early morning television." Oh, what a difference a decade makes.

Brooke Shields, before she became funny, introduced the guests on the dais, which was pretty much the most boring part of the evening. Admittedly it's hard to put some pep into intros like, "And now, three of Revlon's unforgettable women—Sandra Zatezallo, Cara Young, and Nastasia," I would explain to you who they were, but everybody forgot. In spite of Jack L. Green, the Friars' Dean at the time, telling the audience to hold back on the applause—after all, you don't want all that clapping for Revlon's unforgettable women holding things up—Brooke paused after each and every intro. The audience, not wanting to make her look the fool, half-heartedly applauded for every person. Sort of sad when Ossie Davis gets the same four people clapping that Eva Donaldson got. Who's Eva Donaldson, you ask? I rest my case. "You changed the list on me," Brooke muttered to Green as she left the podium. What's to change? Did she think she would be introducing the dais of the Victor Herbert Dinner?

Gumbel admitted that he was not a comedian by trade and therefore out of his league at a Friars Club event. He was so right, "I hope you all enjoyed your dinner. We had everything up here on the menu, except the 'Friars delight.' Some of us didn't know what turns a Friar on, so we weren't taking any chances." And to think the Friars survived the nineties with these events.

Motown music maven Suzanne De Passe mentioned the unmentionable, "Working with you is amazing—not always easy—but amazing." Brave girl, that Suzanne. Five Friars ducked after that one in case any fur flew.

David Tebet produced the evening, but Miss Ross was quite active in producing as well—okay, reality check, she ran the whole damn show. Which explains the wonderfully fabulously divine accolades by really rich and powerful people (no, Eva Donaldson was not among them). Their speeches could not have been nicer—which is exactly why you won't be reading them here.

Ashford and Simpson performed "Ain't No Mountain High Enough"—and it was a really, really cool rendition! In spite of the fact that they wrote the song, I think I'd have shied away from performing Miss Ross' signature song in front of her. Then again, I'm a coward. I kept my mouth shut when Barbra Streisand shrieked to me in the Club's elevator once that IT WAS REALLY SMALL! She was talking about the elevator, people!

Impressionist Jim Morris provided the only comic relief for the evening, but maybe that's just because he did impressions of Ronald Reagan and George Bush, who are certainly no strangers to comic relief. "Before I left office I gave George Bush words of advice and that is, 'George, if and when you meet with Mr. Gorbachev, whatever you do, don't stare at that spot on his head. It changes shapes and colors, it's mesmerizing, it's like a mood scar. The KGB put it there. You end up signing silly agreements.'"

Bilal, Hakeem, Khiry Samad, and Tajh are part of a group called The Boys. No, they are not headliners at the Raleigh in the Catskills. They're a singing group whose ages, Gumbel pointed out, collectively add up to fifty-six. When he introduced them to perform, Diana piped up (a little too quickly, it would seem), "Bryant, I don't think they're here. If they're not, I would like to ask if my girls . . . Rhonda, Tracee, would you come up to the stage, and my father, my sister, would you come to the microphone. The Boys have been doing a video all day, and I think they're somewhere in town but they're very close to being able to perform for us. In the meantime, we've got to spend a little time. And I'd like my children and my family to say something to you. They want to, so I'd like them to." Whatever Diana wants, Diana gets. That was a pretty quick solution Miss Ross

Richard Pryor and Robin Williams look ahead toward less fires and more Friars.

Rob Reiner defines all the words in his list of dirty words for Billy Crystal.

Chevy Chase tells Robert DeNiro that he just saw Berle's penis in the bathroom and it's THIS big!

Whoopi Goldberg and Ted Danson— you really didn't expect us to print the *other* picture did you?

David Hyde Pierce and Kelsey Grammer—who loves you, baby?

Jerry Stiller is serenaded by Jason Alexander.

The eighth wonder of the world—Aretha Franklin in a tutu.

Sylvester Stallone waxes eloquent with John Travolta and Kelly Preston.

Candice Bergen, Barbara Walters, and Freddie Roman can't wait to hear what Hugh Downs will have to say at Barbara's Dinner.

Drew Carey can't understand why Jack Carter is going on about a license plate and Bobcat Goldthwait.

came up with to fill that void there. In case you're hanging onto every riveting moment of this evening, The Boys never did show. Guess it got past their bedtime.

For all of her hard work, Miss Ross received the Friars Oscar (a beefy bronzed monk as opposed to the Roast's crystal, flamed one); a certificate of her new honorary membership; a diamond watch; and a contribution of $25,000 donated by the Friars to various children's charities of her choosing. So maybe this was a worthwhile night after all. "I know you spent your money and your time here with me and I have never felt worthy for you to be here with me. I started off with the Supremes and with Motown, and I really feel I have not really done enough in my life to deserve an honor. But I do want to thank you for being here." Miss Ross then broke into "Reach Out and Touch," and the entire ballroom was waving and swaying—how Arsenio Hall-ish of them. She really did inspire everybody to reach out and touch—but these were the days you could do that and not be hauled into court.

CLIVE DAVIS TESTIMONIAL DINNER – 1992

(Oh, my achin' back!)

ROGER MOORE, *Toastmaster*
DAVID BROWN
HELEN GURLEY BROWN
SAMMY CAHN
TITA CAHN
CY COLEMAN
BETTY COMDEN
FRANCIS FORD COPPOLA
KENNY "BABYFACE" EDMONDS
ARETHA FRANKLIN
KENNY G
MARK GOODSON
ADOLPH GREEN
JOHN HEARD
JENNIFER HOLLIDAY
WHITNEY HOUSTON

CHARLES KOPPELMAN
MATHILDE KRIM
ROBIN LEACH
SUSAN LUCCI
BARRY MANILOW
JERRY ORBACH
FRANCIS W. PRESTON
MARTY RICHARDS
CHUCK SCARBOROUGH
BROOKE SHIELDS
MARTHA STEWART
JULE STYNE
DAVID TEBET
CHERYL TIEGS
DIONNE WARWICK

Any event where the highlight is Aretha Franklin performing in a tutu has got to have the Friars' name on it. Oh, some souls might disagree and say that would be Weight Watchers' annual production of *Swan Lake*, but in this particular instance, it was the Friars Dinner in honor of Clive Davis. As president of Arista Records, he commandeered the careers of Aretha, Whitney Houston, Kenny G, Barry Manilow, Dionne Warwick, and a gazillion other talented and colorful musicians. He is the original music man, and this night was dedicated to just that—music. Nothing more. Nothing less. Just music. Music, music, music. Oh boy—that music was coming out of their asses, there was so much music.

The Master of Ceremonies was Moore, Roger Moore. He is one of the more sophisticated emcees to have graced a Friars dais, "He is going to witness what was revealed at the Earth Summit. That the Friars Club is the largest single source in North America for greenhouse gases," said television news anchor Chuck Scarborough in his as-sophisticated-as-they-get introduction of Moore. The Toastmaster from across the pond was quite witty, actually, "CD does not stand for compact disc. CD stands for Clive Davis." Wonder how many times Clive has heard that one? Wonder how many times Clive has paid people to say it?

The fact that you have just basically read the laughs for the evening should clue you in that comedy took a backseat to the music—a very rare occurrence, but it does happen. Kenny G was the hot new act in town, and he played "Forever In Love"—you remember that song, it's that whiny off-key-sounding saxophoney one. This was a monumental musical moment for the Friars (the kings of overstatement). "It's the first time we ever performed that song," announced Kenny, "it's from an album we just got through recording. And it will be released whenever Clive says it will be released. I'd like to dedicate it to you, Clive." The song actually became a huge hit, even bigger than "Here's To The Friars."

Barry Manilow was there, as was his fan club. Yes, Barry has a fan club, and it seems the bridge-and-tunnel contingency spared no expense and purchased a table for the event. "He's not a homosexual, Mr. Dougherty, he's gifted," was what I was told by the president of the group when she made her table arrangements.

Like I asked? Now that someone obviously in the know has put that nasty rumor to bed, he's free to wed Lisa Marie Presley. Clive certainly commands a lot of lovin'—or maybe it's just fear. In any case, his accompanying journal was literally the fattest in the history of the Friars, chock full of accolades and testimonials. But Dionne Warwick wins the "I broke my back to be here" award, hands down (just not on her back, please). She hurt her back, severely, at the LA airport while waiting to board the plane to New York. (Don't they have luggage carriers out there?) Did she miss her flight? Yes. Did she miss the show? No way, San José! Just a few hours and a $20,000 private plane ride later, she was warbling "I Know I'll Never Love This Way Again" with Barry at the piano. She didn't look all that well, but her voice sure wasn't in pain. Cousin Whitney Houston (what the hell is their family relationship anyway?) joined her for "That's What Friends Are For." Doesn't Whitney usually claim to have a sore throat and bail out of these things? Clive must really rate. Or maybe she figured it wouldn't wash, seeing as Dionne was singing with a broken back and all.

Aretha Franklin, however, attired in bustier and tutu, gets the "My, isn't she comfortable with her body" award. Surrounded by svelte ballet dancers, she sang "Natural Woman" while dipping in between their pirouettes and pliés. It was quite a sight. Now make it go away!

BARBARA WALTERS TESTIMONIAL DINNER – 1994

(These people are journalists?)

CANDICE BERGEN, *Toastmaster*	ROBERT IGER
ROONE ARLEDGE	STACY KEACH
SID CAESAR	DR. HENRY KISSINGER
OSCAR DE LA RENTA	LOUIS MALLE
SAM DONALDSON	DARREN MCGAVIN
HUGH DOWNS	MAUREEN MCGOVERN
FRANK GIFFORD	JIM MORRIS
KATHIE LEE GIFFORD	MIKE NICHOLS

JOY PHILBIN
REGIS PHILBIN
FREDDIE ROMAN
DIANE SAWYER
BEVERLY SILLS
LIZ SMITH
SHARON STONE

JULE STYNE
DAVID TEBET
MARLO THOMAS
JOE WILLIAMS
NANCY WILSON
MORTIMER ZUCKERMAN

Barbara Walters' father, Lou, was a nightclub owner—the Latin Quarter—and an active member of the Friars for many years. Owing to this connection, the Friars Club holds a very special place for Ms. Walters—it may not be in her heart exactly, but tucked somewhere inside she gets all fuzzy when she thinks about the Friars. Well, as fuzzy as someone who interviews dictators and makes people cry can get.

In any case, she was thrilled beyond compare that the Friars chose her as their Woman of the Year in 1994. In that year, the only obvious candidate to serve as emcee was Candice Bergen, who opened with praise: "What can I say about a television journalist who has used her brains and her talent to rise to the very top of her profession. A woman who has received every award her industry has to bestow. A star of a successful television newsmagazine who can talk with kings and presidents and yet remain down to earth and human. Simply, that I love playing her and I hope *Murphy Brown* goes on forever. But enough about me—we're here tonight to talk about another journalist at the top of her profession. Someone else I hope goes on forever, Barbara Walters."

The night did belong to Barbara, beginning with her being escorted through the kitchen of the Waldorf-Astoria in her full length, ruby-red gown—she was a vision amidst the dirty dishes and stark-white uniforms of the food service staff. There were speeches and testimonials and high praise up the wazoo from journalists—who sometimes can be a bunch of real unfunny people. "Freddie Roman is not really here because he knows Barbara Walters, he's keeping an eye on nobody carting off the cutlery—I could have left that one out, couldn't I?" Oh boy, could you have, Hugh Downs!

Jim Morris' impressions are uncannily authentic, especially

his Henry Kissinger, who happened to be just two seats away from the podium. Holding up Kissinger's book, he said, "I had Dr. Kissinger sign it before I did my act, just in case I bombed. But then again, you bombed in Cambodia, didn't you?" There may have been a moment or two before the audience realized the impact of the remark. "At that instant," recalls Morris, "I was thinking what a rare opportunity this is to score a jab. I was thinking about all of the people who had a problem with his policy during the Vietnam War and when I delivered the line, I knew that it was an explosive line and I just knew that the chips would fall where they may." While the crowd didn't turn on him, what was Kissinger's reaction? Morris had to seek the answer elsewhere. "I looked over at Kissinger and I saw him turn to say something to Beverly Sills, and I knew it had to be something about what I said. So after the Dinner I asked Beverly Sills what he said and she said, 'Well, he leaned over to me and said, 'I should have seen it coming.'" As for the book, which was signed earlier . . . Dr. Kissinger, who Morris warned would be the butt of a joke or two, seemed to be quite the clairvoyant: "To Jim Morris, before the execution, every good wish. Henry A. Kissinger."

Seeing as Morris had already thrown caution to the wind at this staid affair, he took yet another fork in the road of Friars comedy by doing an impression of Richard Nixon, who had been buried a week earlier, "Henry, I do want to say it was very eloquent last week, I never knew you cared so much." According to Morris, "This, I think, was more ballsy than the bombing remark. I mean, he wept at the guy's funeral."

This was the first event after the Whoopi Goldberg Roast— oh, you haven't read about that yet, have you? Well, Bergen said, "Ted Danson was supposed to be here tonight, but he's off doing a command performance at the Nelson Mandela inaugural." Actually Barbara also mentioned that Roast, "Whoopi Goldberg in the fall and me in the spring—it's what they call in show business 'variety.'" Stop moaning, you already know what she's talking about, so just keep reading; Ted's time will come.

Kissinger, who sounded just like Jim Morris, pretty much solidified what everyone already knows about Walters and her journalist mind-set, "I acted, at times, as her talent scout. I once arranged for her to interview a president of a country. It was all set, when one day the chief of staff of that president called me up and said he had had a phone call from Barbara, who told him that she had an opportunity to interview the lady who had been, shall we say, involved with Mike Tyson, and that she would have to drop the president and she was sure that the president would understand. The chief of staff inquired of me what it was that he had missed that would help his president to understand." It's all about gossip and ratings, prez, understood?

Bergen had never hosted any event like this before, and she did quite well. If only she could have remembered to go back to the podium after each speaker, she would have been perfect. At one point, after Hugh Downs finished speaking and the laughs from his boffo comedic delivery died down, the audience just stared at the empty podium. It finally dawned on Candice that she had a job to do. She jumped up and said, "I'm sorry! It's my first time doing this and I keep forgetting!" I just thought that was cute; that's why it's here.

You want cute and funny for real? Diane Sawyer, in retaliation to the tabloids, which had been having a field day with a feud between her and Barbara over career and financial status, sang a parody to the tune of "You Made Me Love You":

You made me ruthless. I didn't want to do it, ambition drove me to it.
You made me greedy. I couldn't bear that you net three million more than I get?
Your tiny skirts with those legs on display. Started me thinking, Lorena Bobbitt's way—I'm so embarrassed
Desperate to beat you, I thought I'd do what you do. I slept with Roone and Hugh, too
Scheming for interviews, where they schmooze and then end in boo hoo hoos
Gimme, gimme more airtime, it's the air I breathe
I hate to tell my story—you know, All About Eve
I even married a Jew!

Funny, no?

After getting her gold watch, Barbara said, "I heard a story this winter that a colleague of mine told and when I heard it I knew exactly why it was that I was being asked to be here tonight and to have this wonderful tribute. So I will tell it to you although, as you know, I don't sing or dance—but I'm going to try with one story. It's about this perfectly wonderful man who died and went to heaven. And St. Peter was there and he said, 'You are such a good man and we don't get men like you here all the time and we would like to do something very special for you. Is there anything that you want, now that you are up here?' The man said, 'As a matter of fact, there is one thing. I would like to see the Blessed Mother.' St. Peter said, 'Well, that just can't be done. That's just asking too much.' The man said, 'All my life I've wanted to see the Blessed Mother. I have only one question that I would like to ask her. If I could just ask her this one question?' Suddenly, there was the Blessed Mother, and she said, 'My son, I very rarely see anyone but I understand that there is one question that you want to ask me. What is it?' And he said, 'Well, you know, Blessed Mother, all my life I have seen you, from the time I was a small child, in frescos and paintings and sculptures and stained glass windows, and I've always wondered, why do you look so sad?' And she said, 'We wanted a girl.'" C'mon, you gotta hand it to her—that was cute.

JOHN TRAVOLTA AND KELLY PRESTON TESTIMONIAL DINNER – 1997

(Kelly who?)

LARRY KING, *Toastmaster*	FYVUSH FINKEL
DANNY AIELLO	LOUIS GOSSETT, JR.
LAUREN BACALL	JACK L. GREEN
THE BEE GEES	MARIEL HEMINGWAY
JOY BEHAR	ANTHONY HOPKINS
HARRY BELAFONTE	LAUREN HUTTON
SID CAESAR	HARVEY KEITEL
NORA EPHRON	SALLY KELLERMAN
JENNIFER FLAVIN	ALAN KING

ARNOLD KOPELSON
ANNE KOPELSON
SHIRLEY MACLAINE
MACE NEUFELD
ERIC ROBERTS
FREDDIE ROMAN
RAY ROMANO
JEFFREY ROSS

KYRA SEDGWICK
SYLVESTER STALLONE
ABE VIGODA
HARVEY WEINSTEIN
DEBRA WINGER
SEAN YOUNG
THE VILLAGE PEOPLE

Larry King was the Master of Ceremonies. She had Harry Winston's diamonds on, and he had a new Friars' watch—which he later sent back to exchange for another "sportier" one, but that's neither here nor there. John Travolta and his wife, Kelly Preston, it was noted in the press, were the first to be so honored by the Friars as a couple. That's true—if you don't count Douglas Fairbanks and Mary Pickford, who had a tiny "do" in 1920. And, as we have learned, who has complete records from that era? You also shouldn't count Benny Fields and Blossom Seeley, a very funny vaudeville couple who had some celebratory thing for a show they did, but it's a time that's long behind us. Steve and Eydie really don't count because theirs was in the sixties and nobody remembers what the hell went on in that decade what with the mushrooms and dope and all. But John and Kelly were the first for the nineties, and they were the sweethearts of the night.

"We've been honoring people for over fifty years, dinners of the greatest stars," said Alan King to the happy couple. "We've never had younger or more attractive guests of honor than you two. Absolutely. The Friars is not really known as a daycare center; in fact, the hit song from your film *Saturday Night Fever* has become our anthem 'Stayin' Alive.'" But he did spice things up a bit, "I've been here forever, and I have never seen such a high-powered dais in my life. Obviously, you don't have too many black friends. We should have rented a few, something."

Harry Belafonte, however, didn't want the audience to go home with the wrong impression about either the guests of honor or Alan, "I know you're not going to defend yourself tonight," he said to Travolta, "with a remark that was made earlier that cast aspersions on your being. There was a remark made by Alan King, one of the great racists." Belafonte then went on to relate a story about King helping him to coordinate an event for Martin Luther King in Harlem—it was a nice, funny story and, no, King is not a racist. Neither is Travolta, as Belafonte talked about his compassion for people of color. Belafonte also told his version of the Friars' black experience. "Let me tell you something about the Friars. Their first black members were Al Jolson and Eddie Cantor. And they thought they had ended the racial question. When they discovered they hadn't, they went out and got one of the finest and greatest artists of the world by the name of Sammy Davis, Jr. But they met with him first, and now you know why Sammy Davis, Jr., turned Jewish—just so he could become a member of the Friars. Then they thought they would broaden the format and let Italians have some comfort zone within the Friars, and they called Belafonte. They heard my song "Day-O" and assumed I was Italian!"

This night had the Bee Gees, and they sang "How Deep Is Your Love" a cappella because they had just intended to speak and not sing. And the point of that would have been? The group The Village People were also there, but they didn't speak—they just sang "YMCA" and "Macho Man." But as Jeffrey Ross commented during his comedy routine, "I thought I was lucky to be on the show. The Village People? I mean, twenty years ago they sang "YMCA," and last night they stayed at the YMCA." He also voiced the question on many people's minds on this night that they were honoring a former sweathog, "*Welcome Back Kotter* was my all-time favorite show when I was a kid, and with us tonight are two former castmates on the dais—and Gabe Kaplan in the kitchen." Actually Gabe was selling real estate in Utah, or something.

Ray Romano put things in perspective, as is his wont, "Am I the only one that thinks Kelly Preston is going to be on the phone tomorrow with her friends going, 'Oh, it was John this, John that, John this.'" Then again, John's career had had its ups and downs, to, as did Romano's, "The first week that I started working at the Cinemart Movie Theater in Forest Hills was the week *Saturday Night Fever* came out, so it's a great privilege for me to be here. The sad part of that story is I was an usher when *Pulp Fiction* came out, too. It wasn't a smart career choice, but it was steady—I didn't have to make a comeback."

Speaking of comebacks, John and Kelly had a little finish to the evening planned, which would have been a disaster if Larry King had had his way. At the start of the show, when King approached the podium, the teleprompter paddles that were framing his face immediately bothered him, "Why are these things here? Does anyone have prepared remarks? Can we take these away?" The problem was, someone did have prepared remarks, but it's not like John and Kelly could jump up and *say* that. Jack Green, who produced the gala event, saved the day and said to leave them, but King was still a little confused, especially when some know-it-all said they were for security purposes. "Security for who?" He then launched into a not-terribly-amusing joke about Al Gore. But at least the Travoltas' finale was secure.

The two huddled at the podium, dripping with sweetness:

JOHN: Congratulations, honey.
KELLY: Congratulations, John.
JOHN: Honey? Did you hear all the nice things they said about us tonight?
KELLY: Yes, I did.
JOHN: Don't you just love us!
KELLY: They made us sound like so much fun! Maybe we should spend more time with ourselves?
JOHN: You know, I actually think the Friars helped save our marriage!

The two then launched into song—yes, folks, another parody, courtesy of the Friars Club: "It's very clear, our love is here to stay / not for a year, but for ever and a day / tonight we were laughers and criers / we ended up Friars / They really saved the day / 'cause our love is here to stay. / I love you, Friar Kelly. I love you, Friar John." I love the fact that the Testimonials for the '90s are finished and we can get on with the Roasts!

CHEVY CHASE ROAST – 1990

(A whole new world)

DAN AYKROYD, Roastmaster	DARREN MCGAVIN
KEVIN BACON	ROBERT MERRILL
RICHARD BELZER	LORNE MICHAELS
MARK CANTON	DENNIS MILLER
DICK CAPRI	ROBERT MORTON
DANA CARVEY	KEVIN NEALON
MARTHA J. CLINE	LEROY NEIMAN
PROFESSOR IRWIN COREY	PAUL NEWMAN
NORM CROSBY	PHYLLIS NEWMAN
BEVERLY D'ANGELO	JERRY ORBACH
CLIVE DAVIS	TONY ORLANDO
ROBERT DE NIRO	TONY RANDALL
RON DELSENER	PAUL REISER
DAVID DINKINS	PAUL RIGBY
DONNA DIXON	AL ROKER
CLINT EASTWOOD	FREDDIE ROMAN
DR. FRANK FIELD	DIANA ROSS
SALLY FIELD	STEVE ROSS
AL FRANKEN	RITA RUDNER
JOE FRANKLIN	CHUCK SCARBOROUGH
VINCENT GARDENIA	JOHN SCHER
GILBERT GOTTFRIED	MARVIN SCOTT
ELLIOT GOULD	NEIL SIMON
JACK L. GREEN	MICHAEL SPINKS
PHIL HARTMAN	JONATHAN TISCH
ROBERT KLEIN	JACK WESTON
ROBIN LEACH	ALAN ZWEIBEL
BUTCH LEWIS	

Some people review the *Encyclopedia Britannica* to find out about world history, others just have to attend Friars Club Roasts. Throughout the years, the comedians have always based much of their humor on current world situations, and Chevy Chase's Roast in 1990 was no different. The Gulf War was under way and Americans were pretty touchy about things, which explains Roastmaster Dan Aykroyd's opening remarks,

"Last year, there was a piece by some overpaid puff columnist in one of your local bankrupt New York tabloids about how he attended the Friars Roast and how he was forced to endure a couple of hours of the most shocking, foul, lightning-blue chatter he's ever heard in his life. This journalist was offended, morally upset, and seemed to be shaking his head over the whole thing. Well, pal, if you're here now, put on your Walkman because today the filth is gonna fly. And for some very good reasons, and those reasons are 200,000 navy, army, and airmen in camouflage sitting in some Saudi desert pisshole protecting the very freedom we are gonna exercise today." The applause in the room took forever to die down, and when it did, Aykroyd went to work, "That freedom is the inalienable right to take out our dicks and piss on the most overrated, overpaid actor in the history of show business. Chevy Chase, a comedian with all the charisma of the Hillside Strangler."

Aykroyd had a field day with the Roast venue, which gave him the opportunity to talk about his former *Saturday Night Live* costar in ways his mother certainly never taught him. "Chevy Chase is Hollywood's foremost brownnoser and locker suck. For the lead role in *Caddyshack*, he blew Jon Peters' pet pit bull and even though Peters had nothing to do with *Fletch*, Chevy went back and blew the same dog because he enjoyed it so much the first time."

This Roast was the first one that allowed women to be seated on the dais and, even more important, the first time a woman comedian actually performed as a Roaster, "My husband got the call, and I was out of town," remembers Rita Rudner, "They said Paul Newman is going to be there and Neil Simon and he said, 'OK.' He didn't know what a Friars Club is, he's from England; he just thought it would be fun to meet those people." What Rita didn't realize was that she had to perform in a venue that was unlike any she had done before, "I knew it was dirty, but you don't really know the level until you're in the room. I'm no Mother Teresa here, but all of a sudden as it progressed it got worse and worse and it was very funny, but it got very degrading, especially towards women. I was stuck there with my friend Dennis Miller and we were each going, 'What are we going to do? I don't know what am I gonna do. I have my little ballet jokes here.'" Someone doesn't sound like she was having much fun, that's for sure. "You have to go to the level of the room; you can't go to a different level. Once it's on a raunchy level, you can't bring it back. That's a rule in comedy."

Another rule is to take Excedrin before you embark on a journey into history, "My head was pounding, and I was getting a terrible headache, and it was my turn," Rita remembers. To mark the auspicious occasion, Chevy allowed nature to call and left the dais, "I gotta take a big crap." There Rita stood, ready to make history, and the guest of honor was nowhere to be found. "I'm not going to take it personally that Chevy just left," she said, and just started without him. "People have been telling me, 'Rita, this is very, very dirty, filthy, really disgusting,' so I've prepared something this afternoon I hope is appropriate. Hello, cocksuckers! How the fuck are you?" If you're not familiar with Rita Rudner and her persona, then you may not be aware why the audience was in hysterics. She is a very calm, soft-spoken person—picture Marilyn Monroe's voice with Bambi's wide eyes. According to Freddie Roman, "The audience was taken aback a little bit, they were. They didn't know what to expect; they were not sure. Her persona is a soft-spoken comedienne." They got over it, though, as did Rita, "So women are here now, huh? I have to say, we're in the locker room and we're on the moon and someday, God willing, we'll mean something at the box office. Because right now we don't. The most shameless attempt to get people in to see women at the box office I think was *Steel Magnolias*. I know, Sally, you're here, but I've never seen so many women crammed together on a poster. It looks like an ad for a lesbian picnic. It's a hard thing for me to do here . . . fucking . . . I figure I'll throw that in every once in a while."

Eventually all nightmares end, as did Rita's, "I remember that my approach worked and I had a tremendous migraine on the way back on the plane and I thought, this isn't for me. I've been invited to a few Roasts since, but it's not my style and it's not who I am and it's so hard on me that I was just glad to escape."

Norm Crosby today admits he had a problem with the newest visitors to the Roast, the ladies, "There is something about looking out into the audience and seeing a whole bunch of women looking up at you saying 'fuck.' I remember Sally Field was on the dais. I was so embarrassed for her, 'cause I knew it wasn't her thing." But when his turn at bat came that afternoon, Norm adjusted, "Chevy and I were there in Monterey last year. Clint Eastwood had a wonderful benefit to restore a church that was damaged in the San Francisco earthquake area. It was a gay church, Our Lady of Perpetual Ointment. For those of you who don't know, a gay church is very much like a regular church, except that every other person is kneeling."

Dennis Miller kept the flavor of the afternoon moving along and even picked up some new words, thanks to Rita, "Nice to be so far down in the program that the word cocksucker is passé. Milton Berle's cock is so big it makes me think he stole that, too." Almost forty years later, and still with the Berle cock jokes—will it never end?

Here are some of Freddie Roman's musings, "Chevy, you are to acting what panty hose is to finger-fucking. . . . I want to say one word in honor of David Dinkins. This is a man who brought Nelson Mandela to New York this summer, and Mandela became the first black man in the history of New York City to stop traffic without a squeegee in his hand. . . .Who could ever forget Sally Field when Burt Reynolds was going down on her and she said, 'He likes me, he really likes me!" Just for the record, this was Sally's first and last Friars event—can't imagine why.

Revenge is always sweet for these guests of honor, "I'm not a stand-up comic, and I think you know that by now. But I am a stand-up fucking guy. I always thought the Friars Club was a bunch of sweaty, washed-up, borscht-belt comics, smoking cigars and recycling cock jokes sitting on donut cushions, hoping their rugs won't slip into the urinals every time they squeeze a drip. But I was wrong. There are very few toupees today. Rita Rudner, I was a little bit late. I just happened to walk by you as I came in and you were just starting your monologue and it made me think about the Knicks. I don't know why it made me think about the Knicks. And I thought to myself, what's the difference between Rita Rudner and the Knicks and it came to me that, really, the Knicks shower after every fourth period." No wonder she had a headache.

But Chevy had more to say, "This is supposed to be fucking dirty; I heard nothing dirty. I was gonna hear jokes like, you know, a little kid in the fourth grade says, 'Hey dad, I got the biggest cock in the fourth grade, is that, 'cuz I'm black?' 'No, son, it's because you're nineteen.' That's what I thought I was gonna hear. I didn't hear any of that shit. I thought I was gonna hear, 'What's the difference between Roseanne Barr and a bowling ball? I don't know what the difference is; well, if I really had to, I'd eat the bowling ball.' I just don't get it. Let me just say to all of you fellas, you're all really not as good as I am and it's a shame, but that's why I'm here and you're all just sorta looking at me." I have a feeling lots of people just sort of look at Chevy.

RICHARD PRYOR ROAST – 1991

(The original fried Friar)

ROBIN WILLIAMS, *Roastmaster*
DANNY AIELLO
PAUL ANKA
KEVIN BACON
HARRY BELAFONTE
TOVA BORGNINE
ALLAN BREGMAN
DAVID BRENNER
MATTHEW BRODERICK
KEITH CARRADINE
CHEVY CHASE
PAT COOPER
NORM CROSBY
CLIVE DAVIS
BRIAN DENNEHY
DAVID DINKINS
KEIR DULLEA
AHMET ERTEGUN

MICHAEL FUCHS
VINCENT GARDENIA
LOUIS GOSSETT, JR.
DICK GREGORY
CHARLES GRODIN
ARTHUR HILLER
REGINALD HUDLIN
WARRINGTON HUDLIN
QUINCY JONES
L.L. COOL J
ALAN LADD, JR.
SUGAR RAY LEONARD
BUTCH LEWIS
ROBERT LOGGIA
LEE MAJORS
LORNE MICHAELS
MR. T
WARREN MOON

KEVIN NEALON
PATRICK O'NEAL
JERRY ORBACH
ANTHONY QUINN
JOAN RIVERS
FREDDIE ROMAN
HERBERT ROSS
RICHARD ROUNDTREE
MERCEDES RUEHL
GEORGE SCHLATTER
MARTIN SCORSESE

BOBBY SHORT
SINBAD
ROD STEIGER
ROBERT VAUGHN
BEN VEREEN
ABE VIGODA
MARSHA WARFIELD
JACK WESTON
GENE WILDER
STEVIE WONDER

Do you think the dais got a little out of control? Remember how Maurice Chevalier's Roast had, like, five names on his dais list?

Richard Pryor is an amazing individual—both for his talent and for his personal struggles. He was also the perfect candidate to honor with a Roast. It was an event that almost didn't happen. When the Friars approached Pryor to be the guest of honor, it was not yet revealed that he was suffering from multiple sclerosis; however, he did agree to take on the Friars' comics. Then, a few months before the event, he had to undergo heart surgery. The Club was unsure if their annual tradition would have to be cancelled unexpectedly—but like everything else in Pryor's life, he won the battle, for the moment at least. He was ill and weak, yet he allowed himself to be verbally castrated at the hands of the Friars. More people know about Pryor's personal life than they do about his career, thanks to his front-page trials and tribulations. It should come as no surprise to anyone that to the Friars Club's bottomless well of comedians, the word "sympathy" is as foreign as the word "sincere." Which would explain Roastmaster Robin Williams cutting to the chase, "It seems strange to have a Roast for a man who did it to himself. We are here today to honor a man who believes not only that black is beautiful, but that black is flammable. This is truly the hottest man in show business." There will be no sweet 'n sappy songs sung at this event, that's for sure.

When Robin ran out of self-immolation jokes, he pressed on

to other favorite Friar topics, "I remember one night in our wilder days, we woke up nude together, and you turned to me and you said, 'Robin, did I perform a homosexual act?' I said, 'No, baby, Peter Allen is a homosexual act—you just blew me.'"

"Probably the biggest laugh I ever got was at the Richard Pryor Roast," remembers Norm Crosby. It was most likely for this one: "Ladies and gentlemen, it's a very personal treat for me to be here this afternoon, because few people know that Richard and I were little kids together. We played together on my grandfather's farm. We walked in the woods together till we were about eleven years old, and then my grandfather sold him. . . . I'm only kidding; we kept him till he was fourteen." The laughs did take a while to quiet down before he could throw out this little laugher: "Does anybody here know why a Jewish bride walks down the aisle with a great big smile on her face? It's because she knows she has given her last blow job."

New York's mayor at the time was David Dinkins, who must have worked the Catskills when he wasn't getting arrested at rallies, "Despite what some New Yorkers think, I'm not a comedian, I'm just a real funny mayor. I know I'm funnier than Quincy Jones." Um, okay.

Chevy Chase was fresh off his own Roast from the prior (I've been dying to use that word in this section) year. "It's tough to Roast a really good friend. Even harder to Roast a man who's been through three cardiac episodes, multiple sclerosis, eight marriages, countless children of many different nationalities, a sextuple heart bypass, a testicleoptopy, and a microwaving. Hell, Richard's been clinically dead for eight years!"

Joan Rivers was actually very nice to Richard, "I think you're the outstanding living performer today." What the hell is that about? But she wasn't nice about everybody, "There's nothing to say except that LaToya Jackson's father hit me also. That mean bitch—she took her snake and made shoes." Whew, for a minute there I thought Joan had gone nice on us.

Pat Cooper, the angry Italian, closed many of these Roasts and each time he'd put up a fuss about having to do it—but each time he did it brilliantly. His tirades were perfect endings to some great afternoons, "The suit that Robin is wearing is my mother's drapes." Oh, yes, that suit! It was *the* ugliest article of clothing ever worn to a Friars' event, and that includes any time Phyllis Diller was ever on a dais. He's right, too; it was this brown, ugly, heavy-looking wool suit. Yuk! Sorry. Back to Pat: "All these black people that spoke, I don't understand a fuckin' word. . . . Fuck with me! I'll fuck with ya! I love these fuckin' geniuses!. . . . This fuckin' bum made ninety million dollars, I can't get thirty fuckin' dollars a club date! He opened up the door for comedy? When this is over I don't wanna talk to you no fuckin' more!. . . . Richard, you did shit for me!"

It was difficult to watch Pryor during his speech. It was slurred and slow and he didn't look well—but it was also quite touching. Let's face it. Another time, and he would have whipped these guys into shape with raunchy comebacks, but these days he tended to show his warm and tender side, "I was standing in the hall backstage and who should walk in? Anthony Quinn. I don't know if you guys see Quinn a lot; maybe it's not a big thing with you. Anthony Quinn—come on! He just hugged me, he actually hugged me; it was nice, and I was happy. I'm happy now. I'm appreciative!" Sure, from Quinn he got a hug, from Williams he got a Roast—which one would you thank at the end of the day?

BILLY CRYSTAL ROAST – 1992

(One shattered ego)

ROB REINER, *Roastmaster*	HARRY CONNICK, JR.
DANNY AIELLO	PAT COOPER
MUHAMMAD ALI	BOB COSTAS
KEVIN BACON	KEVIN COSTNER
KATHY BATES	NORM CROSBY
ED BEGLEY, JR.	JANICE CRYSTAL
JIM BELUSHI	DAVID DINKINS
MATTHEW BRODERICK	KEVIN DOBSON
JOHN BYNER	DR. J.
GIL CATES	ROGER EBERT
JAMES COBURN	MICHAEL FUCHS

PETER GRUBER	LORNE MICHAELS
CHRISTOPHER GUEST	JERRY ORBACH
ROBERT GUILLAUME	REGIS PHILBIN
BUDDY HACKETT	KEVIN POLLAK
HARRY HAMLIN	ANTHONY QUINN
NORMAN JEWISON	TONY RANDALL
HARVEY KEITEL	FREDDIE ROMAN
GEORGE KENNEDY	GARRY SHANDLING
ALAN KING	RON SILVER
ALAN LADD, JR.	SINBAD
BARRY LEVINSON	GENE SISKEL
BUTCH LEWIS	PAUL SORVINO
JON LOVITZ	DANIEL STERN
KARL MALDEN	DONALD TRUMP
JOE MANTEGNA	ROBIN WILLIAMS

When Rob Reiner helmed the proceedings at the Billy Crystal Roast, he tried to do so with dignity, "Maybe I can bring something new to this kind of affair. Maybe we could bring some class and possibly elevate the tone of this kind of function if for no other reason than Billy's wife and mother are present here this afternoon. I'm taking it upon myself to ask the Roasters to show some respect." He got his answer when Buddy Hackett yelled out, "Fuck you!" So much for that idea. If you can't beat 'em, join 'em, "I thought we should get just a few other things out of the way before we start—okay—shit, piss, cum, ass, asshole, asswipe, buttfuck, gerbil, cock, cocksucker, prick, dick, putz, schmuck, jerkoff, whackoff, beatoff, fuck cunt, pussy, twat, snatch, cunt-licker, cunt-wrapper, boy, is she a cunt! fuck, fuck you, fuck me, fuck your mother, fuck your sister, fuck a nun, fuck a cow, fuck a sheep, blow the Pope!—I think that about covers it. I'm sorry, Mayor Dinkins, if I've forced you to rethink your speech." Remember when Phil Silvers got bent out of shape over saying "jock?"

Lest you think Reiner was finished for the afternoon, guess again. He still had Crystal to break, "What can I say about Billy? He's my best friend. I think sick twisted Jew just about sums it up. I happen to know he has enormous balls. When I say enormous balls, I'm not talking about strength of character. I'm talking about size and contact of the scrotal sack. This man has huge balls! They're so big, as a matter of fact, that when Janice goes down on him, she has a place to rest her head!"

Garry Shandling was introduced by Reiner as "The only man who fakes an orgasm during masturbation," which paved the way for Garry's quick ad-lib, "Actually, what I like to do after I masturbate is stand up in front of a crowd and tell some jokes." And jokes he told, "Billy will not tell you his penis size until we switch to the metric system. . . . Billy and I are both animal lovers. Billy called me up once and says, 'My dog's penis tastes bitter, do you know what causes that?'" Just to let you know, Billy's movie, *Mr. Saturday Night* opened up the night before this event, so he was a tad preoccupied with things—if this Roast didn't cheer him up, then only drugs would.

According to Reiner, Buddy Hackett used to baby-sit for him when he was a little boy, "I was not your babysitter. Actually, your father and I shared a dressing room and your mother and him were fucking one afternoon in the dressing room and if I hadn't stepped on your father's ass, you wouldn't be here today."

David Letterman was not at the Roast, but he did send a list of "The Top 10 Little-Known Facts About Billy Crystal":

10. Major star in Belgium, where he is considered normal-looking.
9. Now that Ed McMahon has cut back officially, luckiest man in show business.
8. As a child with learning disability, mistakenly joined Jews for Cheeses.
7. First show business job—Siegfried and Roy's oil boy.
6. Installed vibrating attachment to Emmy Award.
5. By strange law, when Alan King dies he's in charge of Sid Caesar.
4. Kept begging producers to change movie to "When Harry Met Barry."
3. Upon hearing of Sammy Jr.'s death, retired his Sammy impersonation for three hours.
2. Hopes one day to be a big enough star to date stepdaughter.
1. Purchased first home from "Comic Relief."

"The Pope can condemn us, but what is he—dressed like Liberace's stunt double?" asked Robin Williams. He asked a lot of other things, too, but this is a little book about Roasts and Dinners, not *War and Peace*.

You ready for more Pat Cooper? "I didn't come here to get laughs, I came here, to be honest, I want a fuckin' job, Billy. . . . Whatever happened to Joe Piscopo?. . . . I'm not bitter, angry, I'm a fuckin' genius, but if I were Jewish, I'd have my own fuckin' show. He fuckin' breaks my balls, I don't understand it, do I have to be a Jew? I'll cut it off, I swear to God I'll cut it off. I'm gonna get a day job and just go about my fuckin' business . . . it's over Billy." Yes it is, Pat.

"I went to the premiere of *Mr. Saturday Night* with great anticipation and some trepidation," announced Alan King from the pulpit (when others stand there it's a podium, but for some reason the word pulpit springs to mind when Alan stands there—as a matter of fact, maybe they should start calling the Friars Club's bar the pulpit in homage to Alan). "And you portrayed an aging, cigar-smoking, shoulder-rolling Jew comic, and as Queen Victoria once said, 'I was not amused.' And the fact that he was a prick didn't sit too well with me, either. I'm sorry that Milton Berle is not here to defend himself."

Jack Palance, who won an Oscar for his role opposite Billy in *City Slickers*, was invited to attend the Roast, but ran into a bit of a snafu—one of his own making perhaps, but a snafu nonetheless. He went into the Grand Ballroom of the Hilton Hotel the morning of the event, "just to have a look around." Then he went out for coffee—never to be seen on the dais or in the ballroom again. He did leave a note though, written on Hilton stationery: "Sorry Billy. But I came by the dais entrance and was told no tickets, no—? Hope you have a great time. Jack Palance. P.S. No one had given me a ticket." Um, Jack? What exactly was in that coffee you left to go have? I mean, let's face it, if Pierre Cossette can get onto the dais, one would think Jack Palance could with ease. Maybe if he spent more time practicing two-armed pushups, he could push his way into things like this a little harder.

Billy was reduced to tears by the end of the afternoon, and it wasn't because he was sincerely touched, "As a kid, my brothers and I and my family, we'd always think about what was said behind the closed doors of the Friars, and you know, you always wanted to know what was going on and now that I've sat through it, it's really no big fuckin' deal. Milton Berle could not be here today; they couldn't get a Depends big enough to fit around his dick. I want to thank all the people who I admired as a young boy and really am repulsed by now as an adult—Pat Cooper. Pat, if it wasn't for Columbus Day, you'd never work. Buddy Hackett, I love Buddy Hackett, but I tell ya buddy, my mother thinks you're an asshole, and so do I.

"What can I say about my dear friend Alan King that hasn't been said about bigger people. Rob, I thought you did a fantastic job and when he's not directing great movies, he is Sebastian Cabot's stunt man. True story, when he was fourteen years old he was thrown off the set of the *Dick Van Dyke Show* for grabbing Mary Tyler Moore's ass. What he doesn't tell you is that two weeks later he was arrested for going down on Morey Amsterdam. I can't say enough about Robin, I love him dearly, but Robin, you know, I host the awards, you just lose them." You have to admit, the '90s brought their own, how do you say, je ne sais quoi, to these Roasts. Which may explain. . . .

WHOOPI GOLDBERG – 1993

(The face that launched a thousand "Holy Shit's!")

TED DANSON, *Roastmaster*	NATALIE COLE
KEITH ADDIS	ROBERT DE NIRO
ANITA BAKER	MICHAEL DOUGLAS
ED BEGLEY, JR.	ROGER EBERT
SHARI BELAFONTE	MICHAEL FUCHS
HALLE BERRY	JACK L. GREEN
JOSEPH BOLOGNA	ROBERT GUILLAUME
LORRAINE BRACCO	JASMINE GUY
MATTHEW BRODERICK	ROBERT HALMI
DAVID BROWN	JAMES IVORY
BRAD CAFARELLI	BEVERLY JOHNSON
GIL CATES	HARVEY KEITEL

LARRY KING
ROBIN LEACH
SUGAR RAY LEONARD
BUTCH LEWIS
ISMAIL MERCHANT
RON MEYER
ARNON MILCHAN
MATTHEW MODINE
EDWARD JAMES OLMOS
KEVIN POLLAK
TONY RANDALL
GERALDO RIVERA
CHRIS ROCK

PAUL SORVINO
MICHAEL SPINKS
MR. T
JOHN TURTURRO
MALCOLM JAMAL WARNER
BOB WEINSTEIN
HARVEY WEINSTEIN
MONTEL WILLIAMS
   (for like a minute)
ROBIN WILLIAMS
VANESSA WILLIAMS
SEAN YOUNG

If Sophie Tucker is the jewel in the Friars tiara of Roasts, Whoopi Goldberg is the gem. Ted Danson, her boyfriend at the time (well, actually they had just broken up, but it wasn't common knowledge at that point) was the Master of Ceremonies and a fine figure he cut in top hat and tails. The figure that didn't cut it, apparently, was the presence of him standing at the podium in blackface. "This takes a lot of balls to come out here in blackface for someone you care about in front of 3,000 motherfuckin' people," said Whoopi in her speech at the end of the Roast. "I liked it. I don't care if you did, 'cause this was for me, 'cause I'm the queen of New York today, baby!" This should be enough said on the subject, but it was only the beginning.

Maybe if someone had not snuck in a journalist, and if that journalist had not snuck in a photographer, and if that photographer's batteries hadn't been working, then just maybe no one would have known what went on behind those closed doors. Then again, there was always Montel Williams—oh, and this book!

And so begins the tale. The Roast was going swimmingly. The press and photo op were running along at their usual caliber of merriment. Ted Danson, in his de rigueur whiteface, was being the perfect host for the afternoon. The guest of honor was beaming over the attention, and she could not have been more thrilled by the festivities. Cocktails, then lunch—it all went on without a hitch.

Danson left the dais to prepare for the show. Who's to say what made the more striking image—his return to the dais wearing blackface with white lips, or his devouring a slice of watermelon a little later in the proceedings. Contrary to what people would like to think, there were no shrieks. No gasps. No moans. The loudest noise in the room was Whoopi, pounding the table, yelling, "Oh shit! Oh my God! Oh!" Danson, who had also changed into his tux, said, "I wanted to dress elegantly for you, my darling, because you're the most elegant woman I know." He then told the filled-to-capacity Hilton Hotel Ballroom, "I have to share this with you. This morning I was shaving and wondering what I was gonna say this afternoon, and Whoopi was giving me a blow job. We're beginning to set the tone here, ladies and gentlemen." And what a tone it was! "I know comparisons are odious but, uh, I gotta tell ya, black chicks sure do know their way around a dick. I suppose, in all fairness, that's because white girls get toys at Christmas." And he was off and running . . . as was Montel Williams.

The minute Danson walked in, Williams bolted from the dais and made a beeline for Western Union to send the following telegram to Roast Producer Robert Saks, "As a new member of the Friars Club, I attended my first Celebrity Roast fifteen minutes ago. And after the seven minutes that I stayed I was confused as to whether or not I was at a Friars' event or at a rally for the KKK and Aryan Nation. I understand what humor is. I understand what comedy is, and what good and bad taste is. But I am shocked that an organization that I held with such high regard and always wanted to be a member of could sponsor an event that was as disgusting and tasteless as this one. My dues are paid in full, so therefore you have no reason to contact me ever again." Actually, Montel, as a "working performer" your membership is free for the first six months—but it does make for more dramatic license to say you were paid up. It was also sort of interesting that the *Daily News*, which featured a black-faced Danson and smiling Whoopi on the cover of its edition the next day, also had a transcript, verbatim, of Montel's telegram. Wonder where they got that? The Friars had no idea the papers knew about the incident.

When news of the Roast got out, all hell broke loose for both the Friars Club and for Whoopi and Ted. "Part of what Ted's Roasting was, was about being proud of me and proud of who I am. And that he is proud to be my friend and walk before me in life. But Montel missed all that," said an angry Whoopi at a press conference a few days later. "If this is going to be the outcry after each Friars Roast, the Friars will no longer be able to have them. That Mr. Danson came in blackface was my idea. I had a great time and I'm thrilled that RuPaul, dressed as a nun, stood up and humped the podium while screaming, 'Give it to me big, daddy.' I guess Montel missed that." Actually, it was, "Oh shit, oh you motherfucker, goddamn, rip it, rip it, motherfucker, rip it, rip it," but it was probably wise for her to give a sanitized version. I gotta remember that sometime. "Or Robin Williams who talked about my sexuality and said he opened my legs once, looked in, and saw six guys and a Harley. There was a lot that went on at this Roast."

"The thing that aggravated me more than anything else about the furor was that she wrote the lines for him and she was the one that suggested he come out in blackface. And that Montel Williams gets so crazy over it, no sense of humor," says Freddie Roman. "I think it hurt us in terms of getting future guests of honor for a couple of years, there's no question about that. Because of the amount of negative publicity, it hurt us terribly. Now, I think we've recovered from that nicely. In particular because they're on television now, which yes, they're bleeped and edited, but still it comes off very well on the television version."

As Whoopi said, though, there were other things going on, other than Ted's unnatural tan. But he was hard to miss, sitting that way throughout the entire show. "What kind of weird-ass bet did you lose?" asked Bobcat Goldthwait. "Did you really think black people would think that's funny in ninety-fuckin'-three? I'm sure Dinkins is really glad he's here on a reelection fuckin' thing. Maybe, you should just get really fucked up now, that's your only hope." The mayor did get into a bit of a pickle over this one actually, but he certainly maintained his composure and was a good sport about it, "I see you're all subtle as ever, just like always here at the Friars."

But here's some more of Ted: "I tell ya the tabloids, they just won't let us alone. This morning Whoopi said to me, you know, if only we can get Burt Reynolds to fuck Michael Jackson maybe we'd be home free. Maybe they'd let us alone then. It's tough being in the tabloids. I'll never forget the time I took Whoopi to meet my parents, it was so profound, so moving that I wrote it in my diary. I'd like to share it with you—and I hope the tabloids are here so they can get this straight:

June 22nd '92
I was worried about how my parents would react when I brought Whoopi home to meet them, they can be so stuffy and out of touch, but Whoopi fit right in. And after she did the laundry and washed the dishes and dusted and generally tidied up the place—my father, my sweet, sweet father offered to give her a ride to the bus station—and my mother, you remember this, said that was really out of place, Ned, really out of place, especially since she felt Whoopi had missed a few of the spots on the higher shelves. Actually my mother got along with Whoopi beautifully, but that's because my mother's a dyke.

Chris Rock also had a beef with Ted. "You know what's fucked up, is that there's only two rich black women in the whole world and he gets one of them. There's Whoopi and Oprah, and how the fuck did he get Whoopi? You want a black girl, why don't you start lower. Why don't you go to the projects and get some crack girl or some shit and leave her to me. You know, between you and De Niro I gotta fuck Blossom now!"

Kevin Pollak read a telegram from President Clinton: "Dear Whoopi, I'm so sorry Hill and I couldn't be there, I'm sure it would have been fun. I've never Roasted anyone and I'm sure I would've enjoyed saying 'motherfucker' and 'cocksucker.'" He made that up, right?

Kevin Nealon's subliminal character got the best of him with comments like, "Quite frankly, I'm ashamed and embarrassed to be part of this crude and insensitive group led by Mr. Danson. Maybe I can bring a little class and dignity to today's events. I happen to think Whoopi is a wonderful person (big slut); not only is she a wonderful person, but she's also a very talented actress (lucky bitch). And if I, uh, I had my say she would be honored in a different way (butt fuck) you know what I mean?. . . .When I first met Whoopi, I gotta tell you this, there was a lot of things that surprised me about her (transvestite), you know what I mean? She wasn't your typical actress (big phony) there was that something special that separated her from the rest of the pack (body odor)."

Just so you don't think this afternoon was totally void of class, Vanessa Williams sang "The Star Spangled Banner" and blew everyone away—as in her voice! God, you guys! Thank heaven's Alan King always brings a certain elegance to the pulpit, "As the eldest statesman of the Friars Club and the Monitor, it's usually my job to monitor the afternoon. There were twenty-nine fucks; nine motherfuckers; thirteen shits; one cock; four blow jobs; a cocksucker; a dicksucker; a pussy; a cunt; eleven niggers and my hemorrhoids came back during all of this."

Whoopi Goldberg deserves the entertainer of the twentieth century award. She went through a lot by just saying yes to the Friars—and this doesn't even include the Roasting, "I'd like to now get to some of these blow job jokes. I give good head. I make no bones about it. Those of you who have had it know I'm telling the truth—and that's why he got me, Chris, 'cause he knew how to elongate that cumming. Robin, my man, probably the only man on the dais I haven't fucked. This is really nice. I see people I know and I really like. I do." Surveying the audience, she said, "But you all. Who the fuck are you people? I mean really. What did you come here for? This was a very scary experience, because I didn't know what was coming. And you all were very, very light, much lighter than anticipated, dicks and cunts and all this. I want to be the highest paid bitch in Hollywood, and for that I fucked a mouse! Thank you for coming out. I really appreciate it. Thank you."

What can be said that hasn't already been said or written or dissected about this Roast? If you didn't like what you read, well, then you should have stopped reading after the Henry Kissinger Dinner. If you did, cool. If you walked out in the middle of reading it, well, just get over yourself.

STEVEN SEAGAL – 1995

(Bye, bye, Berley)

MILTON BERLE, *Roastmaster*	JERRY ORBACH
DANNY AIELLO	KEVIN POLLAK
LINDA BELL BLUE	SALLY JESSY RAPHAEL
DAVID BRENNER	SAL RICHARDS
DAVID BROWN	ERIC ROBERTS
DICK CAPRI	FREDDIE ROMAN
LEN CARIOU	JEFFREY ROSS
GORDON ELLIOTT	ROBERT SAKS
SCOTT GLENN	IRWIN SCHAEFFER
BUDDY HACKETT	PATRICIA REED SCOTT
ROBERT HALMI, SR.	TERRY SEMEL
LAINIE KAZAN	PAUL SORVINO
LARRY KING	MICHAEL SPINKS
ROBIN LEACH	DONALD TRUMP
KEVIN MEANEY	BOB VILA
ARNON MILCHAN	KEENEN IVORY WAYANS
LILIANE MONTEVECCHI	VERONICA WEBB
JULIUS NASSO	SEAN YOUNG
LEROY NEIMAN	HENNY YOUNGMAN

The year after the Whoopi Goldberg Roast, Bob Newhart bit the bullet and took the honors, with Don Rickles as his Roastmaster. But it wasn't all that exciting, so we'll just move on to Steven Seagal. This Roast was memorable if only for the fact that it was the last time Milton Berle was Roastmaster for the Friars. Almost fifty years had gone by since he presented that tongue to Maurice Chevalier, and here he was wagging his own to this overgrown karate kid. "Laugh it up, Steven, I laugh when you act." Oh, those sweet familiar sounds! "Steven's never said anything bad about me. Oh, he did call my wife, Lorna, a yenta bitch, a pain in the ass, and a lousy hump, but fuck her, that's her problem." I don't care what anyone says, this joke is different because it's the first time he told it with his new wife's name. Then he went into the cunt-shaped-like-a-taco joke that he told at the Willis Roast. Let's face it, there are only about five jokes in the world, and these guys have told them all at every event they've ever performed. But delivery is everything.

While Seagal seems like he'd be a great candidate for Roasting—what martial arts, action hero wouldn't—and his movie *Under Siege II: Dark Territory* had been released that summer, his personality is very different from what he seems. "I'm a private person, shy and quiet. I didn't want to do it, but enough people said I should, so I did it," explains the soft-spoken yet witty actor. He was a good sport, though, enduring such barbs as these from Dick Capri: "When I think of three of the greatest actors in my lifetime, three names immediately come to mind, Sir Laurence Olivier, Spencer Tracy, and Steven Seagal. When I think of three of the greatest movies ever made, I think of *Citizen Kane, Gone With the Wind*, and *Under Siege II*. When I think of three of the most memorable roles that were ever portrayed on screen, I think of Ben Kingsley as Gandhi, Liam Neeson as Oskar Schindler, and Steven Seagal as Gino Filino."

Jeffrey Ross was new to the Roast scene but not new to the Friars ways, "A lot of you don't know me, but I feel uniquely qualified to be up here today, 'cause I'm also a shitty actor." He also learned the tricks of the Friars' trade—shoot every comic in sight, "I was walking around downtown not too long ago and saw Milton Berle in an antique shop—eight hundred bucks." Berle tried to defend himself, but Buddy Hackett cut him off, "Milton, Milton, let the kid work. Don't you remember when you used to?" But seriously, Jeffrey, "What can I say about Steven Seagal that hasn't already been said about Van Damme? I saw your last movie and I left during the previews—is he laughing? I'm afraid to look." He was laughing.

Seagal's good time, however, ended with Gordon Elliott's turn at the podium, "Katie Sagal is the only woman in Hollywood not in litigation with you currently. And speaking of sexual harassment of optometrists . . ." was all it took. "There was a woman at the time, the tabloids had picked up on, she's either, if she's alive, in a mental institution or in prison," says Seagal, "and Milton had told the guys to lay off this topic. But one of the guys got up and mentioned it and, of course, that got in the tabloids. And, of course, that's the reason I didn't want to do it in the first place." Berle remembers, "He wouldn't have done the show unless I was the emcee. And I said, I'll protect you, leave it to me. He was laughing, it was fine. He took all the ribs and all the dirty lines about him, about how can a gay be a big movie star that rides horses and shoots people. Then, when this guy got on, he said something to Steve about him, which wasn't very nice. Didn't fit the situation. Seagal turned to me and said—I think he had a gun on him too, you know Seagal—'Who's that prick?' 'Cause he had a mouth, too, and he said to me, 'I don't want to see him after the show 'cause I'll break his fucking legs.'" Which makes Elliott's closing line even more telling, "We don't hate you because you're beautiful, we hate you because we're very fuckin' scared of you." Be afraid, Gordon, be very afraid. Oh, just for the record, Berle was joking; Seagal didn't really have a gun.

Hackett he could handle, though, "I know that you must have spent two, three thousand dollars on karate and martial arts, and it shows. And about eight and a half dollars on acting lessons, which you should demand your money back. I envy you. Not your career as a great actor, I envy your penis. Not the size of your penis, the age of your penis."

This was also Henny Youngman's last Roast, "Milton, if you had to live your life again, don't do it." Needless to say, he didn't have anything to say about Steven, but that's par for the course and the end of a wonderful, long-running gag.

"I just want to let you guys know the one thing that really hurt me the most was the criticism about my acting. I'm so hurt. I'm devastated," said Seagal. He was kidding, of course. Weren't you, Steven? Don't think that he has only bad memories of the day, because he doesn't at all, "Milton was so brilliant and just so good at the time. I remember, Henny Youngman, it wasn't long before he died, was there. He was so frail, and I watched Berle, who was in his eighties as well, but as Youngman was standing at the mike, I could see Berle holding his belt, steadying him, it was just so touching—blew me away." Wow. What a nice ending to the Roast finale of two of the

Friars' greatest stars. See how everything doesn't have to be goddamn funny! Then again, you already knew that from reading about the Dinah Shore Dinner from 1960.

KELSEY GRAMMER – 1996

(Pick a topic, any topic)

DAVID HYDE PIERCE, *Roastmaster*	ROBERT HALMI, SR.
DANNY AIELLO	SALLY JESSY RAPHAEL
KEVIN BACON	LAINIE KAZAN
ROB BECKER	JANE LEEVES
LINDA BELL BLUE	WARREN LITTLEFIELD
LEWIS BLACK	CHRISTOPHER LLOYD
JAMES BURROWS	TONY LO BIANCO
BOBBY COLLINS	KERRY MCCLUGGAGE
PAT COOPER	PHYLLIS NEWMAN
PROFESSOR IRWIN COREY	MICHAEL NOURI
RICH CRONIN	ERIC ROBERTS
NORM CROSBY	FREDDIE ROMAN
PHYLLIS DILLER	JEFFREY ROSS
DAVID DINKINS	PAUL SORVINO
PERI GILPIN	GERRY RED WILSON
HAZELLE GOODMAN	BOB WRIGHT

"FRASIER ENTERS REHAB" blared newspaper headlines the day before Kelsey Grammer's scheduled Roast. Oh well, it's all in a day's laughs at the Friars Club. Not that his drug and alcohol problems are laughable—then again, let's face it, it was THE DAY BEFORE HIS FUCKIN' ROAST! Oy! When the Roast finally did take place two months later, don't think this little news flash went ignored. "Kelsey had flipped his car and ended up going to the Betty Ford Clinic, and then said, 'Yes, we'll go on and do the Roast.' I think it was a week after he had gotten out of Betty Ford," says Roastmaster and *Frasier* costar David Hyde Pierce. "So it was obvious that if he was willing to do that, you couldn't sidestep that, you couldn't not talk about it." So they talked about it, "Hello, my name is Kelsey Grammer and I'm an alcoholic," is how Pierce opened the show, pretending that his papers had gotten mixed up with Grammer's. And then he talked about it some more, "Our next Roaster is the wonderful comic, Tommy Collins. It's Bobby? Oh, I'm sorry, I just got this note from Kelsey and it says Tom Collins, pronto!" And then someone else talked about it, "I feel I'm qualified to be here because I'm wasted," said Jeffrey Ross, who continued to talk about it, "Two words come to mind, *Cheers*, and 'Cheers.'"

And when they stopped talking about the drinking, Ross moved on, "This poor man Roasts himself." He then shifted gears to another minor—literally—inconvenience that Kelsey had run into, "I won't say Kelsey's girlfriend is young, but when he said, 'I love you,' she said, 'Then buy me a pony.' Have you ever run into Seinfeld at a prom?" Even his costars Peri Gilpin and Jane Leeves announced they had a special guest, Missy, "But she's not here yet because she's not out of study hall." Hazelle Goodman said, "I know you wanted to leave your black sordid past behind you, but I'm here! I met Kelsey when I was thirteen. I was baby-sitting for his girlfriend—she was 11." Freddie Roman was able to jump on two bandwagons with a single joke, "I just had drinks with Kelsey. He had a Shirley Temple—actually it was a fourteen-year old girl." Even NBC Entertainment President Warren Littlefield went down that slippery slope to smut (sorry, I got into this Frasier Crane mode and it just sort of flowed), "Kelsey is so important to our network. He's bringing in our demographics—teens and children."

Littlefield then careened into the car accident segment of the afternoon, courtesy of the guest of honor's recent driving record, "Kelsey truly does love the Viper we gave him; he says it practically drives itself." Gerry Red Wilson approached the podium wrapped in bandages, "I want to let you in on a little secret. I was the other passenger in that fucking Viper. I needed reconstructive surgery on my face and I want to thank Phyllis Diller, on a personal note, for recommending seventy-nine different fucking doctors!" Maybe Kelsey took Lewis Black's advice to heart, "You should move to New York. You can live in this city because God gave us cabs. You can get as fucked up as you want. You wouldn't be in that Viper."

If you're looking for some really good insults, there's always the name game: "Kelsey Grammer, translation from Gaelic means, 'I got a condom on right now!'" said Bobby Collins. Although Littlefield must hail from a different part of the region, "Kelsey's is an ancient Gaelic name, Kelsey meaning 'brave one' and Grammer meaning 'measurement of cocaine.'" Phyllis Diller is still part of the Roast circuit, "We have to move this along because Kelsey's parole only covers the luncheon. Kelsey. What kind of a name is that? To me it sounds like something you take for an upset stomach." Pierce surmised, "Kelsey Grammer? That is a gay person's name. It's a good name for a drag queen." But his real insight into Kelsey's name led into the flatulence portion of the afternoon, "There's a very interesting Norwegian version of Kelsey Grammer, which, loosely translated, means king of farts. And you know? God knows that's true, even as I stand here, I tear up. Kelsey has been sounding that distant trumpet since he was a child and actually even before. His mother had a very easy birth because the gaseous bastard actually propelled himself out of the womb and bounced off a doctor and went down on a nurse." Gilpin and Leeves pulled out of a box of tricks, "A large jar of gas-ex for that nasty little problem. As if anything over the counter could help." They also offered him an enema bag.

These kinds of jokes don't just happen; there is thought and intense research behind them. Just ask Pierce, who was up all night in his suite at the Hilton Hotel, "I remember a lot of our cast and director and people were out there for the Roast, and they were all drinking martinis down in the lobby. I'd go down, have martinis with them, and just see what they thought about a certain area. I remember at one point I was going to do a whole thing about Kelsey farting, so I went down to talk to them about different euphemisms for farting, just to get a catalog of that." Who needs a library for detailed research when you've got a bar full of martini drinkers to lend a hand? The answer, my friends, is breaking in the wind.

When Gerry Red Wilson announced, "Is it hot in here? I'm

sweating like a fag looking at a hot dog—oh, sorry, David." The David he looked at was taken by surprise, "I was not prepared for that," Pierce says. "So I got up afterwards and said, 'Is it just me, or is anyone else here craving a hot dog?' I thought I was in protected territory. It never even occurred to me that I was going to be the subject of a Roast. That just really surprised me and I thought, oh man, I really have to be on my guard ready to hit back." Don't worry, he didn't hit Phyllis too hard.

Speaking of hitting, one really does need to duck when Pat Cooper performs at a Roast, "You gotta be a cocksucker in this business to fuckin' survive. We have two cocksuckers here who are making it, because they crash a car, they drink the shit, they hump a sixteen-year-old—I wanna hump a sixteen-year-old! I never humped a sixteen year old! Every pussy I saw had hair on it, I'm fuckin' mad! Remember one thing, I did *Seinfeld*, baby! Fuck you and your show! You better fuckin' believe it! How long can you do the same shit he done on *Cheers* and they move him over to *Frasier*. I never saw the show, never saw the fuckin' show, don't mean nothin'! You belong on the small screen. Stay small. Look what happened to David Caruso, he's on slides now! Robert Merrill, what can I say, if America goes to war and we lose, you're out of a fuckin' job!" Betcha Merrill didn't see that one coming either.

The one person who should have come out swinging, but seemed quite humbled by all the cheery accolades, was Grammer himself, "Well I'm Kelsey Grammer and I *am* an alcoholic. I've been finding out quite a few things about myself lately, some while at Betty Ford, but I found out some of the most amazing things about myself while I was here. The most comforting of which was that, frankly, I was born with an asshole, and thank you, David, for mentioning how profound an asshole it turned out to be. I do sense some love, even though it's kind of hard to filter out right at this moment." All good things must come to an end, even Roasts, and Kelsey found the end to his perfect afternoon, "There's only one thing I'd like to do and I've been dying to do this all my life. You may remember a performance by Jack Nicholson in *One Flew Over The Cuckoos Nest*. It goes something like this [now folks, this is an audio daily double—you have to picture Grammer imitating Nicholson] 'Doc, that girl was fifteen going on thirty-five. You know what I mean?'"

For Pierce, the experience was certainly, well, an experience, "I really love Kelsey and I wanted to do the best I could in the spirit of the Roast," he acknowledges. "Always, in the back of your mind, the Friars go out of their way to say this is an expression of love, but you wonder, does anyone really believe this or is this just an excuse for savagery?" Finally! Somebody caught on!

DREW CAREY ROAST – 1998

(Friars, you're on the air!)

RYAN STILES, *Roastmaster*	DOM IRRERA
CINDY ADAMS	LAINIE KAZAN
JOEY ADAMS	ALAN KING
LUCIE ARNAZ	KATHY KINNEY
LYNN AHRENS	TSIDII LE LOKA
ABRAHAM D. BEAME	TONY LO BIANCO
JOY BEHAR	LAURENCE LUCKINBILL
BILL BEUTEL	DOUG McCORMICK
MICHAEL IAN BLACK	DARREN McGAVIN
STU BLOOMBERG	ROBERT MERRILL
LINDA BELL BLUE	ALAN MENKEN
BILL BOGGS	JAY MOHR
BRENDAN BYRNE	LeROY NEIMAN
JACK CARTER	SALLY JESSY RAPHAEL
MARGARET CHO	JEFFREY ROSS
PAT COOPER	LIZ SMITH
DAVID DINKINS	WANDA SYKES-HALL
HAZELLE GOODMAN	ABE VIGODA
SKITCH HENDERSON	DR. RUTH WESTHEIMER
DOUG HERZOG	BOB ZANY
CAROLINE HIRSCH	

The time had finally come for the Friars to throw caution to the wind and tackle television one more time. Or is that for the first time? These guys will have your head spinning with their own "who's on first" routine. Let's face it, those previous attempts at televising were sanitized made-for-TV productions. The Drew Carey Roast, however, went straight to cable. In films, that's the kiss of death; for television, it's a ratings coup. Comedy Central and their *South Park* mentality—which is frighteningly similar to the Friars' mentality, it would seem—was dying to get their hands on the Club's raunchy, raucous Roasts.

The Club, needless to say, had some reservations. It took them almost eighty-five years and a stockpile of Valium to get them to allow women in, so you can only imagine what the thought of cursing in people's living rooms did to them. Not to mention the trepidation of the performers. "To me, the fun of that and the freedom of the Friars Club is that it's a private event for those people. Just like there are things I might say to a friend in private that I wouldn't say to them in a public place over a microphone," says David Hyde Pierce. Freddie Roman recalls, "When I approached Paul Reiser to be a Roastmaster for us, he said, 'Freddie, I have a deal with AT&T that nets me an awful lot of money and I don't think they would be happy with my doing it." Red Buttons is pretty adamant about it, "I refuse to do that, because of how I feel doing that kind of material in front of women and I just won't do it. I dropped out. They've asked me and I said no." Norm Crosby says, "I don't understand the fact that now we're showing them on TV. Some of the heavyweights have declined, Red wouldn't go, Hackett wouldn't go. I have an image. I don't want these people to tune in to TV and hear me saying four-letter words and filth. Yet, at the same time, I want to perpetuate the Roasts."

The beauty of the Friars Club is their resilience and ability to adapt to changing times (not to mention sweet business deals). Alan King; Freddie Roman; Ken Greengrass, the producer of the Roasts at this time; and comedian Jeffrey Ross, saw the writing on the wall and when Comedy Central called, they answered. (It's a different kind of answer from when nature calls, but Johnny Carson would know about that better than King, Roman, Greengrass, or Ross.) Now, try finding a guest of honor with the usual prerequisites of a tough hide and great sense of humor plus a new catchphrase for the soon-to-be-centenary club—a ratings grabber. It helped immensely that Ross had his hand in the comedy till of resources—in other words, he's not just funny, he knows funny people too. His affiliation with Comedy Central, not to mention his deep affection for the Friars (we're also talking about a guy who just barely turned 30 for heaven's sake!) brought the two entities together better than Dewar's did with scotch and soda.

Drew Carey fit the bill better than most. His hide is thicker than any living species and he had a hit TV show familiar to Comedy Central's demographics (can you imagine Jessel having to fit "demographics" into his Toastmastering duties?). After Ross approached the sitcom star, Carey was ready for his comedy close-up, "I get insulted on my show every week, so you can't do any better than my writers do," mused Carey just before the big event. "My favorite thing to do is to sit around with my comic friends and bust balls. So I'll only be mad if they hold back. It would be kind of insulting if you come to a Roast and you hold back because there are cameras or something. Being a Roaster is more pressure than an honoree because I just have to sit there and take it. They have to be funny." Finally, the secret is revealed!

The television cameras brought a whole new dimension to the Friars' annual event. Comedy Central wanted to do it up big, make a huge splash and produce a true "event." The Friars complied, bowing to "show business," and changed their Roast format from a casual luncheon to a black-tie formal dinner affair, which gave it that "award show feel." Ryan Stiles, who costars on *The Drew Carey Show*, was the Roastmaster of the event after Ben Stiller had to pull out several months earlier, "I probably know Drew better than a lot of other people, and I was kind of doing him a favor. I thought it was kind of strange that a lot of people were hassling Drew, but don't really know him. It's almost like, it's the same speech, but fill in the name here. So that's kind of the impression I got, especially from the older guys, like Jack Carter. They might have used the same speech on Henny Youngman twenty years ago."

"It's a goddamn imposition to fly 3,000 miles to honor a schmuck that lives across the street from me. This wonderful, delightful, cute little adorable gentile, who has done so much for Jews just by not being one, Dean Carey." That was Jack Carter; maybe Stiles has a point.

If anyone feared that the television cameras would clean up the Friars' act, Alan King was there to flush Mr. Clean down the toilet, "I promised you that I would set the tone for this evening. In order to give it some form, I will attempt to do it alphabetically. Under A, asshole, more descriptive and funnier than anus and more appropriate when honoring Drew Carey. Under B, balls, also appropriate for the guest of honor; I've seen his act. Now, the dreaded C word, I wouldn't touch it. I'm gonna move it down to P for pussy. A pussy is not funny, unless it has a cigar in it." The list did go on, until King dared the comedians, "Feel free to say what you will, give this fat-ass a new hole. Let Comedy Central go bleep themselves. Would you believe I wrote this shit on Yom Kippur?"

"Boy, I was worried about keeping it clean for the older folks, but fuck that," said Stiles following King. Joy Behar, who had been Roastmaster at Danny Aiello's Roast the year before, told Ryan, "I hope your experience hosting the Friars Roast was as good as mine was. I have one question, 'Did you have to go down on Alan King also?'" Dick Capri, who told Drew, "I love you but I am seeing other comedians on the side," talked about his life as a single man, "After I got divorced, the first thing I did was put a tampon on top of the TV set to remind me of the cunt who took the VCR." Margaret Cho allowed her apparent low self-esteem to get the better of her, "I think one of the reasons that I'm here is to make it look like you have more women friends. Strippers don't make good public speakers."

For Jeffrey Ross, why just Roast the guest of honor when there is a dais full of humanity waiting to be crushed, starting with Abe Vigoda, "My one regret is that Abe Vigoda isn't alive to see this. Alan King, a man who's been doing comedy so long he lost to Mark Twain on *Star Search*. Dr. Ruth is here. I promised I wouldn't curse, but I want to fuck you so bad. Milton Berle's not here, but his penis is backstage signing autographs." Oh goody, I was hoping there would be a Berle penis joke. But like Jell-O, there's always room for Drew, "Drew Carey is to comedy what Mariah Carey is to comedy. We all know that Drew isn't two-faced or else why would he wear that one. You look like Buddy Holly and Barney Rubble had a baby and then peed on it. I heard ABC is blaming your face for making Ellen gay."

Jay Mohr arrived to the dais late and for some inexplicable reason, changed backstage out of one tuxedo shirt and into another just before he took his seat at the dais. He also didn't have cufflinks or studs for the shirt, so Oscar Riba, on the staff of the Friars Club, loaned him his. I ended up holding the shirt he removed. Jay's act went something like this, "Yea, I'm up, everybody go piss, that's great. What the fuck happened? I'm the first guy up here with a credit. . . . I'm just gonna stall till they come back from shitting." He then proceeded to get into some verbal sparring with Freddie Roman, which sort of came out of nowhere. So after a painful few minutes and as many laughs as Hugh Downs got at Barbara Walters' Dinner, he finished. He must have been preoccupied when he booked from the Hilton Ballroom since Oscar is still waiting for his cufflinks and studs. I can't remember if Oscar said they were his great-great-grandfather's on his mother's side, or if he got them on sale at Wal-Mart. Even so, he never saw them again. As for Jay's shirt—now, where did I put that?

"I thought it was kind of cool that they were trying to get in a younger breed of Friar in there, but some of the younger guys were kind of hacking on the older guys on the panel more than they did to Drew. Jeff was probably the most vicious, and his stuff was hilarious. Even if you think it's vicious, if you see Drew laughing so hard and he's crying, there's nothing you can say. Dick Capri was hilarious, I think Drew laughed at Dick Capri harder than anybody else," says Stiles.

Suffice it to say, when the show aired several weeks later on Comedy Central, it had been whittled down from two hours to one. Not everyone made the final cut (that's correct, Oscar's cufflinks and studs were never shown on TV). The show still needed to be censored, and many of the words were bleeped, but this comedian did win the "I got more bleeps than anybody" award—care to guess who it might be? "I don't know what the fuck this man does? I don't know where he came from? I'm forty years in this fucking business, this guy drinks beer, passes fucking gas, and he gets a series. I drink beer, pass gas, and I got a fucking colon problem! I came here tonight because I didn't believe that this man existed. I never met Mr. Ken Stiles. Ken, fuck Canada! Margaret Cho, fuck Korea! And fuck your rice and your rickshaws! Abe Vigoda, they made fun that you died. You fucking did die! Last Thursday, Abe! I've been at Roasts for big stars, Bruce Willis, Jerry Lewis, we never had to wear a fucking tuxedo! And when I look at this face, I want to grate cheese!" Did you figure out who that was?

"Everybody was really nice to me tonight, I thought," said Carey at the end of the night. "A lot of people don't realize that everything they said tonight was true. I applaud Stu Bloomberg, from ABC. Ellen is a lesbian, she had to go. I take it up the ass, suck cock, I get two shows. You gotta suck some cock to get ahead on ABC. You want to suck pussy, you go to Fox. This is a real honor and I hope next year you get a big star." And so, just like all those other milestones in the Friars' silly sordid past, this one too passed—and just like gas, it too has been repeated on Comedy Central over and over again.

JERRY STILLER ROAST – 1999

(Swan Song)

JASON ALEXANDER, *Roastmaster*	KEVIN DOBSON
BEATRICE ARTHUR	OLYMPIA DUKAKIS
SANDRA BERNHARD	SUSIE ESSMAN
BILL BEUTEL	TOM FONTANA
LEO BLOOM	JANEANE GAROFALO
LINDA BELL BLUE	SPALDING GRAY
BILL BOGGS	ADOLF GREEN
DAVID BROWN	KEN GREENGRASS
DICK CAPRI	PATRICIA HEARST
LEN CARIOU	FLORENCE HENDERSON
DICK CAVETT	ANNE JACKSON
BLYTHE DANNER	LOU JACOBI
LARRY DIVNEY	KEVIN JAMES
LOU DOBBS	JIMMY KIMMELL

ALAN KING
TSIDII LE LOKA
WENDY LIEBMAN
LAURENCE LUCKINBILL
SHEILA MACRAE
BOB MCGRATH
MICHAEL MCKEAN
ANNE MEARA
LARRY MILLER
PHYLLIS NEWMAN
CHRIS NOTH
CARROLL O'CONNOR
PATTON OSWALT
MAURY POVICH

TONY RANDALL
PAUL RODRIGUEZ
FREDDIE ROMAN
JEFFREY ROSS
ROBERT SCHIMMEL
AMY STILLER
BEN STILLER
LARRY STORCH
ABE VIGODA
GEORGE WALLACE
ELI WALLACH
MAX WEINBERG
DR. RUTH WESTHEIMER
LOUIS ZORICH

Jerry Stiller—the manic, out-of-control, out-of-this-world Frank Costanza on *Seinfeld*—could not be any further from his small-screen persona than, say, Pee Wee Herman was to his. All the more reason to put him in the hot seat in front of millions of television viewers, not to mention the Hilton Hotel's Grand Ballroom audience of Friars. His TV son, Jason Alexander, served as Roastmaster and proved quite the versatile emcee, "I was almost an actor, playing the role of the Roastmaster, a la Alan King, a la Johnny Carson, a la Dean Martin, all these guys. It's not really, truly my persona out there," says Alexander of his Friars stint. Well, whoever it was, he brought the house down with his opening number.

It had been a while since the Friars had a good ol' song to rev them up. And at a Roast, Rob Reiner was the last to croon such lines like this one to Billy Crystal, "You impotent Jew." Trust me, that's all you need. So when song-and-dance man Alexander was introduced, he brought the Roast to new heights when he performed a song, written especially for this occasion, in which he deciphered a message left on his answering machine that the Friars were Roasting Jerry— ". . . my phone recorded nothing more. Leaving me excited to the core. I pondered enthusiastically, as I thought of all the Jerrys it could be. . ." He sang through a litany of Jerrys that ran the gamut from, "It might be Jerry Springer. Wouldn't that be some humdinger? We could hurl our barbs and stingers. And give him the Friar finger," to "The big guy Jerry Seinfeld. Now we're talking a gold minefield. He's not only a big winner. He could buy the whole friggin' dinner." Needless to say he was none too happy to discover the true Jerry, "When I heard, I said, 'merde' that's French for shit, I couldn't make any sense of it."

Alan King, in his capacity as Kahuna of the Friars, tried to answer Jason's musical query, "For the past ninety-five years the Friars have been saying 'We only Roast the people we love,' and then proceed to ream 'em a new ass. Drew Carey was a fat, gentile, beer-guzzling cross-dresser. Whoopi Goldberg had a lover that enjoyed wearing blackface. Jerry Stiller and I have been friends for over forty-five years, for those of us who know him, we realize he's a kind, loving husband, devoted father, deeply religious. I have never heard Jerry say a bad word about anyone, or ever utter a profanity. So, those of us who know him, know that he is one of the fucking dullest men I have ever known in my life. Why we are honoring this bore—he wasn't really our first choice but we found out too late that Abe Vigoda was alive. Not only are you fucking dull, you're fucking old." (But he's fucking nice—he gave me a really nice tie once, does that count?)

"Like every Jew," Jason explained in his monologue, "I have dreamed of hosting a Friars Roast since I was a kid. I've also dreamed of sharing a hot tub with Pamela Anderson and Julia Roberts, and lucky me, look which one of my dreams came true." But he also showed his touching side to the guest of honor, "Jerry, I love you and I adore you. I am your greatest fan. I am privileged to have shared a stage with you. I think of you the way I think of my own real father—as an old and seemingly endless drain on my patience and my pocketbook."

"Ben Stiller is here, folks," announced Kevin James. "Look at Ben. He's calm. He's funny. He's dedicated, successful, just about everything you'd want in a professional entertainer. Why couldn't the tree fall closer to the apple?" I have a philosophy— never trust a person with two first names—guess I should have shared that with Jerry, but then again he was busy pondering,

'This was supposed to be a celebration, even though they're rattling my brains. So I had to draw a kind of a picture in my mind, 'this is supposed to be terrific, Jerry,' even when a guy says, 'Nobody stays home to watch you on Monday nights' or the apple line that Kevin used."

You want boyhood dreams? Here's Kevin's: "Florence Henderson is here. She now replaces Barbara Eden as the oldest woman I'd like to fuck." Don't look for any blush on Florence's face, though; she stood up at her place on the dais and enticed him to "C'mon over!" The audience roared with laughter. "Folks, we will run late. I will fuck her. Let's just say my Very Brady Christmas will come early this year." When he left the podium, James walked over to Henderson, threw his body across the table, and started making out with Mrs. Brady. "Amazingly, in that brief moment, Kevin finished," quipped Alexander.

Susie Essman knows just as much about Roasting as any of her male counterparts, which is proof that letting women in as Roasters wasn't such a bad idea, "I'm very hoarse tonight, I have a sore throat. Jerry knows why. I know why. Enough said. It wasn't pretty," was her opening line, but here's her tirade— and watch out dais: "You know Maury [Povich], I've always wondered why you married Connie Chung and then I realized, we all know Jews love to eat Chinese—once a week, right? . . . Paul Rodriguez is here, I know he's glad he is, because just think Paul, if Freddie Prinze were alive, you'd be mowing lawns in West Covina. . . . Chris Noth, I'm glad you're here. You are the only fuckable guy on this entire dais." To Freddie Roman she said, "I wouldn't fuck you with Dr. Ruth's pussy." These images can't be healthy. But unfortunately for Jerry, he wasn't exactly out of the woods with Susie, "I would have sex with you but massaging your prostate is not my idea of foreplay. I envy you that you're married to such a wonderful woman, because she's really incredible. She's had sex with Jerry, she's given birth to Ben, she's the only woman I know who's had Ben and Jerry inside of her." For Alan King she had this to add: "Alan, did you ever think you'd live so long that your prostate would be as big as your ego?" Not only is her Friars membership still intact, but

King admits, "That's my favorite joke. I told Susie, I use it about myself now."

Dick Capri, about whom Ryan Stiles says, "If you had to write a character that was kind of the old Catskills kind of comic, I think that's the guy," gave his rant: "Jason, I never realized what a good-looking man you are, don't ever go to jail. Everyone should have an idol, someone that they look up to, someone they admire. Some folks look up to people like Albert Einstein, Mother Teresa, Dr. Jonas Salk. My hero is Jerry Stiller—I wanna make it big when I'm seventy. I wanna have a son who's doing better than me. I wanna have a wife who's taller and more talented than I am. I wanna have hair the color of Tang. I wanna go from one sitcom to another playing exactly the same character. I wanna have a delivery that's as subtle as a fart in an echo chamber."

Jeffrey Ross made Jerry all comfy, "Congratulations, Jerry, you're the first person the Friars ever Roasted that's not in show business. Jerry Stiller has the face of a star, and that star is Lassie. The only time I ever saw Stiller and Meara perform live was at Henny Youngman's funeral, and Henny was funnier. That reminds me, Abe, I owe Henny Youngman twenty bucks, you mind giving it to him?" For Paul Rodriguez he offered, "Paul almost didn't come here tonight, then he remembered his dad works in the kitchen." The joke heard around the world this night, however, was also not directed toward the guest of honor, instead it made a beeline for one of the dais guests, "I wouldn't fuck Sandra Bernhard with Bea Arthur's dick." She is, to this day, still wondering where in the hell did that come from. Bea covered her face and pointed her finger to Jeffrey, giving him the "You're a very bad boy" look, which is a hell of a lot better than Maude's "You're dead meat" look. Recalling the moment of impact, Jerry admits, "I must say everything goes in comedy as they say."

Alexander also was caught off guard, "I know Bea and I wasn't sure how that would sit with her and I knew she wasn't getting up to talk and I said to myself, 'Boy, someone should really go to bat for Bea. How do you do it?'" He did it this way, "I hope Bea Arthur kicks his ass. And I know that Bea Arthur can kick his ass." Ross and Bea kissed and made up afterward, not to mention Ross sent her flowers, so I guess there were no hard feelings. According to Jerry, "I called her up and I said, 'I had no idea what was going to be said that night and she said, 'Jerry, I had a great time. It was part of the frolic of the evening. It was a lot of fun.' She was as good a sport as one can be." Ah, another insult, another headline in a tabloid—big fuckin' deal.

The Friars spent a hell of a lot of money on Ben Stiller's hair. Have you ever seen Ben's hair? Well, it looked like it always does–sort of that "Lizzie Borden took an ax to it" look. Sandra Bernhard started the hair and makeup trend when she asked the Club to approve a hairdresser for her gig at the Danny Aiello Roast in 1997. Don't even get me started on *her* hair and makeup! If we've learned anything from this, I guess it would be that if you want to have a really expensive coif, attend a Friars Roast and let them foot the bill. But here's the catch; you have to make sure your hair doesn't look any different than before your head was touched. In any case, Ben was having a great time at his father's expense, "If you knew my dad's aversion to anything dirty you'd enjoy it even more. He's a man who loved his handguns even more than his family." Ben didn't smile a whole lot during the show, by the way, but maybe he didn't like all those things said about his dad. His mother, Anne Meara, couldn't have cared less; however, "When it comes to humiliating my husband, you guys are amateurs. My husband, Jerry Stiller, is every post-menopausal woman's wet dream." Who knew?

Robert Schimmel said, "I'm here to honor this man who actually got critical acclaim for an episode of *Murder She Wrote* for playing Angela Lansbury's cunt, cousin, cousin, cunt?" The ONLY reason you were forced to read that is for a little insight into this Alexander comment, "There was one thing that I literally just trashed right before I did it. For the intro to Bob Schimmel, I tried to be the more outrageous comic, more controversial, and I go into this Joan Rivers bit. The line Mike [Markowitz, who helped write Jason's material] had written for me was, 'Every time I see Joan and her chihuahua-faced daughter outside of one of these award shows, I want to grab Edgar's gun, put it in my mouth and follow him straight into

Valhalla.' And I just went, 'That's gonna be in the *New York Post* the next day and out of context, no one's gonna know what the hell this is.' So that's one that I went, 'Wow, maybe not. And as it was coming out of my mouth I said, 'Let me take a little turn off of this one.'"

Paul Rodriguez closed the show. What about Pat Cooper? Or Jack Carter? Who knows? Jerry got Paul, so shut up already. "I don't know you, but I love you. I must, to have come to New York during an outbreak of encephalitis!" Again, just a sampling to segue into Jason's comment: "I knew that by the time I was introducing Paul Rodriguez that he was pissed off. He just doesn't like the Hispanic jokes, the busboy stuff, and I sit here and I say, 'Then why are you here?' If I didn't like the bald, fat jokes, I wouldn't walk into a Friars Roast. I saw a quote afterwards where it was quite clear, he said, 'I didn't know I was going to be the center of attention.'" Then what's the point of even being a comedian, for God's sake.

At every Roast, and Dinner for that matter, there is a huge press, photo, cocktail thing that takes place behind the scenes before the dais guests enter the ballroom. It's been going on, probably since Charles Emerson Cook's and Channing Pollock's suppers, and there's tons of security and all different kinds of people back there. Jason's take on the experience pretty much sums up the moment for everyone, "They had security on me like I was the fuckin' president. I kept going, 'Is there some threat out there that I'm not aware of? Could you just tell me if my life's in danger? Isn't this the way Bobby Kennedy got it?' I had no idea who the hell was going to be there. To be backstage at a black-tie affair with Larry Storch and Lou Jacobi, and to be introduced by somebody to Abe Beame. He sure as hell doesn't know who Jason Alexander is. I had a lovely conversation with Tsidii LeLoka who, for four hours, I thought was Alfre Woodard. I'm thinking what the hell is Ruth Westheimer doing here? What the hell is Patty Hearst doing here? What is this shit? If you could have been in my head, I'm thinking, 'Am I in a Fellini film?' This is like a walking cavalcade of absurdity.

"The guy who really cut through it all is Belzer, and I don't even know him. I'm a fan, but he came over and said, 'Listen, the only person in the room tonight is me. You're working just for me. Remember that.' I went, 'all right, that's what I'm doing, I'm working for The Belz.' This group of people would congregate nowhere else. You would never have them together. No event, no cause, nothing would bring them together. That was my whole behind-the-scenes experience." And folks, this has been yours!

EPILOGUE

When David Hyde Pierce was asked if visions of Roastmasters past danced in his head when he helmed the Kelsey Grammer Roast, he said, "The Friars is such a paradoxical institution. It is simultaneously so raunchy and so crude and so kind of childish, locker-room; and yet, at the same time, it really is a venerable institution with people who are really legends in our business. And a lot of them were there that day—Sid Caesar, Freddie Roman—for that reason, when you're there doing it you're not so much conscious of Johnny Carson and Milton Berle as much as you are of saying fuck and shit." I felt the same way writing this book, only I was well aware of Carson, Berle, and all the boys who made the Friars Club fun—not to mention full of shit.

The wacky world of Friardom was first chiseled into show biz history books a hundred years ago and here they stand today, in prime time, no less. Even those insightful Founding Fathers could not have envisioned the success that would stem from their legacy. Imagine that Cohan-Berlin conversation now:

> GEORGIE: Say, Irv, did you read in the *Heavenly Variety* the Friars are hotter than ever down there?

IRV: Did I! Boy I tell ya Georgie, if I'da known they'd still be goin' strong after all these years, I'da hung around a lot longer and really cashed in on my Honorary Membership.

GEORGIE: I hear ya. But you gotta feel proud that we was there at the beginning—drinking gin, playin' cards, shootin' pool. . . .

IRV: Frolicking without the goils. . . .

GEORGIE: Yeah. Say, Irv, what was we thinkin'?

IRV: God only knows, Georgie. But look at the ol' boys now!

You may not have been privvy to *every* Friars Roast and Dinner that has gone on, but you sure did experience a whole lot of fun times. Maybe in a hundred more years you'll find out what zany doings the Friars of tomorrow will engage in. You can bet, though, no matter what, it will be just as funny and memorable as ever—if the Friars know one thing, it's how to keep tradition alive. Now, in the words of the late, great Friar George Burns, "Say goodnight, Gracie."

ACKNOWLEDGMENTS

A book like this doesn't get written overnight—well, this one did actually, but usually they don't. But it definitely can't happen without the help of a few people, so here they are:

To Jean Pierre Trebot, the Executive Director of the Friars Club, who threw caution to the wind to allow me to share the Club's good times with the rest of the world. He regrets that today, of course, but I thank him for his earlier trust, foresight, and sense of humor. I also appreciate his recounting his own memorable moments to me.

I'm so grateful to the celebrities and behind-the-scenes folks who shared their experiences, good or bad: Jason Alexander, Steve Allen, Buddy Arnold, Milton Berle, Carol Burnett, Red Buttons, Drew Carey, Jack Carter, Dick Cavett, Norm Crosby, Phyllis Diller, Marty Farrell, Jack L. Green, Buddy Hackett, Bernie Kamber, Alan King, Ed McMahon, Jim Morris, David Hyde Pierce, Don Rickles, Freddie Roman, Rita Rudner, Soupy Sales, Steven Seagal, Neil Simon, Ryan Stiles, Jerry Stiller, and David Tebet. Their honesty and openness paved the way for an honest and open book—not a terribly sincere one, but an honest one.

To Dean Ward, who initially found the key that finally opened the Friars' musty doors to create his documentary *Let Me In, I Hear Laughter*, I thank you. It was a valuable source of inspiration and, okay, material, too—is that so wrong? He helped to pave the way so that this book could be written for all to see.

I would like to acknowledge the photographers throughout the years who captured so many Friar moments: Gene Gabelli, Bill Mark, Paul Schumach, and Sam Siegel. Now if only I could find their photos. Many thanks to Paul Rigby for his devilishly accurate caricatures of Friars Roasts. But mostly for making my caricature have more hair than the real thing.

I am indebted to my agent, June Clark, who thinks books grow on trees—oh, they do, I suppose, as well as to my editor, PJ Dempsey, who luckily likes to laugh or we'd be up a creek here.

To the Friars' staff members who shared their own tales of these events—Gianfranco Capitelli, Michael Caputo, and Dale Roth—I thank you. To Oscar Riba, who lent his own Roast memory (not to mention his cufflinks) as well as researching past Roasts and Dinners, I suppose I owe my thanks and a free lunch. *Muchas gracias* to Alison Grambs for her assistance, although she can get her own lunch. To Eve Darcy, who fielded my many calls on topics ranging from Yiddish translations to thesaurus tips, I can't thank you enough.

I am especially grateful to Michael Matuza, who spent a summer in the bowels of the Friars Monastery searching for anything remotely resembling a historical document. I also thank him for listening to tapes of seemingly endless Roasts and Dinners—if he has to listen to "Laugh it up, I laugh when you act" one more time, I'm a dead man.

A final bow to all of the people who had the chutzpah to stand at a Friars' podium and bless us with their funny words of wisdom.

INDEX